PRAISE FOR

BLACK KNIGHTS
AND
FIGHTING IRISH

"A fine retelling of the glory days of Army–Notre Dame football."

—**Johnny Lujack**

"I was happy to share stories of my dad and the great Army football teams of the '40s in this book."

—**Tony Blanchard, Son of Army Great "Doc" Blanchard**

"Richard Cacioppe has captured a moment in time. It's hard to fathom today the magnitude of the Notre Dame–Army football rivalry in the first half of the twentieth century. *Black Knights and Fighting Irish* illuminates why the series took on such importance, recounting not only the thrilling games but also the legendary players and coaches, and the historical context that shaped them, their sport, and their country."

—**Jason Kelly, Author of *Mr. Notre Dame: The Life and Legend of Edward "Moose" Krause***

"Who knew the story of a football game ending in a 0–0 tie could be so engrossing and richly informative. We are lucky Richard Cacioppe did, and we are rewarded by his brilliant narrative that blends history, culture, tradition, and football in a glorious decades-long run up to the fabled 1946 Army–Notre Dame football game. Read the prologue, and you will not stop there."

—General David A. Bramlett, US Army (Retired)

MORE BOOKS BY

RICHARD CACIOPPE

Heaven on Hold
Welcome Home

Black Knights and Fighting Irish:
A Rivalry, a Game, and America One Year After World War II Ended

by Richard Cacioppe

© Copyright 2023 Richard Cacioppe

ISBN 979-8-88824-000-7

All rights reserved. No part of this publication
may be reproduced, stored in a retrieval system,
or transmitted in any form or by any means—
electronic, mechanical, photocopy, recording, or any other—
except for brief quotations in printed reviews, without the prior
written permission of the author.

Cover photograph provided by US Army Photo.

Published by

köehlerbooks™

3705 Shore Drive
Virginia Beach, VA 23455
800-435-4811
www.koehlerbooks.com

BLACK KNIGHTS

AND

FIGHTING IRISH

A RIVALRY, A GAME, AND AMERICA
ONE YEAR AFTER WORLD WAR II ENDED

RICHARD CACIOPPE

VIRGINIA BEACH
CAPE CHARLES

*For Lisa, Meg, Jeannine, and especially Peg,
who have filled my life with happiness and love.*

CONTENTS

Prologue 5

PART I: Triumph and Hope 15

Chapter 1: The Game 17

Chapter 2: The End 21

Chapter 3: God and Country 26

Chapter 4: Early Years of Football 39

Chapter 5: The Rivalry Begins 51

Chapter 6: The Rockne Years 65

Chapter 7: A Crash in Kansas 82

PART II: The Zenith 91

Chapter 8: The Coaches 93

Chapter 9: 1941 118

Chapter 10: The War 127

Chapter 11: College Football Goes to War 133

Chapter 12: 1942 142

Chapter 13: 1943 150

Chapter 14: 1944 164

Chapter 15: 1945 187

Chapter 16: 1946 198

Chapter 17: The Game 215

PART III: The Sunset 225

Chapter 18: The Beginning of the End 227

Chapter 19: 1947 235

Chapter 20: What Happened to Them 239

Epilogue: Extraordinary Men 258

Acknowledgments 274

Photos 276

Endnotes 278

PROLOGUE

THE IDEA FOR this book began in 1985, although I didn't realize it at the time. I was living in Granger, Indiana, four miles from the Notre Dame campus. My family and I were relocated there by IBM from the east coast. Except for my Army assignments, I had spent much of my life in the New York-New Jersey area, where I grew up. In those days, IBM stood for "I've Been Moved," so I wasn't surprised when IBM asked me to move to the South Bend office from my assignment in Endicott, New York. Many fellow IBMers I worked with received assignments to more glamorous locations such as Los Angeles, Las Vegas, Atlanta, and Dallas. I got South Bend.

I knew almost nothing about the Midwest and absolutely nothing about South Bend other than it was the home of Notre Dame. As a good Catholic boy, of course I knew of and rooted for the *Fighting Irish*. As a good Italian American, my fondness for Notre Dame increased when one day I heard a sportscaster announce, "Here come the Fighting Irish onto the field led by Ralph Guglielmi," the team's starting quarterback.

As a tried-and-true Easterner, I didn't know what to expect of life in the Midwest. It turned out to be a very fortuitous move for me and my family. South Bend is situated on the south bend (the southernmost curve) of the Saint Joseph River. At the turn of the nineteenth century, South Bend was a vibrant industrial city, with many rapidly growing manufacturers. The city was once touted as the *Pearl of the Midwest* and destined to overtake Chicago as the most important city in the Midwest. It boasted dynamic and growing companies such as Oliver Chilled Plow, South Bend Watch, Singer Sewing Machines, and of course, Studebaker wagons.

However, when my family and I arrived in South Bend in 1975, the city was a shadow of its former self. The Studebaker Company, the last of those nineteenth century powerhouses, had ended production twelve years earlier. South Bend then was in the very early stages of rebuilding itself.

The city and its environs were, and still are, a wonderful place to raise a family. The South Bend area today has roughly 250,000 residents. It's a fair-sized city, large enough to offer an excellent variety of activities but small enough so that you can get to know many of your neighbors as well as many of the movers and shakers in town. It still maintains those solid, traditional Midwest values that makes raising a family so pleasant.

South Bend evolved from an agricultural community in the 1800s to a manufacturing center in the late nineteenth century and now is a service and innovation hub. What has remained constant throughout is the impact and influence that Notre Dame has on the South Bend area and its residents.

There are many ways that residents can interact with the university's activities. One of my own most unique and interesting interactions with Notre Dame occurred unexpectedly. Army, my alma mater, was scheduled to play Notre Dame in the fall of 1985. Several of the business leaders and others in volunteer organizations took advantage of the opportunity to organize a charity event in conjunction with the game. They cleverly melded the game activities with an elegant evening commemorating the forty-fifth anniversary of the world premiere of the movie, *Knute Rockne, All American.*

The premiere had taken place in South Bend in 1940 at three different theaters simultaneously, and featured personal appearances by Pat O'Brien, Ronald Reagan (yup, that Ronald Reagan) as well as entertainers Rudy Vallee and Bob Hope. The president's son, Franklin D. Roosevelt Jr., was also present for the festivities. It was one of the biggest entertainment events ever held in South Bend.

My job as a graduate of West Point was to bring as many prominent Army participants as possible to the planned festivities.

My first thought was to call Doc Blanchard and Glenn Davis, the two most famous players in Army's storied football history. I didn't get to speak to either player. Glenn Davis's wife said he was not interested in coming to South Bend. Doc Blanchard's wife told me he no longer flew even though he had been in the Air Force for close to thirty years.

Undeterred, I then called Arnold Tucker, who was the quarterback at Army when Blanchard and Davis played. Although overshadowed for much of his football career by *Mr. Outside* and *Mr. Inside*, Tucker was an exceptional athlete. He won the James E. Sullivan Award as the nation's best amateur athlete in 1946 and was elected to the College Football Hall of Fame in 2008. Arnold could not have been more gracious during our phone conversation. He readily accepted my invitation to join in the planned activities at South Bend.

I called General William Westmoreland, who had been superintendent at the Military Academy when I was a cadet. He also was the commander in Vietnam when I served there in 1966. General Westmoreland readily accepted my invitation to participate in the Army-Notre Dame festivities. It turned out that the general had several ties to Notre Dame that he was looking forward to reestablishing. The chaplain of the Notre Dame Army ROTC, Colonel Francis L. Sampson, was a much respected and legendary Airborne padre that Westmoreland had served with earlier in his military career.

And, in an amazing coincidence, Father Edmund Joyce, the executive vice president of Notre Dame, grew up in Spartanburg, South Carolina, where he and Westmoreland had been friends. In fact, Father Joyce had dated Westmoreland's sister before becoming a priest. Both these acquaintances were an additional incentive for the general to accept my invitation to join us at the celebration in South Bend.

The weekend's activities began with a reenactment of the Knute Rockne movie, which was shown in the newly renovated Morris Performing Arts Center, followed by a gala dinner in the elegantly restored Palais Royale Ballroom. South Bend did all it could to show off its sophisticated and cultural past while also showcasing the city's resurgence, which was then underway.

The next day, Saturday, October 18, was a crisp and clear fall day. After dueling band performances and tailgate parties, the sellout crowd of 59,075 fans filed eagerly into the Notre Dame Stadium. It wasn't much of a football game. Notre Dame easily defeated the visiting Cadets, 30–3. However, it was memorable for me since I got to sit next to Arnold Tucker for the entire game. There's nothing like having a West Point, College Hall of Fame quarterback, analyze a football game with you while you're watching it.

That evening my wife and I hosted a party at our house. In addition to many of our friends, we invited Roland Kelly, a local newscaster. He invited Creighton Miller, a star player on the Notre Dame football teams of the early 1940s. Frank Leahy, Notre Dame's coach during the '40s, once described Creighton Miller as the best athlete he ever coached. That's saying something considering the outstanding players that Coach Leahy mentored during his tenure at Notre Dame.

Roland also brought along something that turned out to be very important to the success of the evening. Somehow, he had come across a VHS tape of the Army-Notre Dame game of 1946. Without a set plan, we all crowded into my family room and watched the video. It had no sound, but that turned out to be fortuitous. Roland had attended the game at Yankee Stadium as a freshman student at Notre Dame. Creighton Miller also was at the game after graduation from ND. And of course, Arnold Tucker had played in the game.

As we watched the silent, grainy video, each of them spontaneously described the atmosphere and action of the game that many call the *Game of the Century*. There was not a sound from the fifty people who packed the room. It was a magical hour that couldn't have been scripted any better, replete with impromptu and colorful commentary by those that had been there in 1946.

At the end of the video, the crowd remained in the room hoping there was more. When it was clear there was not, those in attendance scattered to other areas of the house. It was at that moment that the doorbell rang. Enter General Westmoreland and Father Joyce, whom I had invited but didn't think I would see. If there had been any lingering doubt about my ability to throw an interesting party, those thoughts were dispelled as the general and the Notre Dame senior priest made their way through the crowd.

The best line of the evening came from Joyce Kelly, Roland's wife. She and her husband were among the last to leave. As she was leaving, Joyce looked me in the eye and said seriously, "Next time you have a party, try to get some interesting people."

My wife and I basked in the contentment of that warm and entertaining evening for a long time as the impact of watching the video of that monumental game and the description of the aura surrounding that bygone era took hold of me. I have been thinking about it ever since. I finally decided that the story of that game and the giants that participated in it needed to be revived.

I came to realize that the story is more than just a tale of a great football game. It's a social commentary. World War II had ended a little more than a year earlier. And, although much of the world was still suffering, the US was rapidly returning to a time of normalcy. The country had done its part and suffered huge losses along with the other participants but had not been subjected to the destruction inflicted on the countries of Europe and Asia. Because of this the US was able to rapidly return to its prewar activities. It was the first year since the war began that the country could enjoy a concert, a play, or a football game, not as a distraction, but with the full unbridled enthusiasm of a populace finally freed from the worry, bad news, and uncertainty that had plagued them for so long.

One of the key events that reassured many Americans that life was returning to normal was the resumption of the traditional football rivalry between Army and Notre Dame. The teams had played each other continuously from 1913 (except for one year during WWI). In the last two years of World War II, 1944 and 1945, Army had shut out the Irish by lopsided scores, unusual outcomes for the normally hard-fought and close scores, which characterized much of the rivalry.

There is little doubt that the demand of the war had heavily favored the Military Academy and its ability to attract talented athletes while curtailing Notre Dame's ability to build and retain competitive teams. With the return of veterans following the war's end, fans looked forward to the reestablishment of the rivalry, a resumption of the contest between the two football powerhouses unencumbered and untainted by the demands of the war.

The football season of 1946 was progressing like the seasons prior to the war. Instead of playing teams like Louisville Field US Army Air Force, or Melville PT Boats, the Cadets were once again playing formidable college teams. Army had dominated college athletics during the war years. They had won the College National Championship in both 1944 and 1945. During those years they had held Notre Dame scoreless, an unprecedented feat.

At Yankee Stadium, the Fighting Irish were reinforced with returning service veterans, many with combat experience and others recruited by Leahy while he served in the Navy during the war. The common term, *returning veterans* used today, had a very different meaning in 1946. In that year a returning veteran was someone who might have been at Iwo Jima or the Battle of the Bulge. Ironically, fans attending the game accused the Army players of being draft dodgers because they had spent the war years at West Point, whereas the Notre Dame team fielded fifty-three players just back from their war duties. Of course, many graduates of West Point had made enormous sacrifices to the war effort. No one before or since has ever accused West Point cadets of shirking their duty.

Nonetheless, unbridled enthusiasm and partisanship for the two top-ranked football teams in the country were on full display on that November afternoon. The story of the rivalry, the coaches and the players, and their fateful meeting in Yankee Stadium all converged in what became the *Game of the Century.*

The culmination of the story in this book takes place in 1946, a pivotal year in the history of the world. Rarely, if ever, has the time frame of a sporting event been such a key element in the narrative of what happened. However, the setting of the historic game between Army and Notre Dame is an important element in understanding the significance of the events that took place in Yankee Stadium on that November day in 1946.

It's the story of two iconic American institutions whose graduates' sacrifices and commitment to the country are unparalleled. Although similar in many ways, Notre Dame and West Point found different ways to serve the country they loved. Graduates of both schools share values, respect, and love of their alma maters. The call for cadets at West Point to live up to the ideals of Duty, Honor, Country parallel those of graduates of Notre Dame who are called to embrace the university's motto to serve God, Country, and Notre Dame.

This is also the chronicle of a rivalry that dates to 1913. The competition between these two teams over decades produced some of the most thrilling contests in college football.

Most importantly, it's the story of the young men of both schools who sacrificed so much for the country before, during, and after the costliest war in history. The story of the game can't be told accurately without understanding the years leading up to the game and the men who lived through them.

Gradually, starting in 1939, as the country geared up to become the arsenal of democracy, American industry awakened from its ten-year slumber. Jobs became more plentiful and as they did it allowed the population to feel the faint rays of optimism, which had been denied them for so long.

However, just as the country began to enjoy the fruits of the recovering economy, the nation was drawn into the war. Once again, the American people had to put their lives and plans on hold. Although not economic, the results to the American people were the same. They had money but not very many choices because of shortages due to rationing. The one big difference from the Great Depression was that sacrificing for the war effort toward a common goal gave purpose to the hardship this time.

The war years added an additional somber weight to the burden carried by the populace. The ever-increasing casualty notices continually darkened the mood of the people. The arrival of dreaded telegrams from the War Department was a constant reminder of the tragic and gruesome toll that the war was exacting on the country. Everyone was almost immediately aware of the loss of a neighborhood boy when a nearby window revealed that a blue star had been changed to a gold star, signifying that a loved one had been killed in battle.

And after almost four years, the burdens, both physical and mental, were lifted. The country could once again think and dream about a future unencumbered by fear and sacrifice. Almost overnight the country's mood went from worry and fear to optimism and hope. People at last were able to listen to radio broadcasts without hearing worrisome stories about distant battlefields. News of recovery supplanted the grim news that had been the staple for the weary populace. Simple pleasures such as gatherings with all family members present were being enjoyed again.

It is hard today to imagine the great relief, happiness, and unbridled optimism that all 140 million citizens shared at the war's end. Photos and newsreels from the time convey joy and celebration. What they can't show is the inner emotions of pride, relief, unbridled optimism, and faith in a better future, all tinged by the losses of the preceding four years.

It was this environment that provided the dramatic backdrop for one of the greatest games of one of the greatest college football rivalries in sports history.

PART I

TRIUMPH AND HOPE

CHAPTER 1

THE GAME

Duty, Honor, Country.
God, Country, Notre Dame.

THE ATMOSPHERE WAS electric. Even though it was a chilly November day, many of the sellout crowd at Yankee Stadium had arrived early. Army, national champions in both 1944 and 1945, was the favorite. They had defeated Notre Dame by a combined score of 107–0 in the preceding two years. But everyone understood that this year the undefeated Irish would not be a pushover. Anyone who followed college football knew that Frank Leahy, the Notre Dame coach, had assembled an awesome team of talented athletes reinforced by a significant number of returning veterans recently released from the service and players who had transferred to Notre Dame after the war.

The matchup was historic. The Army team of 1946 had dominated college football for the preceding two years with talented athletes who had been exempted from war service during their time at West Point. They were opposed by a Notre Dame team that had not scored against Army in their last two meetings, but who had dominated the series prior to that. For this contest the Irish came reinforced by a contingent of combat-hardened veterans returning from battlefields around the world.

The intense rivalry needed no additional motivation. However, Notre Dame came into the game looking to avenge consecutive humiliating losses, while Army felt the need to prove that its dominance was due to more than just the recruiting advantage it had enjoyed during the war years.

The matchup would be different than the two preceding years. The Army team, hobbled by injuries and the loss of several key players due to graduation or academic difficulties, lacked the depth of talent that had characterized their earlier teams. However, there was no question that Army was still formidable. The most talented backfield duo of college football, Doc Blanchard and Glenn Davis, were back for their final year. Their effectiveness would be enhanced by their gifted and skilled quarterback, Arnold Tucker, and an experienced line.

Notre Dame had so much talent that Coach Leahy, recently returned from the Navy, had encouraged some starters of previous years to seek other opportunities. While serving in the Navy, Leahy had discovered and recruited a handful of talented players such as Jim Martin and George Connor, who would help to establish Irish football dominance in the future. They would be joined by returning Notre Dame players such as John Lujack, Emil Sitko, and Jim Mello, whose careers has been interrupted by military service.

Interest in the game was worldwide. Ninety-five newspapers and wire services vied for vantage points in the crowded press box. They had traveled to the game from twenty states, as well as Australia, Sweden, and England. Twenty photo-news syndicates, five newsreel crews, and twenty-four radio teams joined them. One hundred and fifty thousand viewers in New York, Philadelphia, and Washington, DC who were fortunate to own a new device called a television set were able to view NBC's limited black-and-white coverage of the game. In 2015, sixty-nine years later, 114 million viewers, only 26 million fewer than the entire US population of 140 million in 1946, watched the Super Bowl on their large screen color sets.

Yankee Stadium was filled with 74,000 enthusiastic fans that were lucky enough to get tickets. Tickets officially went on sale in early August, but by late June most of the tickets had already been presold or gifted to VIPs and others. Notre Dame had to refund over $500,000 to hopeful fans who had been unable to qualify for tickets.

Many lucky ticket holders took advantage of the scarcity by scalping their own. An enterprising seller circled the stadium in his automobile with a sign placed in his windshield advertising a $3.30 end zone seat for $200. Someone bought it.

The attending crowd included famous WWII Generals Dwight Eisenhower and Omar Bradley, both of whom had played football at West Point. Both the secretary of war and the Navy secretary were present in addition to about a hundred wounded veterans from the New York area.

Both teams would be cheered on by fans, many of whom had also been tested on battlefields or who had contributed to the war effort on the home front and were now more than ready to enjoy the long-awaited spectacle. For them, it was more than a football game. It was a celebration and a confirmation that the world had been restored to its proper order and life could at last get back to simple pleasures such as the important resumption of the thirty-four-year-old rivalry.

The crowds looked forward to the contest that would remind them of an earlier, simpler time, a time steeped in tradition and hard-fought competition. While stuck in traffic amid the honking of horns in the Bronx, they had to try to remember a time when horses and horseless carriages shared the road. Airplanes were in their infancy, and amazed and curious people went to the airfields just to see the machines take off and land.

There was nostalgia even for the difficult years preceding the war. That nostalgia was illuminated by pride and a strong hope for a brighter future. This Notre Dame-Army clash signaled the rebirth of a rivalry that represented so much more than a football game. It was a hope for the restoration of what had been and what could be again.

But like most dreams of the future this one had unforeseen events that would darken this bright vision. The rivalry, which was so admired and loved by its ardent fans would end soon after this game. The two respected architects of today's game, Coach "Red" Blaik, and Coach Frank Leahy would both be touched by scandal and censure.

But on gameday, all that was hidden from the enthusiastic crowd that jostled its way into Yankee Stadium and was unseen by the millions who eagerly tuned their radios early to make sure they didn't miss a minute of the pageantry.

CHAPTER 2

THE END

"There is no substitute for victory."
— General Douglas MacArthur

IN THE FALL of 1946, the vestiges of the war still lingered. The families of the 407,300 that were killed were still grieving over the loss of their loved ones. Many of the 671,801 wounded were still recovering, some in hospitals and some at home. Many of the eighteen, nineteen, and twenty-year-olds who had made up the bulk of the US armed forces were attempting to adjust to peace. But the balance had clearly shifted.

Every day brought news of further restoration of normalcy and evidence that tomorrow would be better than yesterday. On the day of the big game, President Truman had announced the lifting of war-time price controls on all items except rent, sugar, rice, and molasses. This action and others would result in the unleashing of the US economy. By 1947, half of all the world's manufacturing would be done in the United States.

When the war began in Europe in 1939, the US Army was the nineteenth largest in the world, behind Bulgaria, and was the same size as Portugal's army. As the war increased in intensity in 1940, fully 25 percent of the US population supported the America First Committee, which espoused strict neutrality with the belligerents and a strong policy of isolationism. Charles Lindbergh, an American early aviation hero, was one of the committee's leaders. Many more people were firm supporters of the concept of keeping America neutral and out of the war, but were repelled by the strident rhetoric of the committee and its ties to the American German Bund, an organization friendly to Nazi Germany. Only about half of the country was in favor of giving material aid to Great Britain, Russia, and China, who were still resisting the Axis forces.

A bill to require the country's first peace time conscription was introduced in June 1940, the same month that France fell to the German forces. The proposal became law in September 1940 as the Battle of Britain culminated. The law required all men between the ages of twenty-one and forty-five to register for the draft. If selected, a man was to serve on active duty for one year and in a reserve component for ten years. The first draftees reported for duty in November.

The unrelenting threat of war continued to close in on America as the Axis forces were triumphant everywhere. In Asia, Japanese forces continued their conquests by occupying Indochina in late 1940. In early 1941, the Nazis solidified their hold on Europe. As these events unfolded, it became increasingly apparent that the United States would certainly be drawn into the conflict.

Amid these ominous developments, President Roosevelt asked Congress to extend the term of duty for draftees from twelve to thirty months. The Service Extension Act, complying with the president's wishes, became law in August 1941 after passing in the House of Representatives by just one vote.

So it was then, by a series of fits and starts, that the country was reluctantly nudged into preparedness for a war it refused to acknowledge even though much of the world was already aflame.

It appeared that the grim war news from around the world was at last motivating the US government toward greater preparedness. The civilian population, and the recently conscripted soldiers, however, still lagged the president and others in the government who now embraced a more urgent need to get the country ready for possible entry into the war.

However, this new commitment was even less popular among

the earlier draftees who were nearing the end of their previous obligation of one year. The letters *OHIO* were found written on walls throughout the Army camps, which had sprung up around the country. The message from the new soldiers was clear. They would go *Over the Hill in October* because they didn't share the newfound urgency with the country's leaders. These service members also felt they had been deceived by the promise of the Selective Service and Training Act of 1940, which had committed them to only one year of active service.

On December 7, 1941, all doubt about US involvement in the war was erased with the Japanese assault on Pearl Harbor. The country was instantly united by the sneak attack. Even The America First Committee, which had so adamantly opposed America's involvement in the war, now joined the patriotic fervor sweeping the nation by closing its doors on December 10, signifying an end to its previously strident isolationist position.

The Japanese attack presented a strategic dilemma for President Roosevelt. He and his War Department had long planned for a *Germany first* strategy, perceiving that the Nazi threat was by far the most serious. After Pearl Harbor, however, the American people were almost unanimous in their demand for revenge against the Japanese Empire. Fortunately, Hitler solved the president's problem by declaring war on the United States on December 11, 1941.

The country was thrust into a war which it had anticipated but was not prepared for. Not only was the US Army woefully small, but it was almost totally lacking in effective equipment, which would be needed in the war. During maneuvers, newly drafted soldiers trained with stovepipe mortars and light trucks with signs designating them as tanks. The soldiers, sailors, and airmen who fought the country's early battles paid dearly for the lack of equipment and foresight of its leaders.

In the Pacific, in battle after battle, the inferiority of equipment and lack of air power enabled the battle-hardened Japanese forces to defeat the defending American forces. In the first half of 1942, the US suffered crushing defeats at Guam, Wake Island, and in the Philippines. The only meaningful bright spot in the early days of the war was the miraculous and stunning US Naval victory at Midway in early June.

After these depressing early defeats, it took the US over eight months to launch its first offensive of the war at Guadalcanal in August 1942. With great effort, the Marines were able to land a division of about 14,000 men on Guadalcanal and several offshore islands.

Considering that the US Armed Forces would ultimately number almost four million by the end of 1942, the US lacked efficient transportation and supply systems during the first year of the war. Worldwide support systems would be needed to sustain a force of over sixteen million service men and women three years later.

Three months after the invasion of Guadalcanal, the US launched its second offensive of the war. Operation Torch was the combined Anglo-American invasion of French North Africa and our initial entry into the European Theater. It was a substantially more ambitious American endeavor than Guadalcanal. This joint operation was comprised of over 100,000 men, mostly American, landed in three locations along the Northwestern African coast. Still, even this effort paled in contrast to the millions of German and Soviet troops then locked in combat in Russia.

The American forces in both the European and Pacific Theaters licked their wounds and learned quickly from these early battles. Ineffective and poor leaders were replaced. Tactical doctrine was continually refined so that the prewar theories of the planners were revised to reflect the harsh realities of the actual battlefield. Improved logistic and support systems ensured that the fighting men were well supplied with the updated equipment now pouring out of America's factories.

By the time of the D-Day invasion in 1944, the American Armed Forces were much improved, and an Allied victory seemed more assured. In Europe, the Russian forces had held the Nazis and were now quickly regaining the ground they had lost in 1941. The Americans, British, and Canadians were poised to invade the European continent. In the Pacific, Naval, Marine, and Army units were forcing the Japanese to relinquish territory they had taken so easily early in the war.

However, as the pace of Allied advances increased, so too did casualties. As the hope of victory and the end of the bloody conflict increased, so did the number of War Department telegrams notifying families of the loss of a loved one. The number of KIAs grew from 53,517 to 167,276 in 1944. The awful pace of casualties continued to increase right up to the end of the conflict. Almost 75 percent of all US KIAs of WWII occurred in the last year of the war.[1] It seemed ironic and frustrating that the weakened Axis forces were inflicting greater and greater casualties on the victorious Allied armies. War weariness was setting in, not only among the fighting men, but also among those on the home front.

After the race across France and the rout of the German army in the fall of 1944, there was a glimmer of hope that perhaps the war in Europe would conclude by year's end. The Battle of the Bulge dashed that optimistic thought. Once again, newly arrived green American troops performed poorly. Fortunately, this time there were enough battle tested American units to first seal the Bulge and then drive the Germans back. However, there was concern among senior officers after the quick surrender of a few American units at the battle that soldiers were increasingly reluctant to fight as the end of the war drew near.

Despite these temporary setbacks, it was becoming increasingly apparent as 1945 began that a victorious end to the war was now possible. The American people, after years of anguish, sacrifice, and hardship could sense the approaching victory. But it wasn't here yet. Not yet.

CHAPTER 3

GOD AND COUNTRY

"This will have the best possible effect upon the men," he said. "It will be very gratifying, and will do much toward conciliating our people."
—Robert E. Lee to Ulysses S. Grant[2]

ALMOST 800 MILES separate the compact 1,261-acre campus of Notre Dame in Indiana from the sprawling 16,000-acre military reservation that houses the US Military Academy in West Point, New York. This disparity in physical size masks the similarity between the two institutions.

Both enjoy reputations that far exceed what would be expected of schools with such small student bodies. West Point, for most of its 219-year history, has had a student body of less than 2,000. The last increase of the Corps of Cadets occurred in 1964 when the authorized strength almost doubled from 2,400 to its current size of 4,400. Notre Dame's undergraduates number around 8,000.

Additionally, both West Point and Notre Dame were founded as institutions for men only. Notre Dame admitted women in 1972, West Point in 1976. Both had a Catholic women's college right outside their gates, Ladycliff College in Highland Falls, New York (closed in 1980) and St. Mary's College in South Bend, Indiana.

Both Notre Dame and the Military Academy were established in originally remote areas, away from major metropolitan centers. West Point is sixty miles north of New York City. Notre Dame is approximately a hundred miles east of Chicago. These cities are close enough for the students to visit when they have extended time off, but not close enough for surreptitious visits by all but the most daring. Because both were founded before the advent of railroads, river access was important. Both were founded close to nearby rivers. West Point is on a point of land where the Hudson River makes a sharp turn to the west. Notre Dame is close to the location where the Saint Joseph River takes a slight bend in a southerly direction before it courses its way northward to Lake Michigan.

However, the most important attribute shared by these two institutions is not physical. It is more of a spiritual link. Both exhort and expect their students and graduates to embrace and commit themselves to goals more important than themselves. West Point's motto of *Duty, Honor, Country,* has for many years been a beacon guiding the Corps of Cadets to devote itself to selfless service to the country. Equally inspiring are the words etched above the doorway to the Basilica of Sacred Heart, which calls on the student body of Notre Dame to dedicate itself to the principles of God, Country, Notre Dame. The achievements of both institutions have been driven by their similar commitments to these higher values. These lofty goals have helped to guide the graduates of both schools to gain worldwide respect for their alma maters.

Their mutual commitments to such lofty ideals have also resulted in a rich history that both schools share on athletic fields and on the battlefields of America's wars. Their story is one of intense competition, common cause, and dedicated service to the country.

"From the headwaters in the Adirondack mountains, the Hudson River flows due south with hardly a twist or turn for more than 200 miles through a beautiful valley of green pastures and forest clad Granite Hills. Then, after slipping through a narrow gap between two particularly lofty, broad shouldered peaks called Storm King and Breakneck Ridge, the stream collides with a flat-topped promontory towering almost 200 feet above the waterline.

Over the ages the stratum of hard rock has resisted the constant corrosive power, forcing it into an abrupt right angle bent to the east. Scarcely a quarter mile farther on, the Hudson, having flanked this indomitable barrier, makes another ninety-degree turn as it resumes a southward course for some fifty odd miles to the sea." [3]

Upon this beautiful and dramatic promontory overlooking the Hudson River stands the United States Military Academy. However, it is not the physical beauty of this site that made it one of the most iconic and historic locations in America. It is the exploits and contributions of its many graduates to the country that have made West Point so intertwined with the fate and destiny of the United States.

From its beginning, West Point's destiny has been inseparably and closely woven into the fabric of America's own destiny. Early in the War for Independence, it became clear that fortifications were needed at West Point to prevent the British forces from controlling the Hudson. Control of the river would enable the British to sever the New England colonies from the rest of the recently established nation. Fortifications were built on a strategic promontory at a point where the river made two dramatic turns. Sailing ships would have to slow to navigate these twists, enabling a well-placed fort to pummel the slowed vessels. A giant chain with links two feet long and weighing half a ton each was attached to log rafts and secured to ensure that no ships could slip by the fort. A brigade of continental troops was assigned to West Point to further defend and enhance the defense of this vital location.

American troops have occupied the site since that day, making it the oldest continuously occupied US Army post in the world. Benedict Arnold, earlier a heroic American general, recognized the strategic value of West Point. He managed to get himself appointed commandant of the post in 1780. Arnold then proceeded to sabotage efforts to strengthen the position and corresponded with the British to hand over the fortifications, ordnance, and garrison.

The plot was discovered and thwarted but not before becoming the epitome of treason to the country. His name has become synonymous with betrayal. It is truly ironic that Arnold's final act of perfidy against his country should have taken place at the very location that would spawn an institution whose hallmark would be to produce graduates who would consider it their sworn duty to render honorable service to the nation.

With the war's end, the new nation grappled with trying to balance its aversion to having a professional standing army to defend itself. In November 1799, Alexander Hamilton proposed a plan to the secretary of war, that a Military Academy be established to instruct all branches of service, even the Navy, in military fundamentals. He sent a copy of this proposal to former President George Washington at Mount Vernon. "In the last letter he ever penned—on December 12, 1799, two days before his death—Washington replied that the establishment of such an institution 'has ever been considered by me as an object of primary importance to this country,' and concluded with the hope that Hamilton's arguments would prevail upon the legislature to place it on permanent and respectable footing."[4]

Washington did not live to see the creation of the institution he had recommended. Almost two-and-a-half years after his death, on March 16, 1802, Congress passed an act establishing the US Military Academy. West Point's birth and the early years of the republic are firmly intertwined. Its founding was only thirteen years after the ratification of the Constitution. Two of our most famous Founding Fathers, Washington and Jefferson, played important roles in its establishment. There is probably no other institution of higher learning in the country that has such rich and historic bonds to our country.

The early years of the academy were uncertain and difficult as it tried to carve out a role for itself in a country that had disdain and mistrust of a permanent and professional military. It received its broad and vague mission when Congress, on March 16, 1802, passed an act establishing a Corps of Engineers that was to include ten cadets sent to West Point.

★ ★ ★

The first few years were chaotic and disorganized. It was Sylvanus Thayer, a graduate of the class of 1808, later hailed as the father of West Point, who in 1812 established a formal education system and code of conduct which formed the foundation of the institution that exists today.

In its earliest years, West Point graduates sallied forth to perform important missions for the fledgling country with little recognition—defense of its frontiers, protection of settlers moving into new lands, and development of much needed engineering projects such as building bridges and canals and surveying the recently acquired vast Western lands.

It was the Mexican War from 1846 to 1848 that highlighted the importance to the country of the military skills of the graduates of West Point. It also turned out to be a great proving ground for a host of young officers who would become key commanders in a looming struggle that would too soon tragically divide them. Over a thousand graduates of West Point commanded units and served in other roles in the mostly volunteer army that invaded Mexico.

In 1860 Winfield Scott, commander-in-chief of the US Army, made his famous pronouncement on the contribution of West Point graduates to the victories of the Mexican War. This declaration has been memorized by academy cadets ever since.

"I give it as my fixed opinion that but for our graduated cadets the war between the United States and Mexico might, and probably would, have lasted some four or five years, with, in its first half, more defeat than victories falling to our share, whereas in less than two campaigns we conquered a great country and a peace without the loss of a single battle or skirmish."

Between the Mexican War and the Civil War, West Point graduates mapped the vast Western territories, assisted in building the railroads that penetrated the still untamed wilderness and developed the rivers and ports that would improve access and enhance the commercial value of the newly acquired lands.

It was the Civil War that brought the importance of the Military Academy to the attention of the US and the world. Of the fewer than two thousand graduates of West Point before the Civil War, 294 became general officers on the Union side and 151 on the Confederate side. In the sixty-five major battles of the war, West Point graduates commanded both sides in sixty-three of those battles. In the remaining two engagements, West Point graduates commanded one side.

There are numerous stories of West Point officers showing kindness and respect to their fellow graduates during the war who were now in the enemy camp. Perhaps the most poignant and famous of these friendly encounters of former comrades occurred at the surrender of the Confederate forces in the rural Virginia hamlet of Appomattox Courthouse.

General Robert E Lee, commander of the Confederate forces, arrived first at the home of Wilmer McLean, the site of the surrender. By a strange coincidence this same farmer had owned a home near Bull Run, location of one of the earliest battles of the war. McLean had moved his family to this remote location seeking refuge from the war. Now his home was to become a place not only of peace for his family, but for the country as well.

As General US Grant, commander of the Union forces, entered the home, Lee rose to meet him. Grant tried to relieve the tension. "I met you once before, General," he said recalling a time in Mexico when the Virginian had visited his brigade. "I have always remembered your appearance and I think I should have recognized you anywhere."

Lee nodded. "Yes, I know I met you on that occasion," he replied, "and I've often thought of it and tried to recollect how you looked. But I have never been able to recall a single feature." [5] The comment was not intended as an insult, but merely a statement of fact. Grant took it as that.

Grant had not written up anything prior to Lee's arrival. After discussing the surrender terms, Grant penned a document in his order book and passed it to Lee for his review. Lee thought momentarily about asking for a concession for his army. It was difficult for the dignified but vanquished Virginian to make a plea on behalf of his men. Grant made it easier by asking if the Southern commander had any further suggestions as to the final form of the surrender document. Lee hesitated before replying. "There is one thing I would like to mention. The cavalryman and artillerists own their own horses in our army. Its organization in this respect differs from that of the United States. I would like to understand whether these men will be permitted to retain their horses."

Grant overlooked what he later called "this implication that we were two countries," but said flatly, "You will find that the terms as written do not allow this." Lee perused again the two sheets of yellow flimsy. He was asking a favor, and he did not enjoy the role of supplicant. "No," he admitted regretfully, "I see the terms do not allow it. That is clear."

Grant considered the request for a moment. Then said, "I will arrange it this way; I will not change the terms as now written, but I will instruct the officers I shall appoint to receive the paroles to let all the men who claim to own a horse or mule take the animals home with them to work their little farms." Lee's relief and appreciation were expressed in his response. "This will have the best possible effect upon the men," he said. "It will be very gratifying, and will do much toward conciliating our people." [6]

After the Civil War, except for the spectacular defeat of George Armstrong Custer, West Point graduates went about quietly completing engineering projects and maintaining the Army's preparedness. The country's military planners were forced to broaden their scope as the country's focus began to shift from the Western Hemisphere to one which was more international in scope.

★ ★ ★

World War I thrust the country onto the world stage. And West Point graduates again played an important role in that conflict as the country's armed forces grew from 100,000 to over three million. When the war broke out there were 4,900 officers in the regular Army with at least one year of commissioned service. About half were graduates of West Point. [7]

John J. Pershing, class of 1886, was chosen to lead the American Expeditionary Force to France. He drew heavily on his West Point experience. Pershing used the standards of the Military Academy as the model for the fast growing, primarily civilian army. He ordered that, "The standards for the American army will be those of West Point. The rigid attention, the upright bearing, attention to detail, uncomplaining obedience to instruction required of the cadet will be required of every officer and soldier of our armies in France."[8] He knew that his untested soldiers would be closely scrutinized by the battle-hardened and cynical leaders and troops of the two Allied armies who had been fighting for three years.

Pershing also relied heavily on his old classmates and other West Point graduates to lead and staff the Army. Three quarters of American generals were products of the academy; thirty-four of thirty-eight corps and division commanders in France were West Pointers. The impact of Pershing and the untested but enthusiastic American Expeditionary Force (AEF) was decisive in breaking the bloody stalemate on the Western Front. Finally, in 1918 the battlefields of Europe fell silent.

The cost to all junior officers had been high, especially for West Point junior officers. Their training at the academy, regardless of time spent there, had imbued them with a strong ethic of leading from the front. The losses for all non-West Point first lieutenants were thirty per thousand. Among West Point first lieutenants the losses were 195 per thousand.

The war had an enormous impact on West Point. Shortly after the US entered the war in April 1917, the War Department ordered that the class of 1917 be graduated immediately, two months early. The rapid buildup of the Army and the need for junior officers continued to increase as American troops were dispatched to Europe. The next class scheduled to graduate in June 1918 was instead graduated in August 1917. Twenty-one members of these two classes were killed in action and numerous others were wounded.

The War Department continued to view West Point as a ready source of junior officers, regardless of time at the academy. The class of 1919 graduated in June of 1918, one year early. As late as October of 1918, one month prior to the armistice, the War Department uncertain about the war's end, ordered that the classes of 1920 and 1921 be graduated immediately. This last levy had transformed West Point from a military training university to a training camp for officers, similar to the numerous camps that had been established around the country.

That left only the freshman class, which had entered the academy only three months prior. This severed an important link in the education of the new cadets. There were no upper classmen to assist in imparting West Point's traditions and values.

Military authorities continued to make changes to the educational system at the academy by ordering that the course at West Point be shortened to one year. This meant that the current freshman class would graduate in June 1919.

After the war ended some of the officers in the War Department and administration at the Military Academy lobbied to restore the full Corps of Cadets as quickly as possible. The third class, which had graduated shortly before the Armistice, was ordered back to West Point. Because they had already been commissioned and had served in the Army, they continued to wear their officer's uniforms and were segregated from the rest of the corps.

A new class of plebes entered in November of 1918 and joined the existing plebe class, although both classes maintained their own identity.

The old grads and the academy's administration were appalled at the destruction the War Department had inflicted on West Point. They moved quickly to restore the structure of the old system of education and cadets corp. They were aided and challenged by a new superintendent who had made a name for himself in the war just ended-Brigadier General Douglas MacArthur.

In 1836, thirty-four years after the founding of West Point, a young seminarian in France heard an appeal that would change his life and the lives of countless young men and women in the future. This appeal, from a visiting United States bishop, encouraged his young listeners to devote themselves to missionary work in the New World. He described the need to minister to the Natives and settlers of a barely tamed wilderness in the Northwest Territory. In particular, the bishop sought help in a part of the territory, which had become the state of Indiana only twenty years earlier.

The idea caught the imagination of Edward Sorin, one of the seminarians. However, it was five years before Father Sorin became a priest and was able to leave the seminary and put his plan for missionary work into action. He left France in 1841 accompanied by six brothers of the Congregation of the Holy Cross. Sorin was the leader of the group.

After thirty-nine days in steerage, the little band reached the United States. Sorin's arrival in the new land was so emotional that the young priest knelt and kissed the ground. Always short of money, Sorin scrambled around New York to gather the funds he needed to continue his trip to Indiana.

After twenty-four more days of traveling by canal boat, horse and cart, and by foot, overcoming storms and fighting off robbers, the small band reached their destination near Vincennes, Indiana.

The bishop's original plan was to have Father Sorin establish a school in the remote southwest part of the state.

In a short time, the padre and the brothers had such success that they decided that they wanted to now build a college. However, there already was a college in nearby Vincennes. Deciding that he didn't want competition from the ambitious priest, the bishop offered him attractive land 250 miles away near South Bend, Indiana.

Sorin set out this time for his new destination in an ox cart accompanied by the brothers. They reached their new home in ten days. The site comprised 524 undeveloped snow-covered acres with two lakes. When they arrived, they knelt in the snow and dedicated their work to Notre Dame, Our Lady. The only shelter they found was an old log cabin, twenty-four-by-forty feet, with a ground floor that was used as a room for a priest, and the story above which was used as a chapel for the Catholics of South Bend and the neighborhood. The chapel still exists on the campus today and continues to host events such as weddings and baptisms.

Father Sorin and his companions got to work clearing the densely wooded area. In the early years of the college, some students paid their tuition through labor while helping to construct some of the first buildings on the campus.

On January 15, 1844, Sorin received his charter from the state authorizing the establishment of the University of Notre Dame du Lac. The first students came from the residents of the frontier town of South Bend and included sons of plainsman, trappers, farmers, and shopkeepers. Money was always a problem in the early years of the University. Father Sorin found several creative ways to keep his school solvent. When his students couldn't pay with dollars, he accepted grain, produce, hogs, or furniture as tuition payments.

As the population of the South Bend area grew and the reputation of the new school spread, enrollment increased. The country was growing also. With that growth came regional differences and animosity. Less than twenty years after the founding of Notre Dame, the country faced its most serious threat in its short existence with the outbreak of the Civil War in 1861. When war broke out, Notre Dame also became involved. Students and alumni joined the fighting on both sides. In addition, religious members of the Congregation of Holy Cross also volunteered for more peaceable pursuits such as chaplains and nurses.

In October 1861, the Indiana governor asked Father Sorin to provide twelve nuns to serve in field hospitals during the war. By the end of the war eighty nuns, 40 percent of the congregation's sisters, would serve as field nurses. Caring for those suffering the grievous wounds of late nineteenth century warfare was grim work for these charitable and devoted women.

In addition, seven Holy Cross priests served as chaplains in the Union Army during the war. Two of them died from yellow fever and a third was so weakened by the war that he died several years after the war ended.

The most famous of these priests was Father William Corby, who served as a chaplain with the famous Irish Brigade, which saw extensive duty during the war, from the first Battle of Bull Run in 1861 to Appomattox in 1865. During the critical battle of Gettysburg, Father Corby had his most famous moment, later commemorated by statues at both the battlefield and at Notre Dame. The soldiers of the hard-fought Irish Brigade arrived at Gettysburg on the second day of the battle after a difficult thirteen-mile march. Father Corby stood atop a large rock and gave the assembled troops general absolution as they prepared to charge the Confederate lines.

"My eye covered thousands of officers and men," he later wrote in his *Memoirs of a Chaplain Life*. "I noticed that all, Catholic and non-Catholic, officers and private soldiers, showed a profound respect, wishing to receive at this fatal crisis every benefit of divine grace . . . .. My general absolution was intended for all . . . .. Not only for the brigade, but for all, North and South, who were susceptible to it and who were about to appear before their Judge."[9]

The statue outside of Corby Hall on the campus of Notre Dame recreates this dramatic scene by showing the heroic chaplain with his right hand raised symbolizing the absolution he administered on that historic battlefield. Of course, the students at Notre Dame taking note of the raised right hand, irreverently call the statue *Fair Catch Corby*.

Corby became president of the university after the war. As such, he instituted military training at the school in 1880. By the onset of World War I, military training had become a requirement for most of Notre Dame students. After the US entry into the war, approximately 2,200 of the university's students entered the service. Forty-six were killed in action. Their names are memorialized at the *God, Country, Notre Dame* entrance to the Basilica.

World War II would see enormous sacrifices from Notre Dame graduates as well as a significant contribution to the war effort from the university itself. From their earliest days, the leaders at both West Point and Notre Dame were interested in keeping their young charges healthy and active. Controlling the exuberance of their all-male student bodies was a challenge. The development of a new sport—football—soon caught on at both schools.

CHAPTER 4

EARLY YEARS OF FOOTBALL

I shall slug (give a punishment tour to) the first Army player who leaves the field in an upright position.
—Colonel Hawkins, West Point Commandant of Cadets

GAMES WHERE ONE team tried to advance a ball or other object past an opposing team date back to early Greek and Roman times. However, it wasn't until the nineteenth century that athletic contests resembling American football emerged. It was soccer and its offspring, rugby, that laid the foundation for the development of modern football.

In 1876, Yale and Harvard began to play a rugby-like game instead of the soccer style version being played on college campuses. The Harvard-Yale version quickly caught on because it allowed players to run with the ball, an enhancement that had great appeal to the young men drawn to the game. It was a fast-moving game. Like rugby, early rules prohibited members of the team with the ball from running interference in front of the ball carrier.

Several colleges continued to experiment with many variations of the game until 1869, when Rutgers and Princeton played what effectively became the first intercollegiate football game. It was different in many respects from the game played today, but it was an important landmark because it standardized the rules. Under these rules, each team had twenty-five players. Scoring involved kicking the ball only. By 1875 the touchdown was invented, which would soon become the dominant means of scoring.

In 1876, an association of Harvard, Yale, and Columbia formed a committee that refined and formalized these early rules. As more teams joined the association, football as we know it today began to emerge. Earlier rules had specified that each team would be allowed three downs to get five yards or lose ten yards before relinquishing the ball.[10] A field goal counted five points and a touchdown four. It was not until 1909 that a touchdown was changed to six points and a field goal three. Despite these rule changes, the game still resembled rugby as momentum and mass movements of the players around the ball were still the key elements of the game. It was the emphasis on these characteristics that made the early game so dangerous.

In addition, protective equipment for the players was either inadequate or non-existent. Head gear was not required, so wearing a leather-padded helmet was optional. Players placed rubber or felt pads under their jerseys to pad their shoulders. A jersey with canvas trousers was the most common uniform, with long socks to cover the players' legs. Leather shoes with hard leather cleats were the standard footwear.[11] Since the sport was known for its ruggedness and appealed to the toughest players, many participants openly shunned the use of any protection.

After a series of highly publicized football injuries and deaths, several people throughout the country called for the permanent banning of the game. It was clear that some rule changes designed to protect the players would be needed if the game were to continue. In 1910, a committee convened to explore rule changes to minimize injuries. Earlier attempts at reform had failed to significantly reduce the dangers of the brutal early contests, so the appointment of this committee was met with skepticism.

Conflicting opinions about the need to retain the forward pass was a particularly thorny issue. Many on the committee favored eliminating passing in any form. Walter Camp, who had coached the Yale football team to a 67–2 record from 1888 to 1892, worked tirelessly to retain the forward pass and implement other rules changes instead.

On May 13, 1910, the committee announced the new rules. Henceforth, each team must have seven men on the line of scrimmage, a significant change from the previous practice of allowing players to gain momentum by starting the play several yards off the line. This significantly reduced the dangerous collision, which occurred when both teams rushed toward each other from several yards away once the ball was snapped. Additionally, interlocking interference (arms linked or hands on belts or other grips placed on uniforms) was prohibited. And, most importantly, the forward pass was preserved. However, no pass was allowed beyond twenty yards. Rules prohibiting interference on pass and kicking plays were also added.

Not everyone was pleased by these changes. Many of the coaches of college teams predicted that the new rules would either not be accepted or would result in the death of the game. An article in the *Houston Post* on September 11, 1910 predicted that, "None of the Yale sharps thinks that the new rules will live a fortnight after the playing schedule begins, and it is believed here that within a week after the college squads report for practice such a howl will go up from the players that the rules committee will issue a hurry call for a meeting and after some of the clauses of the code which are perplexing, contradictory, or impracticable (sic). That the code should exist as it stands till the close of the season seems unbelievable here."

Fortunately, some of the more thoughtful and influential coaches embraced the new changes. Coach Glen S. "Pop" Warner of the Carlisle Indian School announced that he was very pleased with the revised rules. He believed that the changes removed the necessity of having to play abnormally big men on the line thereby giving smaller squads who had trouble recruiting larger players a better chance to develop strong teams.

It was a dynamic time for college football, as many college teams were developing their own versions of the game while trying to adapt to the frequent variations promulgated by regional and national rules committees.

Surprisingly, football arrived late at West Point. It wasn't until 1890, twenty-one years after the birth of college football, that the spark was lit. Part of the reason for the late arrival was that cadets had a full schedule preparing for their future assignments as officers in the US Army. Horsemanship, fencing, boxing, and wrestling gave the Corps of Cadets all the physical training they needed. At least that's what the academy's leadership believed.

The initial tentative step establishing football at West Point was nurtured and developed by the efforts of Dennis Mahan Michie, a cadet. Michie was the son of Peter Michie, class of 1863, who was professor of philosophy at the academy and a veteran of the Civil War.

Young Michie had played football at Lawrenceville Prep School in New Jersey and was interested in starting a team at West Point. An avid reader, he had been following the development of the game at other colleges through the newspapers. While on leave, he ran into a friend of his from his prep school days who now attended the US Naval Academy. The two young men concocted a plan to circumvent the official chain of command at both academies by having the midshipmen issue a football challenge to the cadets. A letter soon arrived at West Point from Annapolis formally requesting a game between the two institutions.

After a short discussion, and with the support of Michie's father, superintendent Colonel John Wilson accepted the challenge. Realism soon intruded on the enthusiasm of young Michie and his prospective teammates, however. Navy had been playing football for eight years. During their most recent season in 1889, they had lost only one game.

Nonetheless, the *Sons of Slum and Gravy* as these cadets called themselves, embarked on an aggressive program to get ready for the big game scheduled for November 29, 1890. However, the preparation had to be conducted only when it didn't conflict with the already full military and academic schedule of the cadets.

Dennis Michie was both coach and trainer. The only time he could use to get his team ready was on Saturday afternoons when bad weather canceled the dress parade. This only gave him two-and-a-half hours to condition his players and teach them the fundamentals of the game.

His team members also got up a half hour before reveille every day "for a run around the Plain, down and back Flirtation Walk, over past Thayer Hall, around the supe's headquarters and then back to the barracks in time for reveille."[12]

The players had to buy their own uniforms, which consisted of white-laced canvas jackets and white breeches, black woolen stockings, and a black woolen cap with a dash of orange to it. The Corps of Cadets even had to put up half the money for Navy's $275 travel expenses by authorizing a charge of fifty-two cents to be made against each cadet's store account.[13]

As the big day approached the excitement built, especially among the military communities. A special rail car was reserved for officers and midshipmen from Annapolis. A large party of officers from the Navy yard in Philadelphia and the north Atlantic squadron joined them. The fans from West Point were augmented by a train load of Army fans from numerous bases along the Atlantic coast.

On game day, the sun was shining brightly. The Navy team took a train up from New York and then was ferried across the Hudson to the grounds of the Military Academy. "On their way up the hill, they took a goat from the yard of a non-com for a mascot."[14]

Hospitality was the order of the day for this rivalry between the services. A luncheon in the officers' club was provided for both the visiting Army brass and their counterparts in the Navy. This was followed by a musical performance by the West Point band before the assemblage moved toward the playing field.

As the fans made their way into the stands, Navy and Army uniforms were on full display. Gold braid and shoulder straps were in abundance. The crowd numbered about a thousand. Only women had seats, which had been borrowed from nearby classrooms.

Lest there be any doubt about the importance of the game, the West Point Commandant of Cadets, Colonel Hawkins gave the Army players a very short pep talk. "I shall slug (give a punishment tour to) the first Army player who leaves the field in an upright position."[15]

From the opening kickoff it was clear that Navy's experience, developed over the preceding eight years of playing the game, would overpower the enthusiasm of the rookie Army team. The well drilled Middies' signals also befuddled the landlubbers from Army. Red Emerich, the captain and star of the Navy team, shouted out the nautical commands. "Splice the main brace," when the ball carrier plunged over center. "Tack ship," he roared, and a halfback zoomed around right end. "Wear ship," he called out as and he went slicing in the opposite direction. "Anchors in sight," "Veer chains," "Reef topsails," and "Savez the bobstay" were other Navy signals.[16]

The Army responded with its own drill commands. "Front into line, gallop, march! In battery heave! As skirmishers, march!"[17]

It was a brutal contest. Some in the crowd sarcastically could see some unintended benefits. "If this game could only be introduced in the Army," said an officer after a particularly lively scrimmage in which four men were laid out. "Promotions would not be so slow. It's quicker than old age and seems to be more fatal."[18] When it was over, the visitors from Annapolis celebrated a clear and resounding victory over the novice Army team, 24–0.

The day after the defeat, Michie and his teammates began to prepare for a rematch. They recruited a former Yale star, Harry L. Williams, who was teaching at a nearby school, to coach the fledgling Army team. Hard work and Williams's coaching paid off the next year when the Cadets of West Point traveled to Annapolis and administered a convincing defeat on the Middies, 32–10.

It was clear that the Army-Navy rivalry had become a popular activity, not only for the cadets and the middies, but also for members of both services and the country. From the outset, passions about the annual game were strong between the services. A particularly nasty display of those passions caused a brief interruption in the series from 1894 until 1899, when a near riot erupted in the Army-Navy club in New York City after an admiral and a general engaged in an overly intense argument after the 1893 game. Although he didn't live to see it, it soon became clear that the efforts of Cadet Dennis Mahan Michie would have a long-lasting impact on both West Point and college football.

After graduation from the academy in 1892, Michie remained at West Point and coached Army to a 3–1–1 record. He was killed at the Battle of San Juan Hill on July 1, 1898, during the Spanish American War. He was the first in a long line of Army football players who made the ultimate sacrifice for the country. Their commitment to the nation and their reputation as warriors is celebrated still today by a quote from General George Marshall. "I want an officer for a secret and dangerous mission. I want a West Point football player."

The football stadium at the US Military Academy, completed in 1924, is fittingly named after the *Father of Army Football*, Dennis Mahan Michie.

College football arrived at Notre Dame in the form of a visiting Michigan squad on November 23, 1887. The game played that day was not even a shadow of a whisper of the hard-fought and thrilling games the two teams would play in years to come. Actually, it wasn't truly a game at all in the competitive sense that would characterize Notre Dame football from that point forward. Notre Dame students had been experimenting with intramural soccer-style football before the arrival of the Wolverines.[19]

According to *The Scholastic*, the campus newspaper, "The home team has been organized only a few weeks and the Michigan boys, the champions of the West, came more to instruct them in the points of the Rugby game than to win fresh laurels. At first, to render our players more familiar with the game, the teams were chosen irrespective of college." After a short scrimmage, the players were reorganized by the school they attended.

The Scholastic's description of the game continued. "On account of time, part of only one inning was played, and resulted in the score of 8–0 in favor of the visitors. The game was interesting and, notwithstanding the slippery condition of the ground, the Ann Arbor boys gave a fine exhibition of skillful playing." *The Scholastic* continued with perhaps the most understated hopeful prediction ever made about sports. "The occasion has started an enthusiastic football boom and it is hoped that coming years will witness a series of these contests."

The two teams played two more games the following spring. Notre Dame lost both games. Finally, on December 6, 1888, Notre Dame claimed its first of many future victories by defeating the Harvard school of Chicago (no relation to the New England Harvard) 20–0.

The team's first away game was played at Northwestern, a hundred miles from the Notre Dame campus in 1889. According to Notre Dame lore, it was at this game that the team got its nickname, *Fighting Irish*. Frank Fehr, the team's center at the time, recalled the circumstances. "We were leading Northwestern 5–0 at the half only to hear the Northwestern fans chanting 'Kill the Fighting Irish. Kill the Fighting Irish' as the second forty-five-minute half opened. From that time on, the name stayed with Notre Dame athletic teams. Funny thing about it—we had only two Irishman on the squad. We never had over two Irishman on the team at the same time the first three years we played."[20] This nickname would not become permanent until much later. For many years the Notre Dame team would be known as the Ramblers because of the difficulty they had in securing a permanent place in a conference.

These were years when football schedules were beginning to morph from games arranged between coaches to a more structured system that established conferences. In 1896, Northwestern joined eight other schools to form the Western Conference. Notre Dame played some of them when their schedules permitted. When Michigan withdrew from the conference in 1905, Notre Dame applied to replace them. The Irish were told by conference officials that they were too small. The implication was that they couldn't measure up to the other teams in drawing power.

Several subtle factors were underway that would propel the Fighting Irish to national prominence. The first was that Notre Dame had, from its beginning, drawn students from all sections of the country. This was important for two reasons, which still exist today. As football grew in popularity across the country, Notre Dame had a broader field from which it could recruit. Also, as one of the preeminent Catholic universities in the nation, it held a further attraction for many young Catholic men. Then as now, many Catholics across the country found the allure of attending and playing for one of the premier institutions of their faith very attractive. It was an especially attractive option for these young men since many sections of the country were still hostile to Catholics.

As Notre Dame students returned to their towns and cities, they brought with them an admiration of both the university and their fledgling football team, planting the seeds of what would become a national following.

Another important factor helped to elevate the Notre Dame football to national prominence. Until 1896 Notre Dame had a series of part-time coaches not well-versed in the key attributes of the game. The program drifted without purpose under these untalented mentors. Although Notre Dame had winning seasons in 1894 and 1895, it was against teams such as Illinois Cycling Club, Indianapolis Artillery, Chicago Physical and Surgical, Northwestern Law, and Rush Medical, a schedule clearly not designed to attract favorable attention from some of the football programs Notre Dame hoped to play.[21]

In 1896, the university hired the first of a series of coaches that would change the trajectory of Notre Dame football. The first of these was Francis B. Hering. When he arrived in South Bend, Hering brought with him a wealth of football knowledge and experience that had heretofore been missing in the fledgling program. Called by many the Father of Notre Dame football, Hering had earned letters under Amos Alonzo Stagg at Chicago University and had coached at Bucknell. These credentials permitted him to take over all aspects of the Notre Dame football program his first year. He was coach, captain, and quarterback of the 1896 team, a clear indication that the eligibility rules of the time were not yet clearly defined nor followed.

Hering was a poet, orator, and magazine writer, but his impact on the football program is the contribution for which he is rightfully remembered. He strengthened the schedule by adding teams such as Chicago University, Purdue, DePauw, Michigan State, Illinois, Michigan, and Indiana. Although his tenure was short, in three years Hering's teams compiled a record of 12–6–1, including wins over Michigan State, DePauw, and Illinois. [22]

Under the leadership of several coaches who followed Hering, the *Fighting Irish* entered the turn of the century as a team to be reckoned with. From 1900 to 1903, Notre Dame compiled a record of 28–6–4, including an undefeated, once-tied season in 1903.

In 1909, the Irish strengthened their schedule further by adding Pittsburgh and Miami of Ohio, which they defeated that season. They also defeated powerhouse and undefeated Michigan that year by a score of 11–3. That game resulted in a feud, which caused the two teams to break off athletic relations for more than thirty years. It was not until 1942 that the football teams played again. The feud stemmed from accusations from Coach Yost of Michigan that Notre Dame had used ineligible players in the game. During those years, player eligibility was ill-defined and was applied unevenly by many teams.

Knute Rockne, as a player at Notre Dame, described the eligibility environment he encountered when he first became involved in college football in 1910. "I had sat at the foot of a learned tramp athlete whose name then was Foley, although he had played for many schools under many aliases. He was typical of young men who roam the country, overflowing with college spirit, regardless of the college. His tongue teemed with professional jargon. He opened my eyes to a state of affairs in college football which has since been reformed—of the journeyman players who leave new names behind them wherever they went and live to a ripe, old age, from foot to mouth, so to speak, taking loyalty and sometimes talent with them to whichever Alma Mater would give them the best break."[23]

Nonetheless, football at Notre Dame continued to grow and flourish in the early years of the twentieth century. Enthusiasm for the game on the Notre Dame campus was greatly enhanced in 1908 when brothers Michael and John Shea wrote the "Notre Dame Victory March." Its words inspire its fans to:

Cheer, cheer for old Notre Dame,
Wake up the echoes cheering her name,
Send a volley cheer on high,
Shake down the thunder from the sky.
What though the odds be great or small
Old Notre Dame will win overall,
While her loyal sons and daughters
March on to victory."

The march is one of the country's most well-known of all college fight songs. "In fact, so many Americans can recognize 'The Notre Dame Victory March' that it is considered one of the nation's four best known songs—along with "The Star-Spangled Banner," "God Bless America," and "White Christmas."[24]

As the team's exploits and reputation grew, it became clear that

Notre Dame's aspirations were bigger than the regional arena in which they played. Several events were underway that would set the stage for the birth of one of the great rivalries in college football.

By the early 1900s college football was facing a critical crossroad. The sport was becoming increasingly popular with a fan base that was growing exponentially. However, the significant number of injuries and deaths occurring during games was shocking and unacceptable to many of the college administrators of the participating schools. The 1905 season had been one of the deadliest in the sports' short history. Nineteen players had died from injuries sustained in the game, triggering committees to establish rules for safety.

Initially, passing was frowned upon. Passes had to be thrown outside a box five yards wide on either side of the center and no longer than twenty yards. Passes had to be completed in the field of play so no pass could be thrown into the end zone. If a pass was not touched by either team, the passing team lost possession of the ball, regardless of the down. These early revisions penalizing use of the pass discouraged many coaches from incorporating an aerial strategy into their game plan.

As these rules continued to change and evolve, so did the coaches, at least some of them. Some coaches weighed the risks of passing and rejected its use in favor of their previously successful ground game. Others, such as Amos Alonzo Stagg, John Heisman, and Pop Warner, embraced the new rules and creatively adjusted their offensive and defensive strategies. This rapidly changing and fluid environment would favor the bold.

CHAPTER 5

THE RIVALRY BEGINS

At the moment when I touched the ball, life for me was complete.
—Knute Rockne

HISTORY IS REPLETE with many incidental events which turn out to have significant consequences. This is true in international affairs as well as in our personal lives. It was also true of the seemingly haphazard events that led to the pairing of the Army and Notre Dame football teams in 1913. No one at the time could imagine that this initial game would become the cornerstone of one of the most exciting rivalries in college football.

Just prior to the 1913 football season, Notre Dame hired Jesse Harper as athletic director and coach of its football team. Harper was a graduate of the University of Chicago where he played both football and baseball under Coach Amos Alonzo Stagg. Following his graduation from The University of Chicago, he took a job selling map books. In 1906 Harper became the athletic director of tiny Alma College in Alma, Michigan about fifty miles northeast of Grand Rapids. He remained there for three years achieving some success by guiding the baseball team to a championship in Michigan, while also defeating the University of Michigan baseball team.

He then moved to Wabash College in Indiana where he coached baseball, football, basketball, and track. In his four years at Wabash, Harper came to the attention of several schools, including Notre Dame, because of his success as a coach. While at Wabash he defeated Purdue three of his four years and gave the Irish a scare, losing to them only by a score of 6–3. The hard-fought game must have had an impact on the Notre Dame administration since they hired him soon after. Hiring a coach that was successful against the Irish was a formula they would use again. Ara Parseghian, while at Northwestern, defeated Notre Dame four years in a row before becoming head coach at Notre Dame.

There are two versions of how that fateful first meeting between the Army and Notre Dame football teams came about. Both revolve around Jesse Harper, the new coach. One version from Francis Wallace who wrote the book, *Notre Dame from Rockne to Parseghian*, attributes the initiative for the game to Coach Harper shortly after he arrived at Notre Dame. One of Harper's first tasks was to beef up the schedule and broaden Notre Dame's exposure beyond the Midwest. "I was looking for games, he told me (Wallace, the author), when I sat down and wrote a few letters. He got answers from Army, Penn State, and Texas." This version is supported by the fact that both Army and Texas were added to the schedule for 1913.

Jim Beach and Daniel Moore in their book, *The Big Game*, detailing every Army-Notre Dame game from 1913 to 1947, report a different version. They wrote that before the 1912 Army-Yale game both coaches mutually agreed to discontinue the series because the annual game between their teams took too much out of the players. The Army team, therefore, found itself with an open date on November 1, 1913. Harold Loomis, the cadet football manager wrote a number of letters to Eastern colleges trying to fill the slot.

"Those that answered said that they were filled. Then he wrote to every college he could think of. Into the spring he still had no game, and at last, he got a bite from Notre Dame, a letter signed by Jesse Harper, who had been hired as the new head coach but was still at Wabash College in Crawfordsville, Indiana."[25]

Regardless of the origin of the invitation, the first momentous meeting of the two teams was scheduled for November 1, 1913.

Army was coached by Lieutenant Charlie Daly. Daly had been a star when he played first at Harvard and then at Army, where he had been an all-American. He graduated from West Point in 1905 and served as an officer for one year before resigning his commission. Before returning there as coach, he had served as assistant to coach Percy Haughton at Harvard and had been appointed fire commissioner of Boston. In March 1913, Daly requested that he be reappointed to the Army so that he could coach the Cadets. Under his leadership, Army was enjoying an undefeated season prior to meeting the Irish.

Contrary to common myth today, the Army team of 1913 was very familiar with the forward pass. Their passing offense was rated the best in the East. Only two weeks prior to the Notre Dame game, they had barely defeated Colgate "using a series of clever forward pass plays."[26] Four weeks after they played Notre Dame, Army defeated Navy at the Polo Grounds 22–9. A newspaper at the time highlighted the skill of Army's passing game. "The repeated ease of the forward pass by the Cadets opened up the play to a far greater extent than the more conservative line attack and runs of the Middies, thus furnishing the spectators with many brilliant football pictures and the Army vehicle of victory."

There's no doubt that playing in the East against such a well-known team as Army was a significant step for the Notre Dame football program. The Irish made sure they would be ready. Gus Dorais, the five-foot-seven-inch, 145-pound quarterback, and Knute Rockne, the Notre Dame end, had roomed and worked together in 1911 and 1912. During the summer of 1913 they both worked at Cedar Point amusement park in Ohio.

Dorais explained their summer workout. "That summer of 1913 at Cedar Point, Rock and I practiced more than we had ever practiced before. Rock perfected his method of catching passes without tension in his fingers, wrists, or arms and with the hands giving with the ball just as a baseball should be caught."[27]

"Perfection of the forward pass came to us only through daily tedious practice," Rockne once said. "I'd run along the beach, Dorais would throw from all angles. People who didn't know we were two college seniors making painstaking preparations for our final season probably thought we were crazy. Once a bearded old gentleman took off his shoes to get in on the fun, seizing the ball and kicking it merrily with bare feet, too, until a friendly keeper came along to take him back to where he belonged."[28]

Bonnie Skiles, a waitress in Cedar Point's Grill Room, was more interested in the fleet young catcher of the passes than she was in the innovative football being demonstrated on the beach. A romance soon developed between Bonnie and Knute that resulted in marriage some years later with quarterback Dorais as best man.

Two changes helped to make the Notre Dame passing attack so effective. "In 1910 there were two accepted methods of throwing the forward pass. One was to lay the ball flat and sail it with an underhand motion giving it a spin; the other was to hook the hand over the end of the ball and give it a discus hurl through the air, wobbling it endwise."[29]

Dorais was a baseball player, so at first, he threw the football like he threw a baseball. In addition, further rule changes in 1912 altered the ball specifications to allow a slightly longer and slimmer model that was easier to throw.[30] After many hours of practice, he was able to refine his throwing to adapt to the size and shape of the football. If you watch old films of Dorais throwing the football, you can see that he still imparted a side-arm cast to the ball.

Almost fifty years later, American football would introduce a version of the forward pass to English Rugby. In 1958, Pete Dawkins, Army's all-American halfback amazed the rugby world by using a "torpedo throw-in" during a scrum when he was a student at Oxford.

Several days before the inaugural Army-Notre Dame matchup, eighteen players, a team manager, and coach Harper, boarded the train for the trip east to West Point, New York. To save money, they took an all-day commuter coach to Buffalo where they then switched to sleeping-car accommodations. Each player carried his own uniform and equipment. The Notre Dame commissary had made sandwiches for the team to eat on the trip.

When they arrived at West Point, they were greeted cordially and treated with great hospitality. They ate in the mess hall with the cadets and slept in Cullum Hall, an elegant building used for social events.

At game time, the Notre Dame team had only a short walk from their lodging in Cullum Hall to the field right outside the building. Army's Michie Stadium would not be built until 1924. The crowd of 5,000 non-paying fans had gathered in the bleachers to witness the contest between Army and the little-known team from the Midwest.

Both teams were unsure of what to expect. Although not overly confident, the Army team expected the game to be a breather, certainly not as challenging as playing Yale, the team that Notre Dame had replaced on the schedule. To get a better picture of the Irish capabilities, Coach Daly of Army had sent one of his former teammates, Captain Tom Hammond, to South Bend the week prior to the Army game to scout out the Midwesterners. Notre Dame was scheduled to play Alma College, one of Coach Harper's previous employers.

What he saw was a convincing 62–0 Irish win. Notre Dame scored four touchdowns on short passes. However, most of the scoring came from running plays. The lopsided game with Alma did not require the Irish to utilize the more open style of play they would employ against Army. Because of that, Captain Hammond became convinced that the ferocious line play on both sides of the ball and a strong running game were the Irish strengths. Therefore, Army prepared a defense against power plays and prepared their own offense on what they considered their superior strength of blasting a path through opponents with the surging force of the wedge.[31]

Captain Hammond's scouting report convinced the Army coaching staff that the Irish wouldn't be a pushover. They also believed that the visitors had a squad of big men. In fact, the Army team outweighed their opponents by fifteen pounds per man.

There was a philosophical difference between the coaches that would turn out to be a significant factor in the game. Many sports fans today believe that the forward pass was introduced during the 1913 Army-Notre Dame game. That belief stemmed chiefly from fictionalized versions of the game. The movie, *Knute Rockne, All American*, was a major contributor to this misconception. The forward pass had been legalized by the rules changes of 1906 and had been further strengthened by a liberalization of the rule in 1913 when the restriction on passes beyond twenty yards was removed. In 1913, coaches were still trying to develop strategies that would effectively incorporate these evolving rules.

Strategically, most coaches, including Coach Daly, believed that the forward pass was a desperation play. Therefore, the Army coach was cautious in his instructions to his quarterbacks. "You may use it at the last minute or two of the first half when deep in your opponent's territory. The forward pass is a hazardous weapon and must be used sparingly."[32]

Tactically, there was also a major difference between the two teams on how the pass was executed. Army passers threw into a zone expecting the receiver to arrive at the correct spot at the right time to catch the ball. Notre Dame took a more open approach. Their passers threw the ball leading the receiver so that he caught it in full stride. Although the Irish assuredly had pass patterns, their air attack was more fluid and more difficult to defend against in the still evolving pass environmental 1913. These differences, both strategic and tactical, would have an enormous impact on the outcome of the game and more broadly on the way college football was played.

For their part, Notre Dame expected a tough game from one of the preeminent teams in the East. At that time Eastern football was considered the strongest in the country. The game would show whether Notre Dame, who was now one of the powerhouses of the Midwest could measure up.

The issue was about to be decided convincingly on that crisp November day near the Hudson River. The team captains, Hoge of Army and Rockne of Notre Dame, met at midfield and shook hands. Notre Dame won the toss and elected to receive. After the kickoff and a short return, the Irish got to work. A combination of Army's hard hitting and early Irish jitters caused Irish quarterback Dorais to fumble on the third play.

Army recovered the ball, but surprisingly was unable to gain a first down. If they hadn't sensed it before, this early stop of the powerful Army backfield must have told the Cadets that this game would not be the breather they had hoped for. After an exchange of punts and another Dorais fumble, the game began to look like it would be a defensive struggle. However, the physical style of Army appeared to be taking its toll on the Irish eleven.

Rockne picked up the narrative of what happened next. "Our attack had been well rehearsed. After one fierce scrimmage, I emerged limping as if hurt. On the next three plays Dorais threw three successful passes in a row to Pliska, our right halfback, for short gains. On each of these three plays I limped down the field acting as if the farthest thing from my mind was to receive a forward pass. After the third play the Army halfback covering me figured I wasn't worth watching. Even as a decoy he figured I was harmless. Finally, Dorais called my number, meaning that he was to throw a long forward pass to me as I ran down the field and out toward the sidelines. I started limping down the field, and the Army halfback covering me almost yawned in my face, he was that bored.

"Suddenly, I put on full speed and left him standing there flat-footed. I raced across the Army goal line as Dorais whipped the ball and the grandstands roared at the completion of the forty-yard pass. Everybody seemed astonished. There had been no hurdling, no tackling, no plunging, no crushing of fiber and sinew. Just a long-distance touchdown by rapid transit. At the moment when I touched the ball, life for me was complete. We proceeded to make it more than complete."[33]

Army fought back. A series of punishing plunges into and through the Notre Dame line plus a pass from Army quarterback Vernon Prichard moved the ball to the Irish fifteen-yard line. It took a few more smashing plays from Army's halfbacks before cadet fullback Hodgson plunged over the line for Army's first score. A missed extra point made the score 7–6 in Notre Dame's favor midway through the first half.

After another Irish fumble, the Army team resumed its relentless pressure on the Notre Dame defense. Two Prichard passes and strong halfback plunges brought the ball to the Midwesterners three-yard line. A holding call against the Irish on the next play took the ball to the six-inch line. It was first and goal, Army.

The Cadets tried three battering runs into the line but were stopped cold. On fourth down, Army quarterback Prichard faked a lateral spreading the Notre Dame defense, and on a delayed buck he scored. After a successful kick, army led 13–7.

After the ensuing kickoff, Notre Dame unleashed its passing attack with short passes to halfback Pliska and longer passes to end Rockne, allowing the Irish to move the ball eighty yards in four plays. With the Army team spread out to defend against the pass, halfback Pliska again plunged through the line for a touchdown. The half ended with Notre Dame leading 14–13.

Coach Daly was one of the more analytical and thoughtful coaches of his day. He was certain to counter the strong Notre Dame passing game. At the start of the second half, the Army team adjusted by using an improvised floating defense anticipating Notre Dame's more aggressive use of the pass. The Cadets moved their ends wide to line up with the Notre Dame flankers. Their defensive backfield drifted with the eligible receivers when they crossed the line of scrimmage.

For a short time, this new defense stopped the Irish.

On Army's first possession they moved the ball to the Notre Dame two-yard line. During the drive, Irish ends Rockne and Gus Hearst protected the flanks, forcing the West Point's backs to batter and bulldoze their way through the center of the line, a style of play they had relied upon.

The biased crowd, sensing a score, was on its feet encouraging the Army to punch it in and take the lead. However, the Notre Dame line stiffened and stopped two rushes. On third down, quarterback Prichard of Army dropped back with perfect protection and lobbed the ball to one of his favorite targets, end Lou Merillat, standing in the end zone. At the very last minute, Notre Dame's feisty quarterback, Gus Dorais, leaped through the air and intercepted the ball.

Notre Dame went on to score three touchdowns through the air in the fourth quarter. When Army spread its defense to cope with the aerial attack, Notre Dame fullback Ray Eichenlaub shredded the cadet line. After the game, the Army linemen felt that it was Eichenlaub's brutal fullback plunges that had caused the most damage to the Cadets by preventing them from concentrating on Notre Dame's passing attack. When the final gun sounded, the score was Notre Dame 35, Army 13. One of the Cadets who sat on the bench and did not get into the game was an injured junior, Dwight D. Eisenhower.

In addition to the game being a significant win for the Notre Dame program, it was also a financial success. The Army Athletic Association had agreed to pay the Irish $1,000 for their appearance. When all costs related to the trip were tallied, the total amounted to $845.50 for all twenty members of the travel team, leaving a profit of $154.50. That's in contrast to the $38 million budget of the 2019 Notre Dame football program.

Despite the hard-fought game, relations between the two teams remained cordial, a fitting start to what would become one of the great rivalries in college sports. After the game, both programs exchanged complimentary letters. Coach Harper thanked the cadets for their hospitality. "The boys appreciated immensely everything you did and have worlds of praise for the Army students and officers. I sincerely hope that none of your men was severely injured in the game Saturday. You can rest assured that all the Notre Dame football men, students, and faculty will be pulling hard for the Army when they play the Navy. When you get ready to arrange your schedule for next year, I'll be glad to take the matter up if you wish to have a game with us again."

The reply from West Point was equally gracious. "Your team made the most favorable impression on the officers and cadets here. And while defeat is of course bitter, still when the winning team is as good as yours and when the members are such thorough good sports and gentlemen as the Notre Dame team showed truly to be, some of the sting of defeat disappears. Hoping that we may have the pleasure of seeing you next year."[34]

It was obvious at the end of the game that a new era of football had been ushered in. The feature of the game that most amazed the sports fans in the East was the length of Dorais' passes. Some of the spiral throws traveled thirty-five to forty yards to the receiver, an unheard-of distance in those days.[35]

One of the most astute observers of the game realized that a sea change in college football was about to take place. "Bill Roper, the former head coach at Princeton who was one of the officials at the game, said that he knew such play was possible under the new existing rules but that he had never seen the forward pass developed to such a state of perfection."[36]

Others also sensed the shift. Football men in the Eastern press marveled at such a concept. "The Westerners flashed the most sensational football ever seen in the east," the *New York Times* reported the next day.[37]

Notre Dame did indeed return to West Point for a rematch in 1914. However, in the intervening year between the monumental Irish upset of Army and the second game of the series, much had changed in the world and at the schools of the two competitors. Several months earlier, the archduke of the Austro-Hungarian Empire had been assassinated, precipitating a cataclysmic war in Europe that ultimately became World War I.

Because of the national defense focus of the Military Academy, the Corps of Cadets paid keen attention to the events unfolding in Europe. Notre Dame was initially more detached from the horrific conflict then in progress. However, each institution would ultimately see many of its sons make the ultimate sacrifice before peace returned in 1918. Thirty-two West Pointers would be killed while forty-six Notre Dame graduates lost their lives.

On a less dramatic level, the teams lining up to play again at West Point on November 7, 1914, were substantially different from a year earlier. Most significantly, both Dorais and Rockne had graduated. Rockne was now an assistant to Coach Harper. Eichenlaub, the huge Notre Dame fullback, was injured and would see only limited action.

Most of the previous year's Army team had returned and was looking forward eagerly to the rematch. In addition, over two hundred members of the six-hundred-man Corps of Cadets had turned out for try outs before the season started. The cadet team was also bolstered by transfers from other schools. West Point recruited players who had exhausted their eligibility at other colleges and gave them three more years of varsity play. Academy officials said they needed the extra time to train officers to fight in wars. For example, halfback Elmer Oliphant, a stocky blond transfer, played three years at Purdue before graduating in 1914. He was a two-time, first-team all-American at West Point in 1916–1917, and entered the College Football Hall of Fame in 1955.[38]

Army's recruiting practices, which added Oliphant to the Army roster, finally grated on the Naval Academy so badly that in 1928 and 1929 Navy refused to play Army. It wasn't until 1937 that Army changed its eligibility code to meet that of Navy. Major General William D. Connor, superintendent of West Point, announced the change on December 7, 1937. "Hereafter the eligibility rules which are obtained at Annapolis and in the leading civilian colleges in the country, will be applied in determining that eligibility of cadets to play up on the athletic teams of the Military Academy." [39] The change meant that Army players were limited to a total of three years eligibility, including play at other schools before attendance at West Point, a rule that would be tested again in a future war.

While at the Military Academy, Oliphant had an unsurpassed athletic career. He was West Point's first four letter man, excelling in football, basketball, baseball, and track. He was the clean-up hitter on the baseball team, alternating with Omar Bradley in his first year. He was also heavyweight boxing champion of the Corps.

Omar Bradley, Oliphant's classmate, was also a standout on the football team. Bradley, a senior substitute who played center, was key to forcing the Irish to run many plays to the outside in the 1914 matchup.

Because of the loss of Dorais and Rockne, Notre Dame's passing game was less effective than the preceding year. Army had also learned to use their own passing offense more effectively while thwarting the Irish aerial attack. Testimonies to Army's effective adoption of the passing game came from an unexpected source. Coach Harper of Notre Dame loved to tell the following story of an incident that occurred many years later. "I was out on the West Coast and was introduced to a Naval submarine commander. As soon as he heard my name, he started cussing. 'You!' he yelled. 'I've been looking for you for a long time. I'm Babe Brown and I was captain of the 1913 Navy team that lost to the Army. And it was your fault, because you're the one who showed 'em how to use those passes." Army, it seemed, had taken all the pass plays out of the Notre Dame book to upset Navy later that year.[40]

The 1914 game was anti-climactic. Army won 20–7 and went on to have an undefeated season and was named by the NCAA as one of three national college football champions for 1914.

By 1917 the war was having a significant impact on the rivalry. Captain Charlie Daly, the coach of Army, was called to active duty. Both the senior and the junior classes at West Point were graduated early to provide officers for the rapidly growing American Army. By August half the Corps of Cadets had left West Point and had assumed their officer duties. Because of these demands, Captain Jeff Keyes, who replaced Coach Daly, had only four returning lettermen.

Notre Dame was also affected by the war. Ten varsity football players enlisted. Enrollment was down 35 percent. Nonetheless, the Irish won a tough defensive struggle with Army that year by a score of 7–2. Coach Harper resigned his job as coach of the Irish at the end of the 1917 season to become partner of a cattle ranch in Kansas.

After a year lapse due to the war, the series was renewed in 1919. Coach Daly had returned to the Army team after his war duties. Because of the commissioning of the classes that had graduated early, West Point did not try to reincorporate these officers back into the ranks of cadets. Only the former cadets of one of the abbreviated classes returned to West Point for a short time to finish their education. The impact of these wartime changes deprived the Army team of the large pool of cadets who had previously provided the manpower for the football team.

Mac McQuarrie, one of the few seasoned Army players, was ill. End, Earl "Red" Blaik, another key starter, had influenza, a deadly disease that year, and would also not be able to play. McQuarrie did play but soon would fade from Army-Notre Dame lore. However, Blaik would return to the series in a different role and would rise to prominence in the years to come.

The year 1919 would mark the first time that a Rockne-coached team would face Army. It would be the start of an intense rivalry with the Cadets. Rockne had become head coach the year before when the Army-Notre Dame series had been interrupted by World War I. The two teams did not meet in 1918. When he became head coach Rockne teamed up with his old quarterback, Gus Dorais, to develop a wide-open, fast offense. His debut in 1918 was not bad considering the impact the war had on his ability to retain players, many of whom had flocked to enlist. In Rockne's first year the Irish won three, tied two and lost only one game.

CHAPTER 6

THE ROCKNE YEARS

If we ever get in another war, it will be good to have those fellows on our side.
—Knute Rockne

WHEN THE SERIES resumed in 1919, Notre Dame was strengthened by returning doughboys. "These are the men Rockne later gave credit for making him a good coach, because they were mature and couldn't be fooled with half-cocked rah-rah hokum that might've worked with younger boys." [41] It was a scenario that would be repeated twenty-seven years later in 1946 when the return of tough veterans from war-time service reinforced an Irish team.

Two names that would figure prominently in Notre Dame football lore took center stage during that year. Knute Rockne would guide the Irish to a 12–9 victory in his first game as head coach against the Army. The Cadets also got to renew their acquaintance with George Gipp, a talented athlete who became Rockne's first all-American and would become an icon in Irish mythology. Army fans and coaches remembered well the trouble the *Gipper* had caused them in the 1917 loss to Notre Dame.

In the 1919 game, Gipp scored one of the Irish's two touchdowns and completed several passes that were key to Notre Dame's only other score, which was enough to squeak by the Cadets. The following year in the 1920 game, it was Gipp again vexing the Army team. He gained 124 yards from scrimmage, threw passes for ninety-six yards, ran back kick-offs for 112 yards, and kicked three points after touchdowns, all of which helped to lead the Irish to a 27–17 victory. Newspapers around the country hailed his football prowess. It was, therefore, a great shock six weeks later when George Gipp died. Pneumonia and streptococcus, before the advent of penicillin and other antibacterial drugs, greatly weakened the star athlete. Many of his fellow Notre Dame students knelt in the snow outside the hospital praying for his recovery. His physical recovery didn't happen, but a spiritual recovery became an important part of Notre Dame lore.

After a 28–0 Notre Dame romp over Army in 1921, the teams played their last game on Cullum Hall Field at West Point on November 11, 1922. The Notre Dame team that returned to the field at West Point that year boasted a 6–0 record having already defeated smaller rivals Kalamazoo, St. Louis, and DePauw as well as football powerhouse rivals Purdue, Georgia Tech, and Indiana. The Irish opponents in those six games were only able to score a total of ten points against the strong Notre Dame defense.

Army seemed to be a good match for the visitors in 1922. The Cadets had five wins and one tie against powerhouse Yale and gave up only thirteen points against their opponents. It was clear that Army athletics was, at last, benefiting from the changes and emphasis that the young superintendent of the Military Academy, Douglas MacArthur, had implemented several years earlier.

After a hard-fought defensive struggle, the game ended in a tie, the first of the series. The 0–0 tie was a fitting end to the contests, which had been played exclusively at Cullum field since the inception of the series in 1913. The growth of the *subway alumni* in New York City, combined with the general post-WWI increased interest in college football, had made the annual Notre Dame visit a very popular event. By the early twenties, it was clear that the interest in the rivalry between the two teams had grown enormously from that first game in 1913 and had gained national attention.

During this period a little known and interesting side note occurred illustrating the continuous intertwining of the two schools and their football programs. Coach Daly of Army was discouraged by the poor performance of his teams in the three preceding years since he had reassumed duties as head coach at West Point. Daly had coached the Cadets earlier from 1913 to 1916 with great success. Although he had presided over the famous Notre Dame loss in their first meeting in 1913, Daly won two of the next three contests against the Irish. He also defeated Navy all four years in his first stint as West Point's coach. His overall record during this period was 31–4–1, with two undefeated seasons and two national titles. However, WWI temporarily ended his coaching career when he was called to active service.

Following the war, he returned to the Military Academy as head coach in 1919. This second stint as coach was not nearly as successful. His teams in 1919, 1920, and 1921 had a 19–9 overall record and lost to archrivals Notre Dame and Navy all three years. Daly was so discouraged by this poor performance that he submitted his resignation to Superintendent MacArthur at the end of the 1921 season. Daly, like all Army football coaches at the time, was an Army officer on temporary duty at the Military Academy. Having spent seven of the last nine years at West Point, he felt that it was time for him to return to his Army duties.

MacArthur discussed the resignation with his staff and suggested that an offer be made to Knute Rockne to take the head coaching job at Army. Apparently, the possibility of recruiting the Notre Dame coach never got beyond the discussion stage since there is no record of anyone approaching Rockne with a proposal. It is difficult to assess the impact such a move would have had on college football. However, it's not difficult to imagine that the impact would have been enormous.

Daly's resignation was rejected by MacArthur. The superintendent felt that some of his own changes as well as the changes the coach had made would have a positive impact on the coming season. In addition, West Point and Notre Dame were actively seeking a new venue to accommodate the increased interest in their football rivalry. Hiring a new coach in the middle of these efforts would only have made these changes more difficult.

The assessments of both the superintendent and the coach proved to be correct. At the end of the 1922 season Army posted an 8–0–2 record. They outscored their opponents 228–27. The Cadets tied Notre Dame and beat Navy for the first time since before the war. But the motivation to return to active military duty was still strong for Coach Daly. He resigned and returned to his Army duties at the end of the season after a total record of 56–13–3 while at West Point.

He was replaced by John J. McEwan, a standout player at West Point and one of Daly's assistant coaches.

Even with the coaching change, there was still interest on the part of both West Point and Notre Dame to broaden the rivalry's exposure. Cullum Field could only accommodate a maximum of 15,000 fans. Both schools were anxious to move to a larger facility but were apprehensive that the game might not attract enough fans to cover the costs of such a major move. They need not have worried. When the game was held on October 13, 1923, the 35,000 seats at Ebbets Field were filled, and another 15,000 people were trying to get inside the stadium. Before the advent of computers and other advanced sales tools, the bulk of tickets were sold on the day of an event, so the uncertainty of the crowd size persisted until game time.

Ebbets Field, home of the Brooklyn Robins, (later the Dodgers) had not been the first choice of the two schools. Both West Point and Notre Dame preferred the Polo Grounds in Upper Manhattan. However, the *Subway World Series* of 1923 pitted the New York Yankees against the New York Giants, making both the Polo Grounds and the newly built Yankee Stadium unavailable.

Prior to the game, Notre Dame Coach Rockne visited the new Army coach, John "Big Mac" McEwan in the dressing room. McEwan had played for West Point against the Irish all four of his years as a cadet. Rockne suggested that the time of the periods be shortened, an option available at the time. In reply, Coach McEwan said, "Mr. Rockne, once a year we get a lesson in football from Notre Dame and we want the full sixty-minute course." [42] The Cadets got the full lesson as well in a 13–0 loss.

The 1924 Army-Notre Dame game was moved again, this time to the Polo Grounds, which could seat 55,000 fans, still not large enough to accommodate all the ticket seekers. In addition, it was the first Army-Notre Dame game to be broadcast by radio, which further extended the reach and appeal of what was already one of the most popular sporting events in the country. The game turned out to be another hard-fought battle won by the Irish 13–7.

The game became immortalized by the stirring words of sportswriter Grantland Rice. "Outlined against a blue gray October sky the Four Horsemen rode again. In dramatic lore they are known as famine, pestilence, destruction, and death. These are only aliases. Their real names are: Stuhldreher, Miller, Crowley, and Layden. They formed the crest of the South Bend cyclone before which another fighting Army team was swept over the precipice at the Polo Grounds this afternoon as 55,000 spectators peered own upon the bewildering panorama spread out upon the green plain below.

"A cyclone can't be shared. It may be surrounded, but somewhere it breaks through to keep on going. When the cyclone starts from South Bend where the candle lights still gleam through the Indiana sycamores, those in the way must take to the storm cellars at top speed. The cyclone struck again as Notre Dame beat the Army 13 to 7 with a set of backfield stars that ripped and rushed through a strong Army defense with more speed and power than the warring Cadets could meet."[43]

Compared to today's players the Irish *cyclone* was very fast but had very little mass. Fullback Elmer Layden was the heaviest of the four backs at 161 pounds. Quarterback Harry Stuhldreher was the lightest at 151 pounds. Right halfback Don Miller was 160 pounds and left halfback Jim Crowley was 158 pounds.

The words may seem overly dramatic and stilted by today's

reporting standards, but at the time they captured the imagination of sports fans throughout the country. Rice's words also helped to catapult Notre Dame Coach Rockne and his team to greater heights of national prominence. The piece also showcased and raised interest in the eleven-year rivalry. That interest continued to grow as the two teams grew stronger over the coming years.

The 1925 game was moved to Yankee Stadium for the first time. It would prove to be the perfect fusion between a great rivalry and an iconic venue. That venue would host the series every year except one from 1925 to 1946. That one exception was in 1930 when the game was played at Soldier Field in Chicago. The now-famous stadium was completed in 1923 at a cost of $2.4 million. The current Yankee Stadium was built in 2009 at a cost of $1.5 billion. It turned out to be a bonanza for the owners of the Yankees.

The building of Yankee Stadium is an interesting story itself. And since the Bronx stadium figures so prominently in the future of the Army-Notre Dame rivalry, it's worth a digression.

For over half of the twentieth century, the New York metropolitan area boasted three teams, the Brooklyn Dodgers, the New York Giants, and the New York Yankees. Until the 1950s, all major league baseball teams were east of the Mississippi River largely because of travel limitations. The advent of extended air travel gave both major leagues the flexibility to play rivals in more distant parts of the country. The departure of the Dodgers to California in 1957 broke the hearts of millions of Brooklyn fans and left the New York area with two teams until the Giants left for San Francisco shortly after, leaving the Yankees as the sole New York team.

The Polo Grounds, home of the New York Giants, was the oldest of the major league New York venues. The first Polo Grounds was built in 1876 and demolished in 1889. Originally built for polo games, it was modified for baseball and leased to the New York

Metropolitans in 1880. The New York Giants, a different team, leased the same stadium from 1883 through 1888. They also played in the second Polo Grounds for part of the 1889 season and all the 1890 season. A third Polo Grounds stadium was built in 1890 and was used until a fire necessitated a rebuilding of the stadium into its fourth iteration in 1911. It was this Polo Grounds that was also the home stadium of the Yankees from 1913 through 1922.

The Yankees started as the Baltimore Orioles. The team had been in the upstart American League and was moved to New York and renamed the Highlanders before being rebranded again as the Yankees. Their stadium, Hilltop Park, was built on one of upper Manhattan's highest points on 165th St. and Broadway which is now the site of New York Presbyterian Hospital.

The Highlanders/Yankees played in that park until the end of the 1912 season when they moved to the Polo Grounds. They shared the stadium under a rental agreement with the Giants. That agreement remained in effect until they were evicted at the end of the 1922 season. While it lasted, having both New York teams share the same stadium created some interesting twists. In 1921, the Giants won the National League pennant, and the Yankees won the American League pennant. This meant that the entire World Series would be played in the Polo Grounds with both teams able to claim it as their home field. Even calling it a subway series was inaccurate because no travel was required for either team. The powerful Giants prevailed over their tenant rivals in eight games. It was the last year that the World Series was a best-of-nine series.

The two New York teams met again in 1922 with both teams still claiming the Polo Grounds as their home field. The Giants prevailed once more, sweeping the series in five games, which was marred by a controversial tie in game two. After several baseball scandals in prior years, Baseball Commissioner Landis was sensitive to the appearance of impropriety, so he mandated that the proceeds from the controversial tie game be donated to charity. In 1923, the

Yankees finally got their revenge by beating the Giants four games to two in their new Bronx stadium.

The ultimate expulsion of the Yankees had started years before. As the Yankees's popularity grew, the owners of the Giants reconsidered their arrangement, terminating the lease agreement with the Yanks at the end of the 1922 season.

Two events hastened the demise of the stadium-sharing agreement between the two New York teams. The first was the addition of Babe Ruth to the Yankee roster in 1920. Ruth quickly exploited the 258-foot right field stands of the Polo Grounds. His mastery of the field attracted the New York fans, enabling the Yankees to outdraw the owners of the stadium. It was a bitter pill for the owners of the Giants.

Booze sales was the second reason why the sharing agreement soured. With the prospect of Prohibition looming, officials in New York became more receptive to reversing the blue law, which prohibited Sunday baseball. On May 4, 1919, the first Sunday baseball games were played in both the Polo Grounds and Ebbets Field. That left Pennsylvania and Massachusetts as the only states that still prohibited Sunday baseball.

The change to New York's blue law was enormously popular. By June, the Giants had already exceeded the attendance for the entire preceding year. However, the Giants had to relinquish half the available Sunday games to the Yankees. It wasn't long before Giants management figured out that they were forfeiting more Sunday revenue than they were getting from their American League tenants.

The owners of the Giants were hoping the Yankees would build their own ballpark in Queens or some other more distant location. Instead, Jacob Ruppert, the Yankee owner, built an attractive stadium just across the Harlem River, several hundred yards away from their former landlord.

★ ★ ★

On October 17, 1925, both Army and Notre Dame looked forward to playing their game in the two-year-old Yankee Stadium. Despite steady rain prior to the game, 80,000 fans shared their anticipation and enthusiasm for the contest. The Corps of Cadets was not able to attend the game because their travel was limited to three football games a season. Yale, Columbia, and the upcoming Navy game had filled that quota, so the dominance of the Irish subway alumni was very apparent. Nonetheless, the few Army fans present were very pleased by the final score of 27–0 in favor of Army.

It was the largest defeat ever inflicted by an Army team on a Rockne-coached team. It was also Coach McEwan's final game against Notre Dame. At the end of the season, he resigned his commission in the Army and therefore his position as football coach at West Point. He had won his last game as captain of the Army team as a cadet, and now he had won this last game as coach, notable achievements in the hard-fought series between the two rivals.

The new Army coach was a 1917 graduate of the Military Academy. "Biff" Jones had played tackle on the Army teams of 1915–1917, so he had been in on the Notre Dame series from its earliest days. The rivalry against the Irish had changed enormously since his playing days on Cullum Field. After service as an artillery officer in France in WWI and other Army assignments, he was once again involved in the competition against Notre Dame. His first effort as coach in 1926 resulted in another close but disappointing loss to the Irish, 7–0. The following year, Jones and his Cadets prevailed over Notre Dame in a convincing 18–9 win.

In 1928 the Cadets were hoping to repeat as national collegiate champions, a feat they had achieved only once in 1914. A convincing win over the Irish would solidify that hope. In addition, Army was anxious to prove that their win the preceding year over Notre Dame was not a fluke. In the previous ten games between the two rivals dating back to 1917 (there was no game in 1918) Army had won only twice and tied once.

Their six-game winning streak coming into the game gave the Cadets confidence about a repeat win in 1928. They were counting once again on Chris Cagle, a junior destined to be a three-year all-American. Cagle had scored two touchdowns in Army's strong showing the previous year.

The Irish, on the other hand, had already suffered losses to Wisconsin and Georgia Tech. Before the season, Coach Rockne had expressed his pessimism about his incoming squad. In a preseason interview, Rockne had called the team his *Minute Men*. "They'll be in the game one minute," he said, "and the other team will score." [44] There was even talk that Rockne had lost some of his coaching magic and was considering a change from Notre Dame and maybe even leaving coaching entirely.

Consequently, the 1928 match-up was shaping up to be key for both teams. Frank Wallace, columnist for the *New York Daily News*, understood the difficulties faced by the underdog Irish. Prior to the game, he predicted that Notre Dame would need speed and high spirit to win. "Rockne must lift his lads into a whirring state of spiritual exaltation and still keep their feet on the ground and their eyes on the ball." [45] It would turn out that it was indeed this spiritual element that carried the Irish to victory that day and in a way that would reverberate for years to come for future Notre Dame teams.

On game day, 86,000 fans showed up at Yankee Stadium to watch the battle between the two rivals. It was the biggest crowd ever to see a football game in the East. Scalpers were asking $25 for $8 tickets, an outrageous markup for the time. [46] The *Daily News* reported even after the opening kickoff, "the crowd continues to pour in and by now there are at least 90,000 people crammed in the stands. An additional 5,000 or more are parked on elevated platforms and every available perch on neighborhood apartment houses from the roofs to the fire escapes and window ledges." [47] Those that came to see a traditional Army-Notre Dame battle would not be disappointed.

The first half was a typical Army-Notre Dame hard-hitting defensive struggle resulting in a 0–0 tie. Despite his description, Rockne's Minute Men had not allowed a score by the strong Army team. It became apparent at the end of the half that the Cadets might wear down the Irish in the second half. But as anyone who knew Rockne would have suspected, the sly old Norwegian had something up his sleeve, a card he had been saving since 1920. When George Gipp had died that year in a hospital, Rockne was one of the few people present at the end. No one knows for sure what the Gipper said to his coach, but Ronald Reagan, who played Gipp in the 1940 movie *Knute Rockne, All American*, gave the alleged last words to great effect. "Someday when the team's up against it and the breaks are beating the boys, ask them to go in there with all they've got and win just one for the Gipper. I don't know where I'll be then, but I'll know about it, and I'll be happy." In the movie, Rockne paused after telling his team in the locker room about Gipp's last words and then added, "Boys, I'm sure this is the game George Gipp would want us to win."[48]

Whether Rockne used that exact quote at halftime is unknown. One thing that is not in doubt is Rockne's ability to deliver an inspirational and passionate speech to his team. Whatever the words, when the Irish came out of the locker room they played an inspired second half.

Army also stepped up their play in the third quarter. A combination of Chris Cagle runs and a forty-yard pass allowed the Cadets to move the ball quickly to the Notre Dame one. A plunge by fullback John Murrell followed by a missed extra point made the score Army 6 and Notre Dame 0.

Notre Dame fought back. The three Irish backs were relentless in attacking the Army defense. Led by Jack Chevigny the work horse, they battered their way through the Army line for short gains. Chevigny was finally able to plunge over from the one-yard line for the first Notre Dame touchdown. Returning to the sideline he threw the ball high in the air as he approached his coach and yelled, "That's one for the Gipper." [49] After a missed extra point, the score was 6–6. The score remained tied going into the fourth quarter.

With third down and twenty-six yards to go late in the fourth quarter, the Irish again began to move the ball. However, crossed signals and an errant center sailed the ball from the Army sixteen to the Army thirty-one-yard line. The ball was recovered by the Irish standout Jack Chevigny. In the ensuing melee, he was injured and forced to leave the game.

With only two minutes remaining, Rockne substituted Johnny O'Brien, a fragile beanpole, for Manny Vezie at left end. O'Brien lined up with his teammates obeying the rule at the time prohibiting substitutes from talking until one play had been run. The ball was then centered to Irish halfback Johnny Niemiec. "He sets his sights for the 6' 2" sprinter dashing for the extreme right corner of the field. That's O'Brien, the fresh end! Niemiec lets go and the ball travels a high, looping trajectory from the forty-three-yard line. O'Brien cuts sharply and then back, taking Cagle out of position and off stride. He looks over his shoulder, makes a lunge as he reaches his long arms for the pass and falls over the goal. It's a touchdown."[50] He would forever be known as Johnny "One Play" O'Brien.

Army desperately fought back, but time ran out before they could score again. The final score was Notre Dame 12, Army 6. After the game a buoyant and relieved Rockne called this team his "greatest—for that afternoon."[51]

In 1929 the intense rivalry took on even more importance, as if that was possible. For the second year in a row, there would be no Army-Navy contest. After thirty-eight years, the two service academies decided to discontinue their annual meeting because of a dispute over recruiting practices at the Military Academy. The Naval Academy restricted its players to three years of total eligibility in college play. West Point had no such restriction, actively recruiting players with college experience. Army star, Chris "Red" Cagle, had played at the University of Louisiana at Lafayette from 1922 to 1925 before joining the cadet team.

This disruption of the series was the third time that the Army-Navy game was discontinued. From 1894 to 1898 there hadn't been a game because of a heated dispute between an admiral and an Army general that resulted in challenges for a duel between the pair. Alarmed by the bad feelings between the two services, the secretaries of War and the Navy mandated that neither team could leave its grounds for a football game. This constraint meant that the two teams could continue playing collegiate football, but not against each other. In 1899, the restriction was lifted allowing the series to continue.

In 1909 there was another brief interruption to the series after Cadet Eugene Byrne died from an injury suffered in the Harvard game that year. Army canceled the rest of its season after the death, dropping the Navy game from its schedule.

The Army-Navy series was reestablished in 1930 after Army agreed to the same eligibility rules as the Naval Academy. Before that happened, however, the 1929 Notre Dame game took on increasing importance for the Cadets. An Army football captain confided to authors Beach and Moore, "We'd lose two Navy games to win one from Notre Dame."[52]

The Army team again featured fullback John Murrell and halfback Chris Cagle, who had met the Irish on three earlier occasions with only one win to show for it. The losses of 1926 and 1928 had been heartbreakers, which the Cadets lost by one touchdown each. The 1927 game had been a solid 18–0 win, giving the Army team reason to believe they were well-matched against the 1929 Irish.

Star halfback Jack Chevigny was gone from the Notre Dame lineup but was ably replaced by Marchy Schwartz. Hard-hitting Schwartz was aided by "Jumpin' Joe" Savoldi at fullback and quarterback Frank Carideo. All three would play important roles in the strong Irish teams of both 1929 and 1930. The close game was decided by one play, a ninety-six-yard return of an intercepted Chris Cagle pass by Irish substitute Jack Elder. Once again, the Army team played an inspired game and still came up short. Neither team completed a pass. The Cadets outgained the Irish on the ground 137–108 yards.

Adding insult to injury, Rockne beat the Army team remotely. He was bedridden in South Bend with an infected leg. His chief aide, Tom Lieb, handled the coaching duties on the field while he and Rockne coordinated game strategy via a phone link that enabled them to jointly engineer a 7–0 Irish victory.

Notre Dame went on to win a national championship that year, an especially significant achievement since the Irish played every game on the road while their new stadium was being built. A new football venue for Notre Dame's growing fan base had long been a goal of the university and especially Rockne. Throughout the 1920s, the Irish had played their home games on Cartier Field, which had outdated wooden bleachers that could hold, at most 30,000 fans.

The Fighting Irish opened their 1930 season in their new $800,000 stadium on October 4. The new red brick facility could seat almost 60,000 fans and included the transplant of the original sod from Cartier Field, the scene of so many Notre Dame victories. Rockne and the team celebrated their new home with a 20–14 victory over SMU. The official dedication took place the next week accompanied by a 26–2 win over Navy.

The 1930 game against Army was played at Soldier Field in Chicago before shivering fans. Every seat in the huge lake-front stadium had been sold in anticipation of a full capacity attendance of 126,000, putting the crowd on track to be the largest ever to witness a college football game. However, the rain, sleet, and cold on game day dampened the ardor of some fans, reducing the number of those attending to about 110,000.

The Irish would be without the services of their bruising fullback Savoldi. Just twelve days prior to the game, Jumpin' Joe had been expelled by the good fathers of the School of Our Lady after it was learned that he was married, an offense then punishable by expulsion.

Savoldi had enjoyed a stellar career at Notre Dame. He was born in Castino Primo, Italy in 1908 and had emigrated to the US with his family when he was eleven, settling in Three Oaks, Michigan, about an hour away from South Bend.

While working for his uncle's construction company toting bricks, he developed an athletic body. After a successful high school sports career, he was recruited by Knute Rockne to wear the Irish blue and gold. He became a starter his junior year, and was the second-highest-scoring player on the championship 1929 team, scoring six touchdowns. His athletic skills on the football field made him a favorite of Irish fans.

A member of the class of 1921 penned a glowing but politically incorrect poem about Jumpin' Joe for the December 1929 issue of *The Notre Dame Alumnus* magazine.

SAVOLDI'S KEED

I wanta' for to tal' to you, I lika' everyt'ing you do.
But I'a lika' best for all.
You gav' Savoldi's keed da' ball.

I nota' know he's old man,
But papers say he's Italian,
I bat he's glad, I ama' too,
Maybe he send some fruit to you.

Deesa Swartz is good, dees' Elder too,
So's all de' resta 'Micka'crew,
So-I t'ink you should, for deesa' fall,
Just geev' Savoldi's keed de ball.

The Irish would miss Savoldi. They came into the game with eight straight season victories following their nine-game winning streak from the preceding year in which Joe played a prominent role. Army, under dynamic new coach Major Ralph Sasse, would not be a pushover. He had rebuilt the team after the loss of many starters from the 1929 team. The heartbreaking loss of the previous year was also a major motivator for the Cadets.

Rockne was ill for this game as well. However, unlike in 1929, he attended, coaching from a wheelchair on the sidelines. The game was another hard-fought Army-Notre Dame defensive battle with neither team able to score in the first three quarters. With five minutes to go, Notre Dame quarterback Frank Carideo, and halfback, Marchmont "Marchy" Schwartz, combined to move the ball into the Army end zone and take a 6–0 lead. Carideo added the extra point, increasing the lead to 7–0 with now less than four minutes remaining in the game.

After failing to move the ball, the Cadets punted, pinning the Notre Dame eleven deep in their own territory. The Army defense dug in and held the Irish for no gain on the next two plays. The South Benders then elected to punt on third down. Frank Carideo, standing on his own ten-yard line, signaled for the snap. As he received the ball, Army's substitute left end Dick King crashed through the Notre Dame line and blocked the kick. The ball bounded to the Irish goal line where cadet guard Harley Trice fell on it in the end zone. The Army fans were ecstatic while the Notre Dame fans sat in stunned silence. The frozen fans who had endured a scoreless game for fifty-five minutes had now witnessed two touchdowns in less than two minutes.

With the clock ticking down, all eyes now turned to a frail, blond, yearling (sophomore) who trotted onto the field. At just five-seven and 140 pounds, Russ Broshous was too small to compete in the rough-and-tumble contact aspect of Army collegiate football. He was, however, Coach Sasse's choice to attempt the tying extra point. His preferred method was the drop kick, a common but not reliable technique at the time. The football in 1930 had a rounder shape than today's ball, making the bounce for the kicker in those days slightly more predictable. Sasse had confidence in Broshous, who had kicked the tying point on a wet field against Yale a month earlier in a 7–7 game.

The Irish loaded the line with nine of their biggest players. Broshous nervously wiped his hands on his jersey and then signaled for the ball to be snapped. He had almost no time to execute as the Notre Dame linemen broke through the Army front and smothered Broshous and the ball. The game was another heartbreaking loss for the Army, 7–6.

Knute Rockne sought out the despondent young kicker in the Army dressing room after the game. He put his arm around the cadet's shoulder, trying to console him, telling him not to allow one failure in a football game to get him down. [53]

The win over Army helped to propel the Irish to a second consecutive national championship, shared with undefeated Alabama. Tragically, Rockne's involvement in the Army-Notre Dame series would end after the 1930 game.

Russ Broshous became a brigadier general and the head of Earth, Space, and Graphic Sciences Department at West Point.

On January 1, 2006, Doug Flutie of the New England Patriots, kicked what may have been the last drop kick in the NFL against the Miami Dolphins, the first such successful kick since 1941.

CHAPTER 7

A CRASH IN KANSAS

I see the day coming when most college teams will be going by air exclusively. As a matter of fact, I'm flying to Los Angeles next week.
—Knute Rockne

KNUTE ROCKNE WAS at the pinnacle of his career by the spring of 1931. His teams had been undefeated in the two preceding seasons and named national collegiate champions in 1929, and again in 1930 when they shared the title with Alabama. Rock's outsized personality and showmanship combined with his success as a football coach made him a favorite of sportswriters and fans across the country. The Notre Dame stadium, with a capacity of nearly 60,000, a long-cherished project of the dynamic coach, had finally been completed in late 1930.

Rockne had written two books and was working on a third. He also wrote magazine articles and had a syndicated newspaper column. He had offers from both the *Chicago Tribune* and the Hearst Organization to become their football expert should he ever leave coaching. Rockne had also made a few film shorts and had been hired by the Studebaker Company, headquartered in South Bend, to be the vice president of sales promotion for the automobile company.

The coach was an innovator who tried to embrace any new technology that could amplify and enhance his own, and his school's reputation. It was no surprise then that the coach decided to head by airplane to the West Coast for a series of meetings.

Shortly before his departure, Rockne had a discussion with the head of the Faculty Athletic Board, Father Mulcaire, who suggested that the coach drop USC from its schedule because it required too much travel time and significantly impacted class time of the football players. Rockne, always a forward thinker, rejected the idea and replied, "I see the day coming when most college teams will be going by air exclusively. As a matter of fact, I'm flying to Los Angeles next week."[54]

Rockne had a full schedule on the West Coast. In addition to meetings with movie executives to discuss a proposed film about Notre Dame football, he also planned to join his good friend Will Rogers for a joint PR appearance at the opening of a Wilson Sporting Goods store. He also scheduled visits to several Studebaker dealers.

His frenetic activities were typical of the constantly moving coach. Before leaving for his West Coast trip, Rockne joined his wife and youngest son in Miami where they were vacationing. He then returned to Notre Dame for a day. After leaving Notre Dame he traveled to Chicago for a dinner with his mother before traveling by train to Kansas City to visit his two oldest sons who were attending a prep school there.

In Kansas City, he boarded TWA flight number 599 on March 31, 1931, for the trip to Los Angeles. TWA, then the initials of Transcontinental and Western Airline, later changed its name to Trans World Airways when the airline became an international air carrier.

The morning of Rockne's departure in Kansas City the weather was cold and drizzly. As the plane lifted off the pilot and copilot were busy coping with the less-than-desirable flying conditions while the six passengers settled into their unbelted wicker chairs with leather cushions.

As the plane proceeded on its initial leg, the weather worsened; the plane ran into a cold front of thick clouds, fog, ice, and low ceilings. Shortly before ten that morning, the Wichita tower contacted the copilot, Jesse Mathias, who answered that he was too busy to talk. The tower persisted. "What are you going to do?"

Mathias gave a terse reply. "I don't know."

Finally, at 10:22 a.m., Mathias radioed their position and reported on the conditions. "The weather here is getting tough," he said. After finding out that the weather at the tower was satisfactory, the crew decided to divert to Wichita.

The tower air controller queried the copilot again. "Do you think you can make it?" he asked. "Can you get through?"

Mathias replied, "Don't know yet. Don't know." [55] Shortly after, the plane crashed near rural Bazaar, Kansas.

A witness on the ground, C.H. McCracken, watched the plane's last moments. He reported that he heard the plane as it circled. "A few seconds after the plane appeared through the clouds a wing came into view. It floated down and landed almost one-half mile east." [56] All eight occupants of the plane were killed. Debris was scattered across the Kansas farmland.

Ironically, the crash site was near the Kansas ranch of old Notre Dame coach Jesse Harper. It was Harper who had recommended Rockne for the head coach's job and argued successfully against those who thought Rockne was not the right man. Harper, when he heard about the accident, saddled up one of the horses on his ranch and rode across the prairie to identify the body.

Rockne's unexpected death quickly became a national story. The fledgling airline industry, which had been only a distant fascination for most Americans, now captured the country's attention. President Hoover sent a telegram to Rockne's widow expressing the sadness of the nation. "I know that every American grieves with you. Mr. Rockne so contributed to a cleanness and high purpose and sportsmanship in athletics that his passing is a national loss."

Nine months after the crash, the Studebaker Corporation announced that it was offering the *Rockne Six* in its 1932 lineup, the success of which was hampered by the Depression.

Analysis and conjecture as to what caused TWA flight 599 to crash were in the news for weeks after the accident. Harris Hanshue, president of TWA Air Express, and Anthony Fokker, the famous designer of the airliner, travelled quickly to rural Kansas to view the crash site.

Initially, there were many rumors and theories about the cause. At first, investigators believed that icing on the wing had been the problem. There even was a story that the plane had been blown up by the mob because a Notre Dame priest had testified against them in a murder trial in Chicago. However, a more thorough investigation by the Department of Commerce, which was responsible for air safety before the creation of the Civil Aeronautics Board, determined that moisture had seeped into one of the supports causing some rot and deterioration that compromised the integrity of the wing. As the plane encountered turbulence above the Kansas prairie the wing vibrated violently and then broke off entirely.

In 1986, a TWA mechanic E.C. "Red" Long revealed that he had inspected the plane several days before Rockne's flight. "He found the wing panels were all loose on the wing and it would take days to fix it. He said the airplane wasn't fit to fly." He refused to sign the log, but an unknown supervisor overruled the mechanic, deciding that the company needed the plane in service. "I don't know who signed the plane off, but they took the airplane," Long told Department of Commerce investigators. "Nobody was safe in that aircraft." [57] Inspecting the internal bracing of the wing was time consuming on the Fokker F-10A. To check the spars, plywood panels forming the outer skin of the plane had to be removed. This was one of the reasons that the plane had been rejected by the US Navy after testing in early 1931.

The high-profile crash had a huge impact on future airline safety. Until the Rockne crash, air accidents had been investigated by the DOC, which did not release the results of their investigations to the public. However, in the wake of Rockne's death, the public demanded transparency. There were calls across the country for more thorough inspections and oversights on the airline industry.

In the years leading up to the Rockne crash, the government's role in air safety had been hotly debated in Congress. One faction believed that the aircraft industry should have minimal interference from the government during its developing years. They cited the freewheeling nature of the railroad industry, which had been relatively unregulated by the federal government for most of its first seventy years of existence. By contrast, only twenty years had passed since the Wright brothers first flight, and many argued the airline business needed lots of leeway to flourish. Shortly after the crash, the *Washington Post* printed an article on the investigation. "Inquiry Is Ordered In Fatal Air Crash—Sweeping Investigation to Include Reason for Wreck Removal." The *Post* disclosed that permission to dismantle the crashed aircraft had come from a Department of Commerce aeronautical inspection supervisor, Richard H. Lees, Jr. He defended his actions, declaring, "We are trying to sell aviation to the public and the wreckage of a plane lying around for people to stare at has a bad effect."[58]

The dichotomy and dangers of the Department of Commerce oversight were clear. It was obvious that changes were necessary. Public outcry over the secrecy of the investigation and the coziness of relations between the airlines, aircraft manufacturers, and federal regulators resulted in the establishment of the Federal Aviation Administration and National Transportation Safety Board. The FAA became responsible for developing and publishing regulations pertaining to air travel. The NTSB became an independent US government investigative agency responsible for civil transportation accident investigation.

The Rockne accident also hastened the move toward all-metal aircraft. Both Boeing and Douglas were working on all metal airplanes at the time of the Fokker crash. Boeing's new design, the twin engine 247, was totally committed to United Airlines, a sister company of Boeing. TWA and American turned then to the Douglas Aircraft Company for a competitive airplane. That request resulted ultimately in the production of the DC-3, the most successful airplane in aviation history. The DC-3 was sturdy, safe, and durable, remaining in service for over seventy years. It was a workhorse in WWII and saw service in the Vietnam war as well.

There is little doubt that these improvements to flight safety would have ultimately been adopted. However, Rockne's death hastened that reform, undoubtedly saving many lives.

The Army-Notre Dame game had always been central to Rockne's career and success from the moment he scored the first touchdown of the series. He presided over the growth of the rivalry from its humble beginnings in 1913 to the national spectacle it became prior to his death in 1931. During that time Army had six head coaches. Notre Dame had two, Jesse Harper and Knute Rockne. Rockne's continuous and steady influence, showmanship, and coaching skills were a major contributor to the success of the series. He also was largely responsible for the warm feelings that persisted between the two schools during his tenure. Marty Maher, the legendary Irishman who served at West Point from 1896 until 1946, was at the academy for momentous years where he witnessed both the growth of Army football and the development of some of West Point's most famous graduates. He knew MacArthur, Eisenhower, Patton, and Bradley, as well as many other senior officers when they were cadets. The plain-spoken Maher recalled the respect Rockne showed after the Army-Notre Dame games. "Rockne always came to our dressing room after a game—win or lose—and he never looked downhearted. He would shake hands, not only with the players who shined, but with those who were expected to shine next year. He was a great winner and a generous loser."[59]

Army coach, Major Ralph Sasse, went to South Bend to pay his respects at Rockne's funeral. While there, Rockne's widow Bonnie took him aside. "Thanks for coming," said the widow. "You know, of all things connected with Notre Dame football, I'm sure Knute was proudest of the game with Army. It meant so much to him. More than once he said to me, 'While I'm here and after I'm gone, nothing must ever happen to the Army game.'" [60] The Rock would surely be disappointed by what happened to the series less than twenty years later.

A poignant footnote: On a night soon after Rockne's death, Cadet Broshous, the kicker who had missed the vital kick in the 1930 game, was studying in his room. He was visited by the Army Coach Sasse, who told the cadet of Rockne's death. Sasse said, "I can honestly say that I am glad you missed that kick. If you'd made it Rock wouldn't have won his last Army game."[61]

PART II

THE ZENITH

CHAPTER 8

THE COACHES

Take all the time you want, Red. But remember, you're a West Pointer. And West Point needs you.
Brigadier General Robert L. Eichelberger-Superintendent of the US Military Academy

THE FINANCIAL IMPACT of Rockne's death on Notre Dame was devastating. Football revenue had funded much of the building on the campus during the late 20s. After Rockne's death, those profits declined precipitously. By 1933 the university's profits from intercollegiate football were only one-third of what they had been in 1930, Rockne's last year.

No one had foreseen the need for an immediate succession planning while the vibrant and energetic Rock was at the helm. Therefore, there was immediate confusion and conjecture as to who might replace him. If there was anyone who might be considered a successor, it was Jack Chevigny.

After his graduation in 1928, Chevigny had stayed on as an assistant coach to Rockne, who treated Chevigny as a son and shared his strategies and use of various formations with his assistant. Chevigny was a part of the coaching staff that helped Rockne and Notre Dame win national championships in both 1929 and 1930.

When Rockne went to the Mayo Clinic a year earlier for treatment of his phlebitis, he asked Chevigny to accompany him. News photos at Rockne's funeral mistakenly identified the young man holding on to Knute's widow as one of his sons. It was Chevigny. In many respects he was a son to Rockne, and by all appearances his protégé.

It was somewhat of a surprise, therefore, when the administrators at Notre Dame chose two men to coach the Irish football team after Rockne's death—Chevigny and Heartly William "Hunk" Anderson, a former Notre Dame lineman who had played for Rockne.

In making the announcement on April 10, Notre Dame president Father Charles L. O'Donnell said, "There is no head coach at Notre Dame. Knute Rockne is always the head coach. Hunk Anderson will be the senior coach and Jack Chevigny will be the junior coach."

It was an ill-conceived idea from the start. Chevigny did much of the work, while Anderson took much of the credit for the early success of the Irish program. When they lost the last two games to USC and Army in 1931, Anderson blamed Chevigny. Disillusioned by the difficult working coaching situation, Chevigny left Notre Dame in 1931 after Rockne's death and the end of the football season.

In 1933, Anderson's team performed dismally, finishing the year 3–5–2, the first losing season for a Notre Dame team since 1888. Even an upset win over heavily favored Army, 13–12 could not save Hunk from dismissal by the good fathers of the School of Our Lady.

After the turmoil and disappointment of the post-Rockne Anderson years, the search committee headed by Father (later Cardinal) John O'Hara wanted a candidate who could restore both harmony and winning to the football program. To do this they reached back to the glory years of the Rockne reign and selected Elmer Layden, a member of the fabled Four Horsemen of the 1924 team.

After graduating from Notre Dame in 1925, Layden became head coach of tiny Columbia College in Dubuque, not far from his hometown of Davenport, Iowa. His successful two winning seasons at Columbia attracted the notice of the administrators of Duquesne University in Pittsburgh. The Dukes had lost every game in 1926 and won only eight of thirty-one games the previous four years.

In his first year, Layden guided the Dukes to a 4–4–1 record, the best record for any Duquesne team up until that time. During his seven years at Duquesne, Layden lost only sixteen games out of seventy. He received national attention when one of his best teams defeated archrival and powerhouse Pitt. His success at Duquesne helped to ensure that he was on the short list of possible candidates to replace Andersen.

Layden was hired as Notre Dame head coach in 1934. He was an excellent choice to restore confidence in the football program, even in the face of a movement to deemphasize athletic programs at the university. However, his first game at the helm turned out to be an ironic and disappointing loss. An upstart Texas team coached by ex-Notre Damer Jack Chevigny defeated the Irish 7–6. For a brief time, it launched Chevigny into the limelight and cast doubt about Layden's coaching skills. However, the fortunes of both men would soon be reversed.

If there was a single characteristic that defined Layden's successful tenure at Notre Dame it was his affability and popularity with his own players and the broader athletic community. He was well-liked by everyone, even his opponents. As athletic director he restored good relations with many of the teams of the Big Ten Conference (then the Western Conference) who had been alienated during the Rockne-Anderson years. During his tenure, he played against or scheduled every team of the conference, including Illinois, Michigan, and Iowa, which had been off the Notre Dame schedule for many years.[62]

The rift with the University of Michigan extended back to incidents that had occurred in 1909. Layden was able to win over Fielding Yost, athletic director at the University of Michigan, who had been a personal enemy of Rockne. Through personal intervention, the Notre Dame coach was able to overcome the long-standing bitter feelings between the two schools and restore the popular football series in 1942.[63]

All of Layden's diplomatic efforts paid off in an important way for the university. Football profits had declined from the highs of $540,000 during the final Rockne years of 1929 and 1930 to only $177,000 during Anderson's last year. Layden was able to halt the slide in his first year in 1934, increasing it slightly to $192,000, even in the face of a deepening depression.[64] By 1939, Layden's efforts increased the profits to $300,000, a key source of revenue that allowed the university to improve its instruction and research activities.[65]

He did all of this while achieving success on the football field. His winning percentage of .783 and record of 47–13–2 makes him one of Notre Dame's most successful coaches. Despite these successes, dissatisfaction and unrest about Coach Layden's tenure began to take hold of the impatient Irish loyalists. Unexpected consecutive losses to Iowa in 1939 and 1940 plus declining gate receipts worked against the coach after seven years at the helm. He resigned unexpectedly on February 4, 1941 to become commissioner of the National Football League.

The Layden years clearly stabilized the Notre Dame football program and brought it back to national prominence. His sudden departure set the stage for the arrival of yet another Knute Rockne protege who would guide the Irish to an even more glorious period that in many ways would rival the years of the master himself.

In 1941 the rivalry took on the indelible imprint of two men who would bring the series to a pinnacle of success and competition. Both West Point and Notre Dame would see the return of two of their own to coach and revive the football fortunes at both schools. The return of both men, Red Blaik at Army and Frank Leahy at Notre Dame, had strikingly similar characteristics.

Blaik was born on February 17, 1897, in Detroit, Michigan. The Detroit Blaiks were descendants of seafaring Scots from Glasgow. His father, William, left Scotland for Canada when he was sixteen years old. He migrated to Detroit where he met and married Margaret

Purcell. They had three children, Douglas, Earl, and Mabel.

The Blaiks soon left Detroit and moved to Dayton, Ohio, where Red's father opened a hardware store. Young Earl was interested in sports from an early age. At Steele High in Dayton, he played football, basketball, and baseball. He weighed just 133 pounds and was not a natural athlete, but he made up for his size and lack of talent with enthusiasm on the playing field.

In 1914 he entered the University of Miami in nearby Oxford, Ohio, where he matured into an excellent athlete, starring in football, basketball, and baseball. It was at Miami where he met his future wife, Merle McDowell, and where he also first learned about West Point.

One of Blaik's fraternity brothers, Jack Butterfield, had attended West Point for one year before being found deficient in academics and separating from the academy. He had played football there during his plebe year and never lost his enthusiasm for the school. Blaik was intrigued by the stories his friend told him about the Military Academy. After Blaik graduated from Miami of Ohio in June 1918, he entered West Point that same month.

West Point was in turmoil due to the rapid expansion of the Army after the US entry into World War I in 1917. The Department of the Army looked to the pool of developing young officer candidates in the Corps of Cadets, depleting West Point's ranks.

In the middle of this maelstrom of change, thirty-nine-year-old brigadier general, Douglas MacArthur arrived to become one of the youngest superintendents in Academy history. MacArthur soon recognized the adverse effect of the war on West Point. "The traditional disciplinary system, so largely built around the prestigious influence of the upperclassman was impossible in a situation where there were no upperclassmen. Cadet officers have never known the example of cadet officers before them, and the body of the Corps had a most imperfect idea of the standards of bearing and conduct which have been characteristic of the cadet for over a century. The old West Point could not be recognized as it appeared in June 1919. It's gone; it had to be replaced."[66]

West Point had always labored under a three-way tension between the academic department, the tactical department, and the traditions of the academy, which had accumulated and become enshrined over the years since its founding in 1802. The academic department is responsible for the scholastic education of cadets, whereas the tactical department is responsible for their military training. They both operate in the shadow of the traditions and values of the academy. All those stationed at West Point would agree that all three legs of the West Point experience are important to the overall success of producing junior and senior officers. They would probably disagree on the relative importance of each.

MacArthur, just returned from the war in Europe, was passionate about the changes he felt were necessary to prepare cadets for the type of warfare he had just experienced. MacArthur's conduct and bravery in the war had enabled him to rise quickly through the ranks, becoming the second youngest superintendent since Sylvanus Thayer. The academic department, somewhat insulated from the conflict, strongly resisted MacArthur's attempts at reform.

Soon after his arrival, MacArthur watched the Corps of Cadets in action during their traditional summer encampment at West Point. Unimpressed by the performance of the cadets, he turned to the adjutant of the post and asked, "How long are we going on preparing for the war of 1812? Of what possible benefit is cadet summer camp."[67]

MacArthur proposed changes he felt would bring the academy more into sync with the country and the nature of modern warfare. "The country's needs had changed—it no longer required a public institution for civil engineers: it did need a cadre of professional soldiers able to lead civilian soldiers in war involving the large masses of society—but the principal remained the same."[68] Initially, he was only able to make small inroads on the hidebound academic department. "He secured such victories as the introduction of the slide rule and the study of economics and the internal combustion engine; World War

I tactics were substituted for those of the Civil War."[69]

The young general also faced enormous opposition from the DOGs (Disgruntled Old Grads) when he moved West Point's traditional encampment from the plain on the academy grounds to Fort Dix, New Jersey, where the cadets could get exposure to Army regulars. He strengthened the honor code and eliminated hazing, a system that had almost killed him when he was a cadet.

Perhaps his most lasting impact during his tenure as superintendent was the emphasis he placed on athletics. His experience in the war convinced him that too many officers were out of shape. "Over there," MacArthur said, "I became convinced that the men who had taken part in organized sports made the best soldiers."[70]

He raised the number of intercollegiate teams from three to seventeen. He proposed building a fifty-thousand-seat stadium with railroad yards for easy access. Congress rejected the idea. Instead, a sixteen-thousand-seat stadium was built in 1924, two years after MacArthur left the academy. "He tried, but failed, to attract a young football coach named Knute Rockne from Notre Dame."[71]

Almost twenty years after he left his position as superintendent, the world was involved in another war. It would remain to be seen if MacArthur's changes fostered by his experience in one war would help the cadets of 1940 to meet the challenges of a new one, should the nation become embroiled in another war.

He established an extensive intramural program that required all cadets to participate in a wide variety of sports, from volleyball to boxing and wrestling. Lest there be any doubt about his strong support of this new system, he codified his philosophy by having an inscription chiseled over the entrance to the gym.

Upon the fields of friendly strife,
Are sown the seeds that,
Upon other fields, on other days,
Will bear the fruits of victory.

MacArthur had been a varsity baseball player and manager of the football team during his cadet days. Consequently, he had great respect for the cadets who had to balance their athletic activities with their heavy academic and military workloads. It was only natural then that he would turn to some of these athletes when he sought allies to help him implement his changes. It was no surprise, therefore, that he chose cadet Earl Blaik to be the head of his ad hoc cadet committee.

Blaik was one the leaders of his class. He was older and more mature than many of his classmates, having already graduated from Miami of Ohio. In addition, he was an excellent athlete. While at West Point, he had excelled at sports. He was an all-American end on the football team, left fielder in baseball, and guard on the basketball team. He won the Athletic Association Saber as the best all-around athlete in his class.

Years later, Blaik could still remember key details of that meeting with the new *supe*. Expecting a formal meeting with a senior officer, he was surprised when MacArthur put the cadets at ease and even offered them cigarettes. At the time, cadets were not permitted to smoke. It was clear to Blaik from this meeting that change was coming to West Point.

Blaik's relationship with MacArthur continued to grow during his time as a cadet. It became a lifelong friendship, with MacArthur taking on the role of mentor and father figure. Even after West Point, the two maintained friendly contact. Shortly after Blaik submitted his resignation from the Army, MacArthur sent him a letter telling him that he (MacArthur) was being reassigned to the Philippines from West Point. He wanted Blaik to join him as his aide. Unfortunately, by the time Blaik received the letter, the paperwork to separate him from the Army was being finalized.

What had united MacArthur and Blaik was their love of sports, West Point, and the tradition of winning. MacArthur's emphatic and uncompromising pronouncement, "There is no substitute for victory," and Blaik's, "The essence of the game is not fun, but the soul-satisfying awareness that comes from communal work and sacrifice," both appeal to the spirit of winning, a central and critical attribute of West Point training.

After leaving the Army, Blaik returned to Dayton. For the first four years there he worked in contracting, real estate, and in his father's business. In the fall of 1926, he took a vacation to Wisconsin and stayed to coach at the university under George Little, who had been the head coach at Miami of Ohio when Blaik played there.

When Army traveled to Chicago to play Navy late in the fall of 1926, Army's new head coach, Biff Jones, asked Blaik to visit him before the game. As a result of the meeting, Blaik became a civilian assistant coach at Army the following season. He remained in the job until 1933. Since the job was part-time, requiring him to be at West Point only in the fall, he returned to Dayton for the rest of the year to manage his business ventures.

Blaik had realized by then that football was his passion. When Army's then head coach, Ralph Sasse, left in 1932, Major Eichelberger, then at the academy as assistant in the administration of athletics, tried desperately to have Blaik named as Sasse's successor. But the tradition of having a graduate on active duty as head coach at Army was at the time an unalterable tradition.

Blaik stayed on at West Point for one more year to assist new head coach Gar Davidson. By then the desire to become a head coach himself had taken hold. When the head-coaching job opened at Dartmouth, Blaik applied. There were 105 applicants, but Blaik was the clear choice of Dartmouth's president.

Blaik imposed his Spartan training and style of play on the Dartmouth football program. It soon paid off. Until his arrival, the Big Green had never won a football game in the Yale Bowl in seventeen tries over fifty-two years. On November 2, 1935, under Head Coach Blaik, Dartmouth defeated Yale 14–6. From 1934 through 1940, Blaik's teams at Dartmouth compiled an impressive record of 44–1–15. The 1937 team was undefeated and won the Ivy League Championship. And he did so with an understated style.

Blaik was a man of few words. For many of his players the coach appeared to be cold and unapproachable much of the time. And as a coach he was mostly silent on the practice field. He watched everything closely, and if someone made a mistake, he would call that player off to the side and calmly explain the correct way of executing the play. He never yelled or scolded a player in front of team members. Years later, when interviewed about the Blaik style of coaching, two of the coach's star Army players remembered his technique. "I never heard him degrade anyone in the presence of anyone else," Glenn Davis said. "I never heard him raise his voice, hardly, in the presence of or to any player." Doug Kenna, another star of the Army teams of the 1940s, noted, "Red Blaik didn't yell." But, he remembered. "Fail once too often and you would never get another chance on his team."

In October 1940, newly minted Brigadier General Robert L. Eichelberger was appointed superintendent at West Point. Shortly after being promoted, he received a congratulatory message from one of his West Point classmates from the class of 1909. "At last they have had the sense enough to promote the two best damn officers in the US Army." The message was signed by George S. Patton, an officer even then not afraid to promote his own cause.[72]

There were several factors that had a significant impact on the fortunes of Army football in the years leading up to the war. One was negative and one positive. Until 1938 West Point had allowed transfers from other schools to have three years of college eligibility regardless of how many years they might have played at any other college. Almost all other schools restricted their players to a total of three college years of eligibility. The Big Ten had refused to play Army from 1935 to 1937 because of Army's stance on eligibility. "Navy broke with Army after their 1927 football game, demanding that the three-year eligibility rule be applied to West Point athletics. Although the two institutions played in 1930 and 1931 for charity, the breach was not officially healed until 1932."[73]

After considerable pressure, Army changed its eligibility standard in 1938 to conform with most of the rest of the other teams by limiting all football players to only three years total college play. "Its immediate impact was to prevent Army from using two outstanding recruits who entered West Point in 1938—Carl Hinkle, an all-American center at Vanderbilt, and John Guckeyson, a brilliant back at Maryland."[74]

The second factor was a restriction that Eichelberger fought hard to change, and which greatly aided Army's ability to recruit players who could be competitive against its rivals. Since 1931 there had been rigid guidelines on the size and weight of all cadets, which had limited West Point's ability to recruit competitive football players. The surgeon general had mandated, for example, that a seventeen-year-old cadet standing six feet tall should ideally weigh 160 pounds and could not weigh more than 176 pounds. A six-foot-four cadet (the height limit for West Point) could not weigh more than 198 pounds.[75] It wasn't until 1937 that a relaxation of the restriction would be allowed with a waiver from the West Point Athletic Council.

One of Eichelberger's first official duties as superintendent was to attend the Army against the University of Pennsylvania game at Franklin field in Philadelphia on November 16. While the new superintendent looked on, the Army team suffered one of the worst defeats in its history, 48–0.

Eichelberger decided then and there that fixing Army's football program was an important part of his mission to prepare West Point for the war he felt was coming. He knew if war came his cadets would soon be in the thick of the fighting. He felt strongly that the team representing the Army had to exhibit the attributes of strength and a winning spirit. The team he had just watched showed neither of these traits.

When he returned to West Point on the following Monday, he called a meeting of the athletic council. He got quickly to the point. "I was impressed, Saturday (he told them) by the way the cadets cheered our team right to the end of that 48–0 beating by Pennsylvania. It looks as if we are developing the finest bunch of losers in the world. By the Gods, I believe the cadets deserve a football team which will teach them how to be good winners!

"Our system of graduate-officer coaching is outdated. We have to go out and get the best coach in the business. We had him here once and we let him get away. It's time we got him back. I'm talking about 'Red' Blaik!"[76]

The board members hesitated. They were aware of Blaik's successful career as head football coach at Dartmouth. But, appointing him would break the long-standing tradition of choosing only a West Point graduate on active duty as a coach. But fulfilling this requirement meant that Army sometimes had to choose officers who coached on a part-time basis. Bill Wood, who coached from 1938 to 1940 in the years preceding Blaik, was a cavalry captain who returned to West Point each fall to coach the football team.[77]

Blaik was a graduate of the Military Academy but had resigned his commission. Eichelberger was hoping that the tradition of having an active-duty Army officer as coach could be overruled.

Eichelberger decided to move quickly. He sent a short letter to Coach Blaik. "If you have not signed a new contract don't sign any until you have talked to me."

Blaik wrote back, "I understand what you mean. I will see you at the Army-Navy game."[78]

The night before the game the two men met in the Army football headquarters in Philadelphia's Ben Franklin hotel. At the meeting the general offered the West Point coaching job to Blaik. Leading his alma mater's football program was very appealing to the forty-three-year-old coach. However, he was hesitant about taking the job. While Dartmouth's football success under his leadership was improving, Army's performance on the gridiron was consistently declining. In 1939, the Cadets had ended the season with three wins, four losses, and two ties. The next year was even worse. The Cadets managed only one win while losing seven games and tying one. During those two years they had failed to score a single point against either Notre Dame or Navy, their two key rivals.

Coach Blaik expressed his concern about taking the head-coaching job to Eichelberger, according to *Gridiron Grenadiers*. "General," he said, "it would be a high honor for me to be the head coach of the football team at West Point. But, I would have to think long before giving an answer. I've been happy at Dartmouth for seven years. My relations there with President Hopkins have been just perfect. We have a beautiful home in Hanover. I doubt whether Mrs. Blaik ever would want to leave it. My boys, Bill and Bob, like it too."

Eichelberger considered the comment for just a moment. "By the Gods, man," he boomed. "We'll build her a finer home at West Point!"[79]

Blaik had always been very analytical and not given to impulse. After thinking a moment, he smiled then became serious and answered Eichelberger. "General," he said, "I must have time to think about this. I just don't know. I must talk to Mr. Hopkins (the president of Dartmouth) and Mrs. Blaik. I'll need at least a month to come to a decision."[80]

Eichelberger replied with his most persuasive and powerful weapon, an appeal to Blaik's sense of loyalty. "Take all the time you want Red," Eichelberger said. "But remember, you're a West Pointer. And West Point needs you."[81]

Blaik pondered the decision for several weeks after the meeting with Eichelberger, discussing the potential change of jobs with both

President Hopkins and his wife.

By the second week of December, he still hadn't made up his mind. He decided to visit General and Mrs. Eichelberger with his wife, Merle, to clear up some open issues and help him to come to a decision.

To try to make sure that Merle Blaik was on board with the change, Eichelberger addressed the issue of moving her family to West Point. The general was certain that the beautiful and historic Hudson Valley would be able to compete well with the location of the home she loved in New Hampshire. "Later on I took Red and Mrs. Blaik up to a ridge near Lusk Reservoir, which I always considered one of the finest building sites on the West Point Reservation. From the eminence one can look down the slope on the Hudson River and across it to the stately hills. I said to Mrs. Blaik: 'We will build you a home here.'"[82]

The general recalled another aspect of the visit years later. "Red is a bit sensitive. He was a little uncertain how he and his family would be received on the post. I suggested he go over to the Officers' Club and have his hair cut by Tom Impell, the widely known raconteur.

'A haircut for a second lieutenant,' I told him, 'takes about five minutes. For the superintendent, about forty-five.' When he came back I asked: 'How long did he take to cut your hair?' He replied: thirty-five minutes.' I said: 'You're in. You'll be about the second-ranking person on the post.'"[83]

Finally, on December 15, Blaik sat at his desk in Hanover and wrote to General Eichelberger on Dartmouth College Athletic Council stationery. Before he was willing to accept the Army offer, he wanted the Military Academy to guarantee three conditions, which he and the general had discussed:

First, the strict physical requirements limiting the size of entering cadets had to be formally changed. Second, he demanded a five-year contract with an annual salary of $12,000 and "quarters as you have outlined them." He expected the Army Athletic Association to pay for his moving expenses and quartering costs until his family moved to the academy. Third, his staff, including, Harry Ellinger, A.F. Gustafson, Roland Bevan, Frank Moore, and Averell Daniel, had to be hired. For each he requested a specific salary.[84]

Eichelberger could guarantee only items two and three. He did not have the authority to unilaterally circumvent the Department of War regulations governing height and weight restrictions on cadet admissions. He, therefore, traveled to Washington to lobby for a change to the regulation. Fortunately, he had a valuable ally in the White House. President Roosevelt's appointment secretary (the equivalent of today's chief of staff). Pa Watson was a graduate of West Point, class of 1908. Wilson had served in the Philippines, Mexico, and the Western Front in World War I.[85]

Watson took on the task enthusiastically. Within a few days, Eichelberger received an official notification to expect, "early approval of our study which will modify the regulations."[86] Although this message was not an official commitment to allow the general to make the change Blaik wanted, it was a strong enough indication to allow Eichelberger to convene a meeting with Blaik on December 22 at the Ritz Carlton in New York.

At the end of a six-hour meeting, Blaik agreed to move to West Point with his entire staff. His gracious statement to the press revealed not only his sadness at leaving Dartmouth, but also his sense of duty in returning to West Point. "I shall always feel close to Dartmouth," Blaik said. "It is difficult to leave, but in these times to return to West Point is not only a challenge but a duty and a privilege."[87]

The Dartmouth director of athletics William H. MacArthur also recognized the powerful draw that the call of duty had on Coach Blaik's decision. "We regret that Coach Blaik has felt it his duty to go to West Point, and congratulate the Military Academy on acquiring one of the best coaching staffs in the country."[88]

Still, it was clear that the decision to leave Dartmouth was a very difficult one for Blaik. Colonel Charles Danielson, then adjutant general of the academy, remarked later, "I've never seen a less happy man than Blaik was the morning after signing. He was a man in a deep fog. All of us, simply by observation, realized how much of a wrench it was for him to leave Dartmouth."[89]

There were other actions being taken at the time that would help the cadets at West Point to prepare for the war, which was drawing closer. In one of the first major expansions of the Military Academy since its inception in 1802, the government purchased an additional 15,000 acres to add to the existing 3,500 acres of the installation. The increase had been authorized by Congress in 1931 but only became a reality in 1939 when war became more imminent. The new land would be used for field training and firing ranges close to the academy.

In October 1941 Stewart Field, in nearby Newburgh was purchased. This enabled the academy to begin an extensive flight training program. In January 1942, the War Department authorized West Point to commission up to 60 percent of its graduates in the Air Corps, a branch of the Army. Cadets who were qualified for pilot training and who desired to enter the Air Corps were designated air cadets after their second year at West Point. These cadets went away to civilian facilities to receive their flight training. As facilities were completed at Stewart Field, the cadets began receiving their basic and advanced training there. Members of the class of 1943 were the first to graduate with their *wings*; those of the class of 1946 were the last. In those years, a total of 1,033 cadets were commissioned into the Air Corps from West Point.

As war approached, the civilian population also took a greater interest in West Point. In 1941, two movies about West Point were released, *West Point Widow* and *Cadet Girl*. Both were lighthearted love stories that featured cadet life in a frivolous way before the war made life at the academy more serious. In early 1942 a third movie, *Ten Gentlemen from West Point,* starring Maureen O'Hara, was released. Although also a love story, the movie depicted the harsh training and hazards of the early days of West Point.

These films, numerous magazine articles—and Army football—allowed the Military Academy to maintain a positive image with the public as it prepared for another war.

Francis William Leahy was born sometime in August of 1908. The exact day is unknown, a mystery, which remains today just like the enigmatic man. Fittingly, his lineage was pure Irish. His grandfather, Michael Leahy, fled the not so green fields of Ireland, which had been afflicted with a blight that destroyed the potato crops of the land and the ability of hard-working farmers to feed their families.

Michael landed first in Peterborough, Ontario. There he married Bridget Torpay in 1861 and subsequently left by wagon in 1869 for Iowa. The young married couple subsequently moved on to Wisner, Nebraska, where Michael became a peace officer at a time when that part of the country was not far removed from the Wild West.

One of their children, Frank, also took an Irish bride, Mary Winifred Kane. Frank had inherited his father's yearning to travel and seek greener pastures. Frank Leahy left his wife and six children and traveled to Roundup, Montana. One of those youngsters, Frank Jr., was less than a year old at the time. Frank Sr. assured his wife that he would send for the family when he got established.

Soon after, the Leahy family traveled by train to Montana to be reunited with Frank Sr. The family moved again after a year to South Dakota, where land had been opened for homesteading. The Leahy family spent their first winter in South Dakota in a tent on the windswept prairie while their home was being built. Finally, in the spring of 1911 the house was completed. Frank Sr. tried his hand at several professions to support his family, all difficult in the harsh South Dakota frontier life.

In addition to his efforts to support his family, Frank Sr. also was a frustrated boxer who taught his boys to be brawlers. "It was common practice for the elder Leahy to stop each of his boys and ask them if they had been involved in a fight at school that day. When they would deny it he would grin malevolently and say: 'Get in one tomorrow. It'll do you some good.'"[90]

When Frank Jr. was seventeen, his father encouraged him to get into the ring with a professional boxer so that he could judge the youngster's pugilistic skills. Young Frank bravely accepted the challenge. He was knocked down six times in the first round. Each time the young amateur rose to his feet and resumed the fight. In the third round, he knocked out the pro.[91] It was clear at an early age that young Frank was a tough and determined young man.

Frank Jr. was enthusiastic about all sports. However, he ultimately gravitated to football because his older brother Gene was a football player of some renown at Creighton University in Omaha, Nebraska. Frank aspired to also attend Creighton. He wanted to play football, graduate from Creighton, and return to coach at the high school in his hometown of Winner.

However, his plans changed with the arrival of a new coach at his high school. Earl Walsh, a Notre Dame graduate who had played with George Gipp and Hunk Anderson, took an immediate liking to Frank. He was impressed by the lad's acute understanding of the strategy of the game. Frank Jr. had become keenly interested in the more cerebral aspects of football because of his older brother's exploits on the gridiron.

Farm work and frontier life ensured that there were plenty of fast, strong boys at Winner High. However, not many had Frank Leahy Jr.'s analytical skills. Therefore, Coach Walsh used him as a signal caller to swiftly read the opposing team's defense and counter it. Impressed with the young man, Coach Walsh recommended young Leahy to Knute Rockne at Notre Dame. By then his older brother Gene had become an insurance salesman in Omaha. He convinced Frank to come live with him in Omaha for a year to gain some maturity and take some courses he might need for Notre Dame.

Shortly after he arrived in Omaha, Frank Jr. approached the

football coach at Central High School and asked to join the team, neglecting to mention that he had already graduated from high school.

Coach Schmidt of Central High quickly determined that the muscular young man was more suited to be a lineman than a tailback. Frank Jr. took quickly to the new role. The local newspapers were soon touting the exploits of the new addition to the team. One of those newspapers soon reached Winner, where a rival coach notified the sports authorities in Omaha of Frank Jr.'s ineligible status.

Young Leahy's second high school career consequently ended rather abruptly. However, he accomplished the primary reasons for his tenure in Omaha. He continued his studies, worked out and gained an extra year of maturity. In addition, during the year his brother Gene had taken him down to the Omaha railroad station to meet the Notre Dame team on its way back to South Bend after having defeated USC. At the station he met brother Gene's old Creighton coach, Tommy Mills, who was now the freshman coach at Notre Dame. Mills would later prove to be a valuable ally in helping to launch Frank Leahy's coaching career.

With his brother Gene's help, Frank Jr. submitted the proper paperwork and was admitted to Notre Dame for the spring semester. In the winter of 1927, he boarded the train in Omaha for South Bend, uncertain about what he might find. He was a frontier youth with very little experience outside of Winner and Omaha. He was driven by three thoughts. He wanted to play football at Notre Dame, he wanted to study coaching under the great Knute Rockne, and he wanted to do both of those things under the umbrella of a strong Catholic environment at The School of Our Lady.

When he finally arrived at the campus, Leahy had lingering doubts about his place in such a prestigious institution. However, his ambivalence soon vanished. Years later, he eloquently described the strong feelings he had when he first walked the campus and discovered that he had found the spiritual environment he was seeking. "Oooooo, I tell you, it was love at first sight. I never felt so Catholic in my life as the first time I saw that school. I never felt so proud to be an Irish Catholic. That may sound awfully strange, but it is true. At the time neither group was wanted. But I saw the school and I knew I was wanted. They could never tell me that being Irish or Catholic was a wrong thing to be in America. And I was determined that if everything else in my life should be a total failure, ah, I would be the truest, finest Irish Catholic I could be. And I would try to show other young men that it was not wrong to be a Catholic in America."[92]

However, coincidental with Leahy's awe and admiration for the school were thoughts that he was not worthy to be part of the Notre Dame mystique. Once again, his own words best describe his insecurities. "In the years ahead, I doubt if any lad who came to the University of Our Lady ever had less confidence in his own ability to make good," he said. "I was simply frozen. There was no place to go except straight ahead. I was totally lost. And if it hadn't been for Knute Rockne, I probably would've gone back down to the train station, put myself on board a coach and got back home to Winner. Chances are I never would've left South Dakota again and nobody would've ever heard of me again."[93]

His first meeting with the famous coach equaled the epiphany he had experienced when he had set foot on the Notre Dame campus a day earlier.[94] The great Rockne, when he first met the shy youngster, soon showed the skills that had made him one of the most successful coaches in the country. His ability to read people, put them at ease and quickly win their loyalty and admiration were on full display. "Feel scared as hell, don't you Frank?" the coach asked. "It's got to be tough. You'll get over that lost feeling in a couple of days. I did. Oh, God, did I feel like there wasn't a friend in the world! There are a lot of other fellows who feel just the same way. In a couple of weeks, when the snow is off the ground and Tommy here has you out on the field with the other freshman, you'll think you never left South

Dakota. If you need to talk to me in the meantime, I'll be around. I'm not one of those coaches who hides in the office. Four years from now when you are a senior, you'll see freshmen like yourself and you'll know how scared they feel. I never forgot."[95]

That first meeting launched a relationship of mutual respect that continued to grow until Rockne's untimely death four years later.

Leahy's story would take many unexpected turns. After moderate success on the freshman team in 1927, he got some playing time at center and tackle on the 1928 Notre Dame varsity. On the undefeated 1929 Irish team, Leahy beat out three other players for the starting right tackle position.

However, an elbow injury in the Navy game that year and a severe knee injury in 1930 preseason practice ended his playing career. He had been counting on showcasing his playing skills during his senior year. However, what appeared to be a devastating loss would provide the mechanism that would ultimately launch Frank Leahy's coaching career.

Coach Rockne had planned an operation on his leg at the Mayo Clinic over the Christmas break in 1930. He invited Frank to go with him to have his own knee worked on. Frank assumed they would have separate rooms at the clinic. When they got to Rochester, Minnesota, he discovered that Rockne had booked only one room for the two of them. For four days while they convalesced, Rockne shared his insights on coaching with his young protégé. Though inspired, Leahy was depressed. Rockne, sensing Leahy's black mood from his injury, sought to understand his pessimism. "Can I ask why you're so discouraged, Frank? You have absolutely no right to be. I thought our Notre Dame players were trained to fight back against adversity. At least that's what I am telling you to do. Maybe I'm not the coach they say I am. What's eating at you? Still fretting because you can't play football anymore. That's foolish, Frank, just damn foolish."[96]

Leahy's despondency was evident in his response. "This knee cost me every opportunity I ever thought I had," he said, looking the other way. "I figured if I really played well my senior year somebody would want to hire me as a line coach. Now I'm getting ready to graduate and I don't have a prospect in the world. They have forgotten all about me."[97]

Rockne listened to the young man intently and then gave Leahy a stack of letters he had just retrieved from the clinic's front desk. He explained that a number of coaches around the country had written to him seeking graduates from the Notre Dame program who might want to get into coaching. He encouraged Leahy to pick the one he was most interested in. After reviewing the letters, Frank chose the request from Tommy Mills, his freshman coach and now the head coach at Georgetown in Washington. Mills had specifically inquired about Leahy. That, and the fact that Georgetown was a Catholic University, convinced Leahy to pursue the job. He quickly accepted Mills' offer to be the line coach at one thousand dollars per year.

Leahy stayed only one year at Georgetown before he was recruited by Jim Crowley, one of Notre Dame's famous Four Horsemen, to be his line coach at Michigan State. Leahy then followed Crowley when he became head coach at Fordham, then a football powerhouse. It was at Fordham that Leahy built his reputation as being worthy of a head coaching job. "If the Four Horsemen of Notre Dame were the most famous backfield unit in the history of college football, then the Seven Blocks of Granite at Fordham are the most famous assembly of linemen. The man responsible for their proficiency is Frank Leahy, an assistant coach whom Knute Rockne once said would someday be a great head coach. Young Leahy has a tremendous start toward that goal."[98]

While at Fordham, Leahy coached a young guard by the name of Vince Lombardi. Lombardi may have been the only player Leahy coached who he felt had too much intensity. "Vincent was so intense. When a play worked against us, he considered it a personal affront. When one of our plays failed, he would come back to the huddle like a madman, looking for the lad who made the fatal mistake. He had a flash-flood temper. He might've been a greater offensive guard if he had simply been able to contain his emotions more. It actually hurt his concentration. I had long talks with him about it and he prayed always to St. Jude that he could overcome this weakness."[99]

In 1939 after his success at Fordham, Leahy achieved the goal he had been striving for since he was in high school: he became head coach of Boston College. There, he took over a losing team and in his first year lost only one game. His second year was even more successful as his team was undefeated in regular season play and defeated Tennessee in the Sugar Bowl.

In February of 1941, Boston College signed him to a new five-year contract. Several weeks later, Elmer Layden unexpectedly resigned as head coach at Notre Dame to become the commissioner of professional football for the princely sum of $20,000 per year. Initially, there were several names mentioned publicly as possible successors to Layden, Leahy among them. However, Leahy was one of two top contenders for the job being considered privately among the key leaders at Notre Dame. After a clandestine meeting with Father Frank Cavanaugh, the future president of Notre Dame, Leahy was hired.

The behind-the-scenes machinations and Leahy's sudden resignation came as a shock to the Boston College community. A week prior to the announcement at a varsity club dinner, it was announced proudly that Leahy had just signed a new contract and would be staying at BC for at least five more years. Leahy himself made warm comments about his affection for BC.

Wikipedia has a description of the vitriolic environment that surrounded Leahy's announcement to leave. I've tried to get the original source of the Wikipedia story without success. Two other sources, *Fenway Park Diaries* and *The Subway Domer* also quote the story.

Here's the Wikipedia version. "He tried without success to get out of his BC contract. He pleaded to the school's vice president.

When that didn't work, he went to the mayor of Boston. Then the governor of Massachusetts. Then, at a press conference, he told fifty reporters what the South Bend Tribune called 'the biggest lie of his life.' Leahy stated: 'Gentlemen I've called you all here today to inform you that I recently received my release from my coaching contract. With the release went the good wishes and benediction of Boston College.' Leahy stepped away, and the buzzing group of reporters battled for phone lines. A phone call came in for Leahy, and he took it. The vice president of Boston College was on the line. 'Coach Leahy,' he barked. 'You may go wherever you want, and whenever you want. Good-bye.'"

Frank's description of the event was far more benign and differs greatly from what was certainly an unhappy parting. "Upon my return, Curley (the BC athletic director) was most upset. He said that he couldn't release me from my contract and that the faculty moderator of athletics, who was, by now, Father Maurice Duella, was out of town, and he didn't know how soon I could get out of it. He indicated that he wanted to try to talk me into staying. I explained to him that I had turned down three offers during the season and two after it, all for more money. The only reason I wanted the Notre Dame job was that it was my Alma Mater and I had, aaaaah, long dreamed of replacing Rockne. He did not seem to understand.

"The release was very slow in coming. There was always some excuse why it could not be issued. The people at Notre Dame were pressing me for a final word. They did not want to be accused of stealing me from another college, especially another Catholic one. The matter of the missing release became crucial. It was necessary to do something. So, I engaged a suite at the Kenmore Hotel and invited the press and sports announcers to come up and have a drink on Frank Leahy. Then I called Curley at Boston College and said, 'I have all the football writers and radio men in town in the suite. I have told them that Boston College has promised me my release to go to coach at Notre Dame. They plan to print it and put it on the air. If I drop out there now, will the release be available? What do the good fathers at Boston College say?'

"Well, what could they say? I got in a cab, picked up the release and was on a train to South Bend within the hour."[100]

Hostile fan reaction was immediate. For weeks after the announcement, the *Boston Globe* printed acerbic letters from fans to the sports editor. "Thank you, Mr. Leahy—For having justified my own belief that you always were overrated, that you took a team hand-made by Gil Dobie (the former coach) and won for yourself fame upon its merits." Another wrote, "The announcement of Leahy's transfer to Notre Dame made the blood in my veins boil to the point of distillation. That is about the rottenest trick that I have imagined any coach would pull, let alone Frank Leahy, especially after that heartwarming speech at the BC varsity dinner last Sunday."[101]

Despite the messy departure from Boston, Leahy was thrilled to take over the job once held by his mentor and idol, Knute Rockne. In the intervening ten years there had been two other coaches, Hunk Anderson and Elmer Layden. However, for Leahy, it was all about inheriting the mantle of the great Rockne.

CHAPTER 9

1941

Blaik barked at him. "You there!" The boy came back to earth with a bang.
"Where are the most football games lost?" he asked. The boy thought for a second and then replied, "Right here at West Point, sir."

WITH AXIS FORCES ascendant across the globe, only Great Britain continued to resist the seemingly unbeatable Nazi forces in Europe and North Africa. In Asia, the Chinese were being constantly pushed back throughout their country by the victorious and unstoppable Japanese forces.

In June, Nazi forces invaded their former ally, Russia, in a move that surprised and shocked everyone. Accurate news of the struggle between these two closed societies was difficult to obtain. So confusing was the situation on this critical front that Americans jokingly referred to any unclear explanation they encountered by commenting that it was as clear as news from the Russian front.

Americans continued to cast a wary eye on the dark events occurring around the globe, but were happy they were not again involved *over there*. Eight years of effort by the Roosevelt Administration and the myriad of alphabet agencies it created had been ineffective in ending the Great Depression. Finally, as the country began to fulfill its role as the *Arsenal of Democracy*, the US economy began to awaken from its ten-year economic slumber. Manufacturing increased to fill defense orders both for the US and its allies. The increase in Americans employed meant that many citizens now had disposable income for the first time in a decade.

This additional income was finally making a national impact on items besides necessities. Retail sales for 1941 were up $10 million, an increase of almost 20 percent over 1940, and $6 million above the 1929 all-time high.[102]

Hollywood offered up a variety of features to match the mood of the ambivalent and divided country. For those that sought temporary relief from thoughts of future US involvement in the widening war there were historical movies such as *That Hamilton Woman* with Lawrence Olivier and Vivian Leigh or thrillers like *The Maltese Falcon* with Humphrey Bogart. *They Died With Their Boots On* and *Sergeant York* helped viewers recall some of the heroes of America's earlier wars.

With the recent passage of the draft, interest grew in military life. But many Americans were not yet interested in the gruesome details of war, so Hollywood offered comedies such as Abbott and Costello's *Buck Privates* and *Keep Em Flying* as well as Bob Hope's *Caught in the Draft*.

Foreign movie makers tried to influence American public opinion with productions of their own. *U-Boat Course West*, a documentary from Germany, provided a sympathetic view of the sea war in the Atlantic from a German point of view. Not to be outdone, the British delivered features such as *49th Parallel* and *Target for Tonight*, two features that highlighted the threat of the Nazis both in Europe and closer to home.

Hollywood stars smoked openly in movies and in photographs of stories about them in the many magazines that closely followed their private lives. Those images helped fuel the rapid rise of smoking. In 1940, the average American consumed 2,558 cigarettes per year, double that of ten years earlier. People smoked in theaters, in airplanes, on trains, at the office, and in college classrooms.[103]

Americans in increasing numbers sought relief from the dismal overseas news by flocking to movie theaters across the country. Theater operators tried to make the movie night experience an elegant and pleasant interlude from the worries of everyday life. Many theaters installed recently developed air conditioning, which offered its patrons a cool respite from the summer heat.

Elegantly uniformed young men and boys assisted moviegoers by welcoming patrons and showing them to their seats. Entry into the theater cost ten cents, seventeen to twenty-one cents for a double feature. Saturday matinees for children who breathlessly followed the weekly trials and tribulations of Batman and Superman, cost a nickel.[104]

The sports world of 1941 had its own constellation of stars. In particular, two major-league baseball players were prominent in the news—one mourned and one celebrated.

On June 2, Lou Gehrig, one of the Yankees's famous *Murderers Row*, died of a little-known and incurable disease of the spine. The disease, amyotrophic lateral sclerosis, now known as ALS, or Lou Gehrig's disease, took the life of the Yankee slugger at age thirty-seven.

Gehrig, who batted cleanup behind Babe Ruth in the New York lineup, was linked often with the Babe on the field, but was totally different from him off the field. Gehrig lived a quiet life and was devoted to his mother. After most games, a Yankee clubhouse attendant recalled that Gehrig would be the first one dressed and go home to his mother.

Because of the onset of the disease, Gehrig retired in 1939 but not before setting a record for playing in 2,130 consecutive games in fourteen years. His record stood for fifty-nine years and was surpassed only by Cal Ripken, Jr. who played in 2,632 consecutive games over twenty-one years.

While the baseball world mourned the loss of Gehrig, it celebrated the streak of another New York Yankee. Joe DiMaggio got a hit in fifty-six consecutive games, a record that still stands. During the streak, which ended on July 17, the *Yankee Clipper* hit fifteen home runs, fifteen RBIs, and batted .408. After the streak ended, DiMaggio confided to friend and fellow Yankee Phil Rizzuto that he would have received $10,000 from the Heinz 57 company if he could've extended the streak one more game to fifty-seven.

In January 1941, Earl Blaik arrived back at his alma mater ready for work. His task was daunting. In 1940 Army had a record of 1–7–1 and did not score against its major competitors. They lost the Navy game the preceding two years and hadn't beaten Notre Dame in a decade. The plebe team, which had a slightly better record of 3–4–1, didn't seem to offer much hope for the future.

Whether or not Blaik was initially unhappy about leaving his successful and peaceful coaching job in the verdant hills of New Hampshire, he took on the Army challenge in his normal intense manner. He started the day at his office on the top floor of the gymnasium early in the morning and worked most of the day either there or on the practice field. He also worked many nights and weekends.

In addition to implementing his own offensive and defensive of schemes on the team, he had the difficult task of instilling confidence in the players and restoring a winning spirit. Coach Blaik loved to tell the following humorous story to illustrate the difficulty he faced when he first got to West Point.

At one of his first training sessions, he emphasized the fundamentals. "No football team can get anywhere without good tackles. Tackle is the position where most football games are lost. You must have . . ."

He broke off. He had noticed one of the players was gazing dreamily into space. Perhaps he was visioning a furlough. Blaik barked at him.

"You there!"

The boy came back to earth with a bang.

"Where are the most football games lost?" he asked.

The boy thought for a second and then replied, "Right here at West Point, sir."[105]

However, Blaik knew that his Cadets would do all that was asked of them. No one believed in working harder than his opponents than Earl Blaik. Starting immediately, he would demand more of his players and form a team around those that responded most aggressively.

In one of his first days back at the Military Academy, Blaik called a team meeting. The players came in their long grey coats expecting a cursory meeting with their new coach. Instead, Coach Blaik moved them to the field house to begin working out.

Blaik's hard work paid off in his first season as Army won its first four games. Coach Blaik was pleased but knew that the schedule he faced in November would be much tougher. First up that month would be Army's old nemesis, Notre Dame, led by their new coach Frank Leahy and a young quarterback by the name of Angelo Bertelli.

It was also Leahy's first season as head coach of the Irish. Leahy quickly established the toughness that he expected of his players and coaches. On a blustery cold northern Indiana day in March, Leahy and his staff met with sports writers for their inaugural meeting of the 1941 season. Leahy wore only a hooded sweatshirt while his assistant coaches wore warm, heavy jackets. The new coach gave the writers his initial assessment of his team and his plans to develop and train them for the upcoming season. He then pointed to his assistant coaches, and said, "My coaching staff, they believe in warmth. See what nice jackets they have on." The message was clear. From then on, the assistant coaches wore what their tough coach from Winner, South Dakota wore.[106]

Leahy's team had only four returning starters. However, he also had several talented non-starters who had significant playing time. Among them were players whose names would become very familiar to Irish fans in the future, notably sophomores Angelo Bertelli and Creighton Miller. Both were talented athletes who excelled in multiple sports. In addition to football, Miller earned a monogram in track. In later years he described how he came to join the track team. One day while visiting track practice, Miller bet the starting sprinter a milkshake that he could beat him. When the bet was accepted Miller went to the locker room and donned a track uniform and track shoes. When he returned Miller defeated his opponent in a sixty-yard dash.

After witnessing the race, Coach Doc Handy invited Miller to join the track team. Miller turned him down because he didn't like practice. He had just finished the football season and was not willing to sign up for a new commitment. The coach then asked him if he would be interested if he just ran in meets.

"I said, 'No practice?'"

"He replied, 'No practice.'"

"I might win a dual meet indoors, that was about the best I could do. But I did win enough points to win my letter, so I became a monogram man in track. At the Michigan State relays some guy got sick, so Doc Handy came up to me and said, 'There's a medley relay; do you know what a medley is?'"

"I said, 'Sure that's where guys run different distances.'"

"He asked, 'Would you run the 220?'"

"I said, 'You're sure it isn't the 440? I'm not running the 440, the track is 440.'"

"He said, 'No it's 220.'"

"I said, 'If it turns out to be 440, I'm giving you the baton when I come around the first time.'"[107]

Bertelli was a star high school football player from western Massachusetts. Because of his strong arm, he was known even in high school as "The Springfield Rifle." Because he also was an excellent hockey player, he initially considered going to several northeastern colleges where he could play both sports. However, Bertelli decided to focus on football and Notre Dame.

Bertelli was not an exceptional runner. It was his passing that had attracted Notre Dame and the other schools that offered him scholarships. But Bertelli's freshman year, 1940, was depressing for the young quarterback. He found himself way down on the roster because Notre Dame in Layden's last year valued running over passing.

Things didn't change all that rapidly for Bertelli even after Leahy's arrival in the spring of 1941. Bertelli was relegated to the seventh team. However, once the coach decided that his team had to pass more in the upcoming season, Bertelli was quickly elevated to the first team and started in the fall. He threw for over 1,000 yards that first season and was second in the Heisman balloting.

Almost all those on the roster of those early Leahy teams would see their collegiate careers shortened or overshadowed by the war that lay just over the horizon. Many of the seniors on the 1941 team would soon be called to active duty. Jack Barry as a Navy Lt. (JG) was in the first wave at Omaha Beach on D-Day. Both Bernie Crimmins and Paul Lillis commanded PT boats and were decorated for heroism. [108] Bob McBride, a lineman in 1941 and 1942 and later a favorite assistant to Leahy, was captured in the Battle of the Bulge. Four members of the 1942 team, Murphy (captain and end), Neff (tackle), Lanahan (center), and Sullivan (tackle), joined the Marine Corps in 1943 and played football at Camp Lejeune under coach and Notre Dame alumni Jack Chevigny. They all later served in some of the most hard-fought battles in the Pacific at Saipan, Iwo Jima, and Okinawa

Despite the looming war, the pieces were in place and the magic of the Leahy years was about to begin. From the opening game in 1941, Leahy's first season had been an unqualified success. The Irish had won their first five games by a combined score of 142–27 and now had their sights set on another national title.

On November 1, over 75,000 eager fans filed into Yankee stadium to watch a rejuvenated and unbeaten Army team take on a strong, undefeated Notre Dame team once again. It was reminiscent of the classic struggles of the 1920s between the two football powerhouses. The game was played in a torrential downpour at Yankee Stadium. The churned and muddy field quickly hampered both the passing and ground game of both teams. Because of the extreme conditions, it was difficult to ascertain each squad's true strength.

Poor playing conditions also made it difficult for each of the first-year coaches to take the full measure of the other. The teams sparred for sixty minutes like two semi-blind boxers who probed for weaknesses and occasionally struck a critical blow without ever being able to deliver a knockout punch. The game ended in a 0–0 tie, a significant achievement for Army and a big disappointment for Notre Dame. Even with subsequent wins over Navy, Northwestern, and USC, that tie was enough to spoil Notre Dames's quest for a national title.

The Notre Dame game marked the high watermark for the Cadets during Blaik's first year. Losses against Harvard, Penn, and Navy, and a slim victory over West Virginia, ended the season in disappointment. The Navy game especially hurt the Cadets. They had not beaten the Midshipmen nor scored against them in the preceding two years. There was little consolation in the fact that Army at least did score in the 1941 game, losing 14–6.

In the preceding five years, the Cadets had scored only twice against the Irish while losing all five games by a combined score total of 13–67. The hard-fought, scoreless tie in 1941 was a fitting start for this first meeting between Blaik and Leahy. It served notice that under these two coaches the rivalry would intensify. It would reach its stunning apex five years in the future, but only after the disruption of a world war that would bring significant change to both institutions.

Five weeks after the Army-Notre Dame game, the Japanese attacked Pearl Harbor. The events of December 7, 1941 would radically change the plans of every American and alter college football in ways unanticipated by everyone involved in the game.

CHAPTER 10

THE WAR

> *We have been stepping closer to war for many months. Now it is come and we must meet it as united Americans regardless of our attitude in the past with the policy our government has followed.*
> —Charles Lindbergh

AS IN PREVIOUS wars, West Point alumni would dominate the leadership of the World War II Army. Of the 155 commanders of units of division size and larger, 89 were Academy graduates. Four of the five generals who ascended to five-star rank were MacArthur, Bradley, Eisenhower, and Arnold—all West Pointers.

On December 6, 1941, debate about America's role in the war then underway in Europe and Asia was robust and passionate. The country was almost equally divided between those fervently espousing total isolation and those advocating aid in varying degrees to the beleaguered Brits, Russians, and Chinese. Leading the opposition against any involvement in the war was the America First Committee. It had several prominent Americans on its board who insured the message of the group would have a substantial megaphone. They included Charles Lindbergh, famed aviator, General Robert Wood, a decorated World War I veteran and chairman of Sears, Walt Disney, and writers Sinclair Lewis and E.E. Cummings. Lindbergh issued a terse statement recognizing that his fervent and passionate stand of a few days earlier was now untenable. "We have been stepping closer to war for many months. Now it is come and we must meet it as united Americans regardless of our attitude in the past with the policy our government has followed.

Whether or not that policy has been wise, our country has been attacked by force of arms and by force of arms we must retaliate. Our own defenses and our own military position have already been neglected too long. We must now turn every effort to building the greatest and most efficient Army, Navy, and Air Force in the world."

Almost everyone knew that sooner or later the US would be involved in the war. Dramatic broadcasts from besieged London by Edward R. Murrow and others as well as the continuous dispatches from battlefields across the globe had told of the unrelenting successes of the Axis forces.

But, like all unthinkable thoughts, the populace pushed thoughts of US involvement in the war to the back of its mind, hoping unrealistically that some unexpected event would occur that would bring the unreasonable belligerents to their senses and allow peace to prevail once again.

However, should that not happen, the US would roll up its sleeves and get into the conflict and quickly end it like it had done only a generation before. The vernacular of the day was clear on that. The overconfident US public felt that the nearsighted Japanese pilots might be running amok against the Chinese, but when they met the might of America it would be a different story. And, apparently those Aryan supermen of Hitler's had already forgotten the licking they took from the doughboys of twenty years earlier. Our fathers had licked their fathers and now we were ready to have our sons lick their sons.

President Roosevelt and other leaders of the government had a difficult task of trying to placate both the isolationists and those wanting to offer aid to those countries facing the Axis forces while trying to ready the country for the war they felt was on the horizon.

Three articles on the front page of the *New York Daily News* on December 6, clearly showed the balancing act the administration was forced to follow while trying to lead the divided country. One article described the obfuscation of the Japanese ambassador in responding to President Roosevelt's inquiry as to the Japanese intentions after that country's occupation of French Indochina. Another article reported that the House of Representatives passed an eight- billion-dollar supplemental bill, which raised total defense spending to sixty-eight billion. This new appropriation would provide funds to raise the army to two million men. Still a third article reported a leaked administration war plan calling for an army of five million to fight Hitler even after the defeat of Great Britain and Russia.

Thus, on one page there was clear evidence of aggressive Japanese plans to widen the war alongside another article indicating the slow awakening of the country to the dangers it faced. The third article, outlining a leaked version of the country's true war plans, drew only an embarrassed and terse response from Roosevelt and Secretary of War Stimson. Such were the difficulties of preparing a reluctant country for a conflict, which was only one day away.

All the debate and division in the country evaporated on December 7, after the Japanese attack on Pearl Harbor. Probably no single event has galvanized and united the country more completely before or since. Enlistments and draft quotas were revised overnight to accommodate the large numbers of volunteers who presented themselves to their local boards and recruiting offices. There were so many volunteers that the secretary of war announced that Army enlistment would soon cease. The fear was that the patriotic outpouring of young men wanting to sign up—such as farm boys—was depriving many war industries of skilled workers. [109] The Army would depend instead on the draft boards to sort out who was needed at home and who could serve.

The impact on college football was immediately and unexpectedly experienced by several teams. Toward the end of the year bowl selections were announced. Duke and Oregon State were scheduled to meet in the Rose Bowl in Pasadena and Fordham would take on Missouri in the Sugar Bowl. Prior to the bowl announcements hardly anyone took note of the planned visit by the San Jose State football team to play a few exhibition games during the first week in December in Hawaii.

The San Jose Spartans were scheduled to play two charity games, one against Willamette University of Oregon and one against the University of Hawaii. All the young men of both the San Jose and Willamette teams were eagerly looking forward to a two-week visit to Hawaii. Instead, they became witnesses to the opening shots of America's entry into World War II.

While having breakfast at the Moana Hotel in Waikiki, several of the players and coaches noticed large geysers in the ocean. They could also hear planes and gunfire but were convinced it must be military maneuvers causing the commotion. They soon heard reports and saw evidence that Pearl Harbor was being attacked by Japanese planes. After the attack, the players sought out the chief of police in Honolulu and volunteered their services. They were given tin hats and shotguns and assigned to police squads led by veteran police officers. They participated in raids on suspected Japanese sympathizers. After a few days they were assigned guard duties in the city.

On December 19, they were evacuated from Hawaii and returned to the mainland. When they arrived in San Francisco many of the young men immediately enlisted.

In the confusion and fears in the days following the Pearl Harbor attack, there were concerns about further Japanese attacks on the West Coast of the United States. Military officials ordered all non-military gatherings to be canceled. The Rose Bowl was one of the victims of this decree. Much to the disappointment of the Duke team, the game's location was changed from Pasadena to Durham, North Carolina.

The Duke team realized that with military commitments looming, they might not be home for Christmas for several years. Giving up two weeks to practice and play in North Carolina was certainly not worth the trade. Therefore, they voted 25–2 against playing the game at all. After a promise from Coach Wallace Wade that he would give them six days off at Christmas, the team agreed to play. Oregon State won the game on January 1, 1942, by a score of 20–14 in a non-Pasadena-like cold and rainy day.

In a short time, many of the eighty or so players who took the field in Durham on New Year's Day were in the military. In chance meetings, several of the participants of that game met again during the war. Charles Haynes of Duke and Frank Parker of Oregon State reunited during their march through Italy with a US infantry unit. Shortly after they met again, Haynes was wounded in battle and left for dead. He was in the open making it too dangerous for his fellow soldiers to rescue him. Some seventeen hours later, Parker, fighting on a nearby hill, heard about his friend being wounded and raced back to rescue Haynes. Parker and another soldier were able to carry his injured comrade to a medical aid station. After several months in a hospital, Haynes returned to his unit. Like so many soldiers of WWII, being wounded didn't mean staying out of the war.

After the war the men reunited at a fiftieth anniversary gathering for the Rose Bowl participants of the game that had been moved from Pasadena to Durham, NC. "Charles Haynes embraced Frank Parker, gave him a hug, told everyone at the reunion, kept pointing out that this was the man that saved his life. As they read the names of the deceased players for Oregon State and Duke, Haynes started to cry and looked across the room at Parker."[110]

Gene Gray, who caught the winning touchdown pass in the 1942 game, survived multiple bombing runs over Europe as a pilot and was later injured when his military plane crashed in Panama. He lost both of his arms. In all, four players—three from Duke and one from Oregon State—were killed in action.[111]

West Point soon became tragically and personally aware of the human cost of the conflict. Hardly a day went by without some notification of the loss of one or more of its graduates. Many of those killed had left less than a year earlier and were known by many cadets still at the academy.

Changes were made at West Point to put it on a war footing. On January 12, 1942, Major General Francis B. Wilby, class of 1905, replaced General Eichelberger as superintendent. Two weeks later Wilby was summoned to the White House to meet with President Roosevelt, whose instructions were clear. He directed the general to minimize cadet losses due to academics and modernize the instruction at West Point by putting increased emphasis on air corps and tank training. Roosevelt, a big sports fan, also directed General Wilby to continue intercollegiate sports for morale purposes until he received contrary instructions from the president.

CHAPTER 11

COLLEGE FOOTBALL GOES TO WAR

We were out of business during World War II. Navy came in and kept us afloat until the war was over.
—Father Theodore Hesburgh President of the University of Notre Dame

AS THE GRIM news from the Philippines, Wake Island, and Guam continued, Americans tried to assess how they would be affected and how they might contribute to the ultimate victory Americans knew they would achieve.

It was clear that fighting a global war would require a huge army and navy. In addition, aircraft production would have to be greatly increased. Ultimately, the number of aircraft produced annually rose from 921 in 1939 to 96,000 by 1944. By war's end over 300,000 planes were built, requiring the addition of large numbers of trained pilots for both Naval aviation and the Army Air Forces. These numbers would greatly exceed all expectations of the war planners at the start of the war.

West Point was doing its part to fill this demand. When the class of 1942 graduated in May, 188 of the 374 members were assigned to the air corps compared to sixty-two in the infantry, thirty-two to field artillery, and ninety-two other ground branches. By July 1942, 255 of the 412 members of the class of 1943, and 315 of the 522 members of the class of 1944 had signed up and qualified for aviation training.[112]

However, the requirement to provide pilots to fill the increasing number of airplanes rolling off the assembly lines could not be met by the service academies alone. In addition, the exponential growth of the US Army required immense numbers of soldiers to be recruited and trained. As the personnel requirements ramped up, the leaders of colleges and universities attempted to discern and anticipate how their activities would be changed by the war and what their role might be. They were rightfully concerned about their ability to survive financially. They knew that the war, to a large extent, would be fought by the segment of the population that was their main source of students. President Roosevelt shared their concerns. In October 1942, the president issued guidance to the military services to develop programs that would utilize the campuses of the country's colleges and universities. His guidance was general but provided an outline for the services to pursue. "Please have an immediate study made as to the highest utilization of American colleges. This is in view of the undoubted fact that the drafting of boys down to and including eighteen years old will greatly deplete all undergraduate enrollment . . . it may be advisable to call in a number of the leading educators. . . .. There is an an enormous amount of equipment in colleges—buildings, athletic fields, etc., which the Army and Navy may be able to use without great changes."[113]

Everyone knew that the job of incorporating the nation's institutions of higher learning into the war effort would be a necessary but daunting task. The president's request was a start. Ultimately over two hundred colleges and universities would host programs for the Army, Navy, Coast Guard, and Marines. The size of the programs would range from two thousand naval (660 marines) students at Dartmouth to sixty-eight at Webb Institute of Naval Architecture in New York. [114] By war's end one Navy program alone would graduate 80,000 cadets and 2,500 instructors.

These programs helped financially struggling universities and colleges to weather the fiscal upheaval brought on by the war. "We were out of business during World War II. Navy came in and kept us afloat until the war was over. Hesburgh vowed that under his watch the football series between the two schools would be kept as long as Navy wanted it continued. To this day, Navy has never wanted to back out."[115]

In early 1942, Notre Dame turned over four of its residence halls on the South Quad—Badin, Howard, Lyons, and Morrissey to the Navy for its V-7 program, which was also known as the Midshipmen School. During that transformation, the Navy constructed a drill hall and a headquarters-classroom building on the north side of the campus, where today's Hesburgh Memorial Library with the *Touchdown Jesus* mural is located. It was dedicated in 1962, after the Navy Drill Hall had been razed.

On July 1, 1943, Notre Dame welcomed 1,851 active-duty trainees, the largest program of its kind in the country. By comparison, Notre Dame's civilian student enrollment was merely seven hundred. Thus, five more residence halls were opened to the sailors: Alumni, Dillon, and Walsh on the South Quad, and Cavanaugh and Zahm on the North Quad.[116]

When these programs were launched, no one knew how they might affect college life or football. Of course, the needs of the services would come first. Any collateral damage to college sports would have to be tolerated as a necessary requirement of the war effort. What emerged was a solution that showed that when the creativity and ingenuity of those involved were applied, preserving sports and winning the war were very complementary. However, the solution would spawn an unorthodox three-legged approach that ultimately saved college football.

The first of these legs was the already existing college football programs. It was clear from the outset that these programs would be greatly strained by the departure of large numbers of players and coaches who either enlisted or were drafted. Because of this, by 1943 approximately 190 colleges had abandoned football. "Starting with the A's, Alabama, Arizona, Arizona State, and Auburn dropped out of big-time football after the 1942 season; in the B's, Baylor and Brigham Young; and so on through the alphabet."[117]

However, all was not grim. For those 131 schools in forty-three states lucky enough to host one of the new military cadet programs on their campus, football was alive and well. Some programs even improved with the addition of the new cadets. In 1943, Purdue, with the assistance of seven navy and twenty-six marine trainees, had a 9–0–0 season good enough to win the Big Ten Championship. This was a significant turnaround from the 1–8–0 record of the preceding year.

Some colleges had conflicting loyalties. The University of Iowa maintained its own team but also hosted the Naval Iowa Preflight Program. When the Preflight team beat the Hawkeyes 25–0, many of the University of Iowa fans booed them.

The Army and Navy took very different approaches to fulfilling the president's guidance. From the outset, the Army was ambivalent about the program it created in response to the president. It had developed the Army Specialist Training Program (ASTP), a successor to the short-lived Student Army Training School (SATS) of World War I. Lieutenant General Leslie J. McNair, commander of the Army Ground Forces, responsible for filling the needs of the Army's ground forces in World War II, exploded when he heard of the plan. "With 300,000 men short . . . we are asked to send men to college!"[118]

The Army hoped to use the program to fill perceived shortages of men having intelligence, aptitude, education, and training in fields such as medicine, engineering, languages, science, mathematics, and psychology. The Army had difficulty competing for men with these skills because the Navy and Army Air Force were more attractive to many of these potential recruits. The program called for selected applicants to attend one of 227 colleges or universities for a period of nine months.

From the outset, the Army expected this program to be a no-frills, intensive training course. Courses such as dentistry, medicine, engineering, languages, science, math, and psychology would be taught. At the end of the nine months, graduates would be considered for Officers Candidate School (OCS) and possible commissioning. The Army made clear that attendance and commissioning were not guaranteed, insisting that the students not be called *cadets*, which might imply they were student officers.

Even though they were on college campuses, trainees in the ASTP group were prohibited from playing varsity sports or engaging in most other campus activities. Their mission was to devote all energy to learning their assigned skill and report as quickly as possible to an Army unit. As the war progressed, the increasing need for more soldiers caused the program to be killed. Because it had been an orphan from the beginning, the 140,000 men enrolled in ASTP had no champion to defend them and their program.

General Marshall, Army's chief of staff, needed replacements for existing units, telling the secretary of war (one of the few defenders of the program) that he wanted to end ASTP to provide critically needed replacements to existing army units. The ASTP was a ready pool of highly qualified soldiers that would fill the need perfectly. If Marshall couldn't get those student soldiers, he would have to disband ten existing divisions to find the replacements he needed for the Army.

Faced with that choice, the secretary of war agreed to cancel the program. To the chagrin of many of the 140,000 students, the announcement was made to liquidate the program on February 10, 1944. The dispossessed participants were sent to units throughout the Army. Sixteen thousand were sent to various locations to work on the atomic bomb. The dispersal of the students ended the Army's brief impact on the colleges and universities of the country.

The Navy took an entirely different approach, which was to have a significant influence on college sports and would become the second leg underpinning war time football. The three most powerful men who had responsibility for the Navy's program were

Under Secretary of the Navy James Forrestal (a future secretary of the Navy and of defense), Captain Arthur Radford, commander of Aeronautic Training, (a future chairman of the joint chiefs) and Commander T.J. Hamilton, a carrier pilot, and former Naval Academy football coach and director of overall flight training (a future admiral and athletic director at the Naval Academy).

They all agreed that intercollegiate sports, specifically football, help to foster the skills and attitudes necessary for the development of successful Navy fighter pilots. The stated purpose of all Naval aviation training was "to master the fastest, most vicious machines in the world—fighting aircraft." The Navy believed that collegiate football provided those that participated with physical and emotional conditioning. It also helped those athletes to develop strength, skill, maturity, stamina, and the will to win. The coaches and the leaders of the program hoped to turn out pilots who would not only enter battle, but would react quickly, remain alert, and aggressively and fearlessly accomplish their missions and return to base, disregarding fatigue, discomfort, or wounds.

This official enthusiastic embrace of the Navy *V* programs contrasted starkly with the lukewarm approach taken by the Army with its ASTP. The Army leaders felt that intramurals could provide the same physical and character benefits as intercollegiate sports. The difference clearly was in the emphasis the Navy placed on the development of the soft skills of character, teamwork, strong desire to win, endurance, and ability to play regardless of pain or fatigue. The Navy felt strongly that these attributes could not be effectively developed in an informal and less rigorous intramural program.

It was ironic that the Army leaders (Marshall included) seemed to ignore the intrinsic, spiritual message embedded in General Marshall's own famous World War II quote, "I want an officer for a secret and dangerous mission. I want a West Point football player." In all fairness, the technical and mental skills required for a member of the Army ground forces were far less than those of a Navy pilot.

The Army Air Force, seeking almost identical skills for its pilots as the Navy required, did embrace a football program similar to that of its sister service.[119]

The Navy programs also produced additional benefits by raising the morale of both Naval personnel and civilians as well as having a positive publicity impact on the Navy flight programs. However, not all Navy leaders were enthusiastic about the V programs. Commander Gene Tunney, the former heavyweight boxing champion, and head of the Navy's aeronautical personnel section, strongly opposed the program. "He opposed the commissioning of 'fat football coaches' and viewed preflight training as 'elitist collegiate play' that slowed combat training, thereby forcing an unfair share of the worst burden on less-fortunate enlisted personnel." [120] Despite Tunney's criticism, the programs flourished and grew.

Football was the most widely known of the sports spawned by the big programs. However, the activities encompassed a wide variety of other sports. During the first year of the program more than 600 football games were played in the intramural, varsity, or instructional phase of training. In addition, there were 4,419 intramural track meets; 9,139 boxing matches; 3,276 swimming meets; 2,828 gymnastic events; 2,000 basketball games; and 875 soccer matches for the approximately 25,000 V-5 air cadets.

By all measures the V programs were a success. The US fleet expanded from seven carriers early in the war to a hundred by war's end. The number of pilots grew from 4,500 to 60,000 to fill the need for pilots to fly the increased production of aircraft, which grew from 3,500 to 41,000. Thanks to these programs and the massive buildup of US manufacturing, which produced large quantities of advanced fighters, the grim defeats of early 1942 were avenged in a spectacular fashion by 1944. In June that year, the Battle of the Philippine Sea, dubbed "The Great Marianas Turkey Shoot" by the jubilant and victorious Naval pilots, US forces destroyed nearly 600 Japanese aircraft, sank two enemy fleet carriers, a light carrier, and two oilers, killing nearly 3,000 of the Imperial Japanese Navy pilots and sailors while losing 123 aircraft and 109 dead.[121]

The third leg of the tripod that supported college football during the war were the teams that represented the many military bases that had sprung up across the country. The mission of these facilities was to train America's rapidly growing armed forces. Ultimately sixteen million men and women passed through these bases enroute to their assignments. Providing trained personnel for the various services was of course the top priority for these posts. The senior leadership of each service determined the schedules and programs to be conducted at each facility.

However, the commanders of these bases wielded enormous power in managing the myriad of issues associated with the personnel on his post. They had considerable latitude when dealing with the service members who came to their facilities, how long they stayed, and when they left. This enabled some ambitious and creative base commanders to recruit and build strong athletic teams. In doing research over seventy-five years after the fact, it's difficult to trace much of the logic of the comings and goings of service members at the various bases. What is clear is that the movement of sixteen million people over the four years of the war created an environment that allowed a system of athletic recruiting to develop on many bases.

Recruiters might show up at a young athlete's home and offer him a much better option than being drafted. And of course, the service academies could offer another attractive option to those men trying to find the best way to serve the country. Many older coaches and players, both professional and college, were also offered these options. Since eligibility rules during the war were almost nonexistent, recruiters had wide latitude in what they could offer prospective candidates.

These wartime programs saved college football, but they did it in a somewhat free-form and Wild West fashion. An AP standings at the end of 1944 provides an interesting insight into how football was changed by the war. The top five ranked teams that year were:

1. Army
2. Ohio State
3. Randolph Field
4. Navy
5. Bainbridge Naval Training Center

Army and Navy were collegiate football powerhouses before the war. There's no question, however, that they both benefited from the wartime recruiting environment. If we count both service academies, four of the top five teams were affiliated with the military, and twelve of the top twenty teams in 1944 were connected to the military.

CHAPTER 12

1942

I won't know until my barber tells me on Monday.
—Knute Rockne

AFTER SUFFERING A series of early defeats in the Pacific, US troops had rallied, helped by the flood of new recruits and equipment. That effort was fueled in large measure by a country that quickly transformed its industries and consumption. IBM now made Browning automatic rifles (BARs) instead of typewriters and accounting machines. Ford was producing bombers instead of cars at its newly built and sprawling Willow Run plant. Rationing of staples such as meat and butter was pervasive throughout the civilian population. Travel in all forms, especially by private automobile, was severely restricted.

Gas rationing was imposed on seventeen eastern states in May 1942 and then nationally in December. A speed limit of thirty-five miles per hour was enforced nationwide. Anyone who tried to circumvent the rationing system was severely punished. A May 23, 1942, article in the *New York Daily News* revealed the story of a socially prominent woman, Mrs. C. Frank Reeves, who was caught hoarding six, five-gallon cans of gasoline in her basement. Her neighbors in the tony Sutton Place neighborhood of New York City smelled gas and reported the hoarder to the authorities. Mrs. Reeves, in addition to the embarrassment suffered by the revelation, faced a heavy fine and confiscation of the gasoline.

Among the most supportive and crucial to the war effort was Army's football alumni. "On November 6, 1942—one day before our invasion of North Africa—of the group of approximately five hundred Army football lettermen since 1891 there were two four-star generals, two lieutenant generals, twenty major generals, thirty-eight brigadier generals, ninety-eight colonels, one hundred-and-five lieutenant colonels, sixty-four majors, twenty-one captains, forty-six first lieutenants, and six second lieutenants. There were also seven who had been killed in action, two missing, three prisoners of war, and only twenty-nine were in civil life."[122]

Of the roughly 10,000 West Point graduates living in 1945, more than 88 percent would serve in the war. Over 500 would be killed, many of those from the war classes of 1941 to 1945.[123]

Only four months after America's entry into the war, the April 1942 issue of *Assembly Magazine,* the magazine published by the West Point Alumni Association for Academy graduates, provided a sad prelude to the sacrifices that awaited academy graduates in the future. Four entries signified the costly commitment of West Point to the country's defense and the enduring and resilient strength of the Long Gray Line. One page listed the early casualties of the war. Another page highlighted those that had already received awards for bravery. Many more pages listed those graduates who had become civilians but had now volunteered to return to active duty when war broke out. A fourth entry memorialized those graduates who had died peacefully after their service to the country in other wars.

One of the many who were cited for bravery was Sandy Nininger, who had graduated less than a year earlier. He was killed on Bataan after volunteering to lead a relief group to help a beleaguered company. He was wounded three times carrying out his mission before he was killed. For these actions he was posthumously awarded the Medal of Honor.

The first full year of the war, 1942, brought chaos and turmoil to football programs across the country. In contrast, the roster at West

Point strengthened and stabilized as many talented young man eagerly sought the opportunity to fulfill their military obligations on the banks of the Hudson River. Because the course of study was now three years, some of them would see wartime service only in the closing days of this war. Many of them would see combat in future wars yet unseen.

This was also a transition year for the Army football program. Military service had not yet stripped America's campuses of many of the young men still playing college football. Army defeated Cornell, Columbia, Harvard, and Princeton in 1942 but lost to Pennsylvania. Their other two losses that season were to the two most important rivals on the schedule—Notre Dame and Navy. The Cadets did not score a point in those three losses.

The senior military leaders were faced with a dilemma when considering whether to play the annual Army-Navy game. Playing the game would raise morale and showcase the two academies. On the other hand, encouraging unnecessary travel for a football game might be viewed as frivolous by the public. Government and military leaders were initially against playing the game at all because of the travel restrictions. President Roosevelt thought the game would be good for morale and directed that it be played with some major modifications.

On November 28, the game was played at Annapolis. Attendees were limited to the Brigade of Midshipmen and fans and newsmen who lived within a ten-mile radius. These restrictions resulted in a sparse crowd of 11,000 instead of the normal attendance of 100,000 of previous Army-Navy games.

The Corps of Cadets was not allowed to travel to the game, so the third classmen (sophomores) and fourth classmen (freshmen) of Midshipmen were ordered to sit behind the Army bench and root for the Cadets. Reports indicated that some of these less than enthusiastic fans sang "On Brave Old Army Team" with fingers crossed. Even Army's mascot was prohibited from traveling. A mule from a nearby dairy farm was recruited to fill in.

President Roosevelt telegrammed both teams emphasizing the teamwork of both services, which were then engaged in a worldwide struggle. "The graduates of the two academies are engaged shoulder to shoulder in the grim game of war. Throughout the world, they are knitting the ties of comradeship which they first formed on the playing fields of the homeland."[124]

The president had been right about his belief that playing the game would be good for the country's morale in this difficult first year of the war. The game was broadcast nationwide by three national radio networks and by shortwave to servicemen worldwide. Over forty million people tuned into the game.

Army, with a 6–2 record, was favored over the Navy team, which entered the game with a record of 4–3. However, the anemic Army offense was once again on full display. The Cadets were unable to cross into Navy territory until the fourth quarter. The game ended in a 14–2 Navy victory. It was clear that Army needed some offensive help. That help was on the way and would soon be incubating in the form of "Doc" Blanchard, Glenn Davis, and Arnold Tucker, and would manifest itself convincingly in the 1944, 1945, and 1946 seasons.

Coach Blaik's second season was a disappointment. His team had failed to score against three major rivals—Penn, Notre Dame, and Navy. However, he had reason to be optimistic. Because of the war, the rule prohibiting freshmen from playing had been suspended for the duration. Army had fielded several promising freshmen. Doug Kenna, Tom Lombardo, Joe Stanowicz, and Dale Hall would be valuable assets in coming seasons. Additionally, events unknown even to the coach were underway that would bring many more talented athletes to the Military Academy. These players would come to be recognized in future years as the greatest Army team in history.

Nine hundred miles west, the country's entry into the war was having the opposite effect on the South Bend campus. Whereas West Point was receiving increased funding and greatly expanded facilities, the administration at Notre Dame was worried about the university's ability to survive financially.

At the time of the Pearl Harbor attack, Notre Dame, then an all-male university, had 3,200 students. Large numbers of Notre Dame students left the school immediately to enlist. In November of 1942 the draft age was lowered from twenty to eighteen, further depleting the pool of potential incoming freshmen. By 1943, Notre Dame faced a 20 percent drop in the student body to the Depression-era levels of only 2,623 students.[125]

Father Hugh O'Donnell hoped that with the advent of a new war, the military would establish new officer training programs on the campus. Prior to the war, the Navy had established a NROTC program for about 150 Notre Dame students. This was a four-year program that would lead to a commission in the Navy for all those that completed the program. However, Father O'Donnell was looking for additional programs. He applied to the Army at the outset of the war seeking to reestablish the program initiated during World War I.

On February 10, 1942, the university received welcome news from the US Department of the Navy; Notre Dame had been selected to host 1,000 sailors each month to a new program that could lead to commissioning in the US Navy. Called the V-7, the program would be revised as the war progressed. However, in its initial phase it called for a one-month preliminary training period at various universities and colleges around the country followed by more lengthy training at other institutions.

Like West Point, Notre Dame worried about its sons that were in harm's way and mourning those already lost in the war. It had already lost eight Notre Dame alumni in the Philippines.

Uncertainty also plagued the coaches of both institutions. If Coach Blaik and Coach Leahy were hoping at the end of 1941 that their second year as head coach would be more tranquil and allow them to settle into their new duties, they would be sorely disappointed. By 1943, both coaches would themselves be in the military. Blaik would become a lieutenant colonel in the Army but remained at West Point. Leahy would become a commander in the Navy and take an assignment in the Pacific that would allow him to both serve the country and help him recruit some of the finest football players then serving in the military, recruits that would help make Notre Dame a football powerhouse after the war.

Leahy had introduced an entirely new offense in 1942. He had observed the Chicago Bears of the National Professional Football League defeat the Washington Redskins decisively 73–0 to win the Professional Championship in 1940. That same season, Stanford defeated Nebraska in the Rose Bowl. Both teams had resurrected the *T-formation* to overwhelm their opponents. The updated T-formation was almost as old as football itself. Amos Alonzo Stagg had introduced it to the University of Chicago in 1892. Army played it in its earliest days.

The T-formation of those bygone days bore only a slight similarity to the new formation. The older version was more a game of power and mass with most of the plays focused on runs between the tackles. As football evolved, greater finesse became more valued. The T-formation was discarded in favor of formations that favored plays to the outside and provided more options for passing. Notre Dame's shift to its famous box by Rockne in the 1920s was indicative of this more fluid style of offense.

This revised T-formation with its myriad of offensive plays was baffling to defenses unfamiliar with it. The backs could rush in three directions. Fakes combined with all the backfield motion made it more difficult to see who had the ball. It could be the fullback running off the guard position or the halfback who slants off the tackle. It might be the man in motion who takes a handoff or a lateral. Or the quarterback could keep the ball after faking a handoff and bootleg or throw a pass. It was these possibilities that stirred Leahy's creativity.

In addition, the Irish had in Angelo Bertelli an excellent passer but not a very fleet runner. In 1941 he threw fifteen touchdown passes and completed seventy out of 123 attempts for 1,027 yards. However, he ran the ball forty-one times, gaining 116 yards while losing sixty yards for the season.

At the start of the 1942 season, the coach delivered the news of his plans to change the offense to his quarterback in his normal direct but diplomatic style. "Ah, Angelo," he said. "Ah, lad, you're looking fine. To get straight to the point, because this concerns you as much as it does anyone. Quite succinctly, lad, you are the finest passer in the nation. You are also about the slowest running tailback I have ever seen since I played the position at Winner High School many years ago. How would you like a situation where all you had to do was concentrate on your passing? You would simply hand the ball off to the others and let them worry about the running."

Anticipating the upcoming wartime player shortages, he continued. "The wear and tear on personnel is lessened because faking and deception are stressed more than naked power. This is it, Angelo, football's future."[126]

Of course, changing the traditional Irish offense after his undefeated 1941 season was not popular with everyone, especially some Irish fans. The coach received this letter shortly after his plan to change the offense was announced:

"You may have been the best coach in the country last year, Mr. Leahy, but junking the classic Notre Dame box formation for the questionable T-formation is, in my humble estimation, a stupid move. You are known as a gambler. Remember a gambler's luck runs dry after a while. The T-formation that Rockne used was far different from the modern Bears's T and you know it. This is a foolhardy experiment. Going to the T after an undefeated season makes as much sense as breaking up a full house to draw for four of a kind. Stand pat, coach, and play the cards you have. That's what a real gambler would do."[127]

He knew that Irish fans were hard to please no matter what the circumstances. Nevertheless, Leahy persevered in implementing the change. Perhaps he remembered the great Rockne's response when asked why he had lost a game. "I won't know until my barber tells me on Monday."

CHAPTER 13

1943

If you go to bed early, don't overeat, save your money, and arise early, you will live longer—or at least it will seem a helluva lot longer.
—Army Coach Herman Hickman

THE BRITISH EIGHTH Army had finally stopped Rommel and the German Afrika Corps at El Alamein in North Africa. The Germans were now in full retreat in that theater after almost two years of hard fighting. The victory in North Africa was followed up quickly by the invasion of Sicily in July. This first invasion of *Fortress Europe* drove Italy out of the war.

On February 1, the German Sixth Army surrendered at Stalingrad, ending a fierce six-month battle that gave the Nazis their first major defeat in Russia. In July, the Germans were dealt another major defeat by the Russians at the Battle of Kursk, the largest tank battle of the war. The Germans never again achieved the strategic offensive advantage on the Eastern Front.

In the Pacific, US Marines were mopping up Japanese forces on Guadalcanal. The situation was improving daily as fresh troops reinforced the weary forces on the island, which was finally declared secured on February 15.

At West Point, events were taking place in 1943 that bolstered Coach Blaik's optimism, as well. In the spring of that year, Blaik was still searching for a line coach to replace his old friend Harry "Fats" Ellinger. Fats had been a hard-hitting guard at Army in the early 1920s and was a West Point graduate, class of 1925. He loved the Army and had hoped to become a career officer. However, he was denied a commission by a medical board because of a heart condition.

Ellinger had spent a few years at West Point as a civilian assistant football coach. When Blaik went to Dartmouth, Ellinger followed, and again followed when Blaik returned to the Military Academy as his line coach. In 1942, Ellinger suffered a fatal heart attack while on a recruiting trip to Washington DC. The normally stoic Blaik was devastated by the loss of his friend and long-time football protégé. He later wrote, "Such a friend and comrade is not replaced."[128]

Perhaps he couldn't find someone to replace his old friend and comrade, but it was vitally important to find a new line coach. Bolstering Army's line play was key to improving the overall offensive game. In his typical thorough manner, the Army head coach made numerous inquiries among his many contacts seeking a candidate; one name kept showing up on many of the responses he received—Herman Hickman.

Hickman had been a star lineman at the University of Tennessee playing on championship teams coached by an old West Pointer, Major Bob Neyland. Coach Neyland held Hickman in high regard. "When one (football writer) said Hickman was 'the best guard the South ever produced,' Coach Bob Neyland snarled, 'Herman Hickman is the greatest guard football has ever known.'"[129] Although he was big for his day at 225 pounds, Hickman was very quick. He could outrun anyone on the football squad except one or two of the fastest backs. He also wrestled and set a school record in the shot put.

After he graduated in 1932, Hickman played professional football in Brooklyn where he won All-League honors at guard. He also wrestled professionally for five years as "The Tennessee Terror." He began his coaching career at Wake Forest and later switched to North Carolina State.

In high school, Hickman had won several oratorical contests and had ever since maintained his love of poetry and literature. Years later, at the height of his and Army's success in 1946, he sat with the famous sportswriter Grantland Rice. Rice asked him about Army's chances of winning the Navy game, which was several weeks away. Hickman without pause, broke into a flawless recitation of the end of Tennyson's *Ulysses* to the astonishment of Rice.

> *Though much is taken, much abides; and though*
> *We are not now that strength which in old days*
> *Moved earth and heaven, that which we are, we are—*
> *One equal temper of heroic hearts,*
> *Made weak by time and fate, but strong in will*
> *To strive, to seek, to find, and not to yield.*[130]

Hickman was a key component of Blaik's successful Army teams of 1944, 1945, and 1946. During his five seasons at Army, he developed six all-American linemen—center Casimir Myslinski, tackles Tex Coulter and Al Nemetz, and guards Joe Stanowicz, Jack Green, and Joe Steffy.

His jovial and folksy manner brought an informality to the team and provided the Cadets with the perfect complement to their serious and taciturn head coach.

Hickman's impact and that of the linemen he coached were obscured by the sensational play of Army's star backs Blanchard, Davis, and Tucker in those years. His coaching and the play of his linemen have been largely overlooked and forgotten by all but the most ardent and serious fans of the game. Hickman and his players would, I'm sure, share the complaint of an underappreciated lineman who once lamented that if you're on the run from the law and need a good place to hide out, become a lineman. No one will ever notice you there.

Army gained with Hickman the wealth of contacts that he had maintained with key coaches in the South, providing West Point an inside track on recruiting many of the most skilled players from this region, which had an abundance of football talent.

Once he saw Hickman at work, Blaik was convinced that he had made an excellent choice. Everyone who saw the new coach at work was astounded by his strength and quickness. Hickman was always ready when needed to lessen the tension with a witty remark. He often shared with others his genial tongue-in-cheek approach to life, which he clearly did not practice. "If you go to bed early, don't overeat, save your money, and arise early, you will live longer—or at least it will seem a helluva lot longer." Or he could offer interesting advice for anyone (like unpopular coaches) that faced censure. "When you are being run out of town, get to the head of the line and look as though you are leading the parade."[131]

Blaik next focused on getting the talented players he needed to build a successful team for 1943. For many of the gifted athletes the coach sought, the stability of a three year stay at West Point was a strong attraction. The incoming plebes of the class of 1946 who arrived at West Point on July 1, 1943, also had to deal with all the changes and turmoil underway as well as to adjust to a very different life than they had just left. Among those plebes was an eighteen-year- old from Bonita, California.

Glenn Woodward Davis was a very talented athlete and much sought-after football recruit. During his senior year at Bonita Union High School he had scored 236 points over nine games, an average of twenty-six points per game.[132]

In an era when most transcontinental travel was by train and films of high school athletes were extremely rare, the link between Davis, Blaik, and West Point was a very unlikely longshot. It all came about because Warren Bentley, a drama professor and friend of Blaik's from his Dartmouth days, was vacationing in Southern California in early 1943. While there, he heard about an outstanding high school football player. After inquiring about the young man, he sent the following note to his friend at West Point. "They say that this kid is the fastest halfback ever seen out there. He's an all-around athlete: baseball, basketball, and track, as well as football. Since I'm told he is interested in going to West Point, I thought you might want to know about him. His name is Glenn Davis."[133]

Davis was highly recruited by West Coast teams. A college scout told his high school coach, John Price, "I have seen everyone of the Coast Conference college teams play and there's not one of them has a back as good as that Davis kid." [134] Glenn and his twin brother, Ralph, were considering enrolling in the V-12 program at USC, which would have given them a tuition-free education leading to a Navy commission.

But Coach Blaik had an important tool in his box of persuasion—an appointment to West Point, which would allow both young men to serve and not be drafted. Both brothers were interested. After securing appointments to West Point from two California congressmen, Glenn and Ralph boarded a train in San Bernardino in May 1943 for the four-day trip east. Their parents loaded them down with sandwiches and lots of reference books so they could study for the validating exam when they arrived at West Point.

They were met at the West Point train station by Coach Blaik, who took them to his home on the grounds of the academy. They stayed with the Blaiks, studying and meeting with tutors until they took the exam, which they passed. On July 1, they moved to the cadet barracks with the other incoming freshmen of the class of 1946 and prepared for the course of study, which had been shortened to three years because of the war.

The first day of July was the beginning of *Beast Barracks*, the grueling six-week indoctrination for all new cadets. The attrition rate during this period for incoming cadets averaged around 20 percent. There are two essential attributes that a new cadet needed to successfully navigate and complete this most arduous period of a cadet's time at West Point. One was to be physically fit in order to cope with the constant physical activities while being deprived of sleep and sometimes even food. The second attribute, equally as important, was to have the right attitude. Plebes were allowed only four answers to any question—"Yes sir," "No sir," "No excuse sir," and, "Sir I do not understand."

Glenn and Ralph had both attributes. First, they were in excellent shape, which helped them to deal with the physical challenges of the training. In addition, their Southern-born parents had taught them to respect everyone and to say, "Yes sir," and "No sir," frequently. They easily accepted the authority of the upperclassmen and officers.

Glenn was unpretentious, soft-spoken, totally without ego, and liked by his classmates. Davis, describing himself some years later said, "'I was the kind of guy who dated one girl all the way through high school and West Point,' which he did."[135] Once when asked about his talent he said, "In high school I only weighed 160 pounds. So it wasn't my size, it was my speed. And God gave me that. I didn't have to work for it."[136]

His self-effacing humor and good attitude undoubtedly helped him get through the rigors of Beast Barracks. Knowing that he was a highly recruited football player also must have helped him to avoid some of the harshest treatment from the upperclassmen.

By the time he graduated from West Point, Glenn's athletic prowess was well known. "Davis won ten letters, four in football, three in baseball, two in track and one in basketball. In fifty-one baseball games for Army he batted .403, stole sixty-four bases in sixty-five attempts, including second, third, and home in an exhibition game against the Brooklyn Dodgers."[137]

With his speed, track probably could have been Davis's best sport had he concentrated on it. In 1947, he ran the sixty-yard dash in 6.1 seconds at Madison Square Garden, beating Barney Ewell who the next year won the silver medal in the 100 meters at the London Olympics. He won the admiration of the other cadets by his performance in the rigorous physical test given to all plebes. The test included a 300-yard run, standing broad and vertical jumps, a rope climb, chin-ups, sit-ups, parallel bar dips, and a softball throw. Davis scored 962.5 points out of 1,000; the average for the cadets as a whole was 550.

The most famous story of his versatile athletic ability occurred in the spring of 1947. After playing nine innings of baseball in centerfield, getting as he later recalled, "a couple of hits," he rushed to the track because Army was short of sprinters. He had not run an outdoor meet that season. In borrowed shoes, he won the hundred-yard dash in 9.7 seconds, then later won the 220 in Academy record time, 20.9 seconds. One of his teammates, Bill Yeoman, later a coach at the University of Houston, told the *Times* in 1983: "There are words to describe how good an athlete 'Doc' Blanchard was. But there aren't words to describe how good Davis was."[138]

His only real challenge at West Point was coping with the challenging academic load, which was heavily weighted with engineering and math. He was as intense about his studies as he was about football. He'd get up at 4 a.m. before reveille to study. "I just couldn't do it all," he told *Sports Illustrated* in 1988. "I was taking five classes every day. I got out of the last one at 3:30 and had to be on the football field at 4:00. I wouldn't get home until 6:30, then I'd have dinner and study."[139]

Despite his efforts, he was found deficient in math in December and sent home. In those days, failing one subject meant dismissal from the academy. He was told he could apply for readmission and take an exam, which if he passed, would allow him to return the following year. He did pass the exam and re-entered West Point for the fall semester of 1944 to join the class of 1947.

When the fall semester of 1943 began, over 85 percent of the men enrolled on the South Bend campus were Navy trainees.[140] The university was certainly happy to have these military students. However, the administration had to remain nimble and flexible relative to the student body since many of these youngsters would only spend one year on the campus before being called away to other duty stations.

For Coach Frank Leahy that meant helping his players meet their military obligations and still retain their eligibility to play football for the Fighting Irish. Notre Dame was not without its own strong allies willing to help Leahy navigate the rules and regulations of the wartime personnel systems. One such example of that significant aid revolved around Bob Kelly, a highly recruited player from Saint Leo's High School in Chicago. Kelly's father, a US congressman, had encouraged his son to attend West Point to fulfill his military obligation.

In January 1943, Kelly and his father took a train to West Point to meet Coach Blaik, who had invited them to his home. Kelly said he planned to enroll young Bob in a prep school in nearby Peekskill, New York, where he could study for the West Point entrance exam along with other recruits. The congressman and his son left Blaik to spend an evening in New York City. During the night, the young man had trouble sleeping. He woke up his father and announced that he wanted to go to Notre Dame instead. The father and son immediately headed to South Bend. When they arrived at the train station they were met by Father Cavanaugh, the president of Notre Dame, and Ed McKeever, a member of the coaching staff. At a meeting in the president's suite in the Oliver Hotel, Cavanaugh explained that young Bob would not be able to enroll at Notre Dame because Blaik was incensed over Bob Kelly's abrupt decision to go to Notre Dame instead of West Point. It's unclear how Coach Blaik learned of the changed decision so quickly.

President Cavanaugh further stated that Blaik had threatened to cancel the Army-Notre Dame series if Notre Dame persisted in stealing another player from Army. "Father Cavanaugh explained the situation, 'We can't take you at Notre Dame. We can't afford to lose that revenue.'"[141]

Now it was Congressman Kelly's turn to be incensed. He called

Blaik immediately. "My son can go wherever he wants to and you, as a military man, are not going to dictate where we can or cannot go. If you do, you won't be at West Point much longer."[142]

Blaik knew that the congressman was a senior member of the Interstate Commerce Committee and had much influence in other matters, including those dealing with the military. He, therefore, wisely reversed course and told the elder Kelly that his son was free to attend whichever college he wanted. He ended the conversation diplomatically by stating that he hoped there were no hard feelings among all those involved.

The Kelly incident had stirred strong feelings with Blaik because just a few months earlier he had lost another star recruit to Notre Dame. John Lujack was an excellent all-around athlete at the Connellsville, Pennsylvania high school where he participated in football, baseball, and track. Henry Opperman, a local resident in Lujack's hometown and an ardent Notre Dame fan, alerted a Notre Dame scout and told him of the young man's significant talents. In those days, before the current NCAA restrictions on contact with athletes, Notre Dame had a large and influential network of alums and friends called *Bird Dogs*. These men, scattered across the country, kept an eye out for young, talented football players. They took pride in alerting the Notre Dame football staff of potential recruits and in securing commitments of promising athletes before other major schools. The scout quickly arranged a tryout on the Notre Dame campus for Lujack. The coaching staff was so impressed by Lujack that they offered him a scholarship on the spot.

However, Lujack's parents thought that their son should consider West Point. They were able to secure an appointment to West Point from their local congressman. Lujack had been highly recruited. "I had a lot of offers and I liked making the trips. They took me to West Point and I never did meet Blaik. The coach who took me on the tour didn't seem too enthusiastic. I was only 160 pounds and I figured that a place like Notre Dame was way over my head." [143]

When he received the Notre Dame scholarship, he quickly accepted the offer. His appointment to West Point was quickly forgotten. However, Coach Blaik would remember Lujack's rejection. He was not accustomed to losing star recruits during the war years, so these back-to-back losses stung the coach greatly.

As the war intensified, recruiting young men to play at Notre Dame became more difficult. The V-12 program at Notre Dame helped Coach Leahy attract and retain some excellent football recruits. However, a majority of Navy V-12 programs would permit a student to stay enrolled for two years—at most—before being sent to a Navy or Marine Corps unit. In addition, during those two years, students might be transferred to other Navy programs at another campus.

In trying to cope with this disruptive churning of personnel, Coach Leahy turned once again to Congressman Kelly, whose son had joined the V-12 program at Notre Dame. At the end of his first year, young Kelly and several other football players were ordered to transfer to other V-12 programs. Before the orders took effect, Leahy called Congressman Kelly to complain about the pending transfers.

The congressman immediately called an admiral at the Naval Bureau of Personnel (BUPERS) to complain about the transfers. He felt it didn't make sense to transfer people from one program to another when they all purported to have similar training. The admiral promised to investigate the situation. Several days later Bob Kelly's orders, as well as those of the other players, were rescinded and they were all allowed to stay at Notre Dame.

After a moderately successful 1942 season where his team had a record of 7–2–2, Leahy was looking forward to a more successful season in 1943. Quarterback Angelo Bertelli now had a year's experience running the coach's new T-formation. He also had a talented backfield with the veteran halfback Creighton Miller and fullback Jim Mello returning. Miller would achieve all-American status at the end of the season. Mello would be called into the service at the end of the season but would return to Notre Dame after two years to play on the 1946 championship team.

Leahy also had sophomore John Lujack playing behind Bertelli at quarterback. For the opening game against Pitt, the coach decided to start young Lujack for the first series because he was from the area and his family was attending the game. When I interviewed John Lujack in 2022 he was ninety-six. One of the stories he recalled about his playing days at Notre Dame was his apprehension in starting at quarterback for the first time. The description of the event by Creighton Miller is even more detailed:

"During Notre Dame's first possession of the ball, we quickly got to Pitt's four-yard line where it was first down and goal. Lujack was still very nervous as he called a 'twenty-two on three.' This was a simple play where the quarterback handed off to the two-back, me, who would go straight ahead for the two hole on the count of three. At the snap of the ball, I ran straight ahead, through a huge hole into the end zone, but there was one thing wrong—I didn't have the ball. It seems that Lujack had spun the wrong way and failed to make the handoff.

"When we got back to the huddle, I said, 'Lujack, I am really a Notre Dame player and on the same team with you—just hand me the ball.' Lujack called the same play and I ran through a big hole into the end zone, but again I did not have the ball. Lujack had turned the wrong way for the second time.

"I got Lujack aside and said, 'John, see the number on my jersey—it's number 37—my name is Creighton Miller and I am the number two back on this team. Believe me, I'm a Notre Dame man. My father was a starting back on the 1906, 1907, and 1908 Notre Dame teams, my uncle Wally was the fullback with George Gipp, and my uncle Don was one of the Four Horsemen. I am truly a Notre Dame man and a member of this team—so just give me the damn ball.'

"Lujack called the play for the third time. This time he handed me the ball and I scored an easy touchdown."[144]

The Irish went on to an easy win over the Pitt Panthers, 41–0.

Their next two games were against Georgia Tech and Michigan, the two teams that had defeated Notre Dame the prior year. They easily avenged the losses by scores of 55–13 and 35–12. Next up was Wisconsin who had tied the Irish in 1942. The final score of 51–0 in Madison, Wisconsin followed by an equally impressive 47–0 win over Illinois, left little doubt that this Notre Dame team was a contender for the national championship.

The Irish then traveled to Cleveland to face undefeated and third-ranked Navy before 78,000 fans. Playing his last game before being called to Marine Corps service, quarterback Angelo Bertelli led Notre Dame to a convincing 33–6 victory. It was the worst defeat for the Middies in the series against Notre Dame. The future Naval officers were held to minus seven yards rushing while the South Benders gained 323 yards on the ground. Bertelli was given a thunderous ovation as he trotted off the field for the last time before leaving to serve his country.

The following week, the Irish returned to Yankee Stadium for their annual meeting with the Cadets. Blaik's team came into the game undefeated but with one tie against Penn. From a vantage point of eighty years of hindsight, the game now seems more important for what it didn't reveal than what it did about the future of the rivalry. What was most obvious to those watching the game was the appearance of two youngsters who faced each other for the first time. John Lujack was very impressive as the heir to the Bertelli throne. He and the Irish seemed not to have missed a beat by the loss of their all-American signal caller only a week earlier.

Glenn Davis, Army's star freshman, had a difficult game. He fumbled twice and threw an interception. Almost no one outside of his immediate circle knew that Davis was having great difficulty meeting the academic requirements of the Military Academy. Davis had come directly from a small California high school where he had not been challenged academically. His scholastic difficulties were always on his mind, even on the football field. "Doug Kenna remembered him (Davis) sitting tensely in the locker room before a game and telling him to relax. 'You don't have anything to worry about. You'll play great.' Glenn replied, 'You know, I don't think I did very well on that last math test.' 'Can you imagine?' said Kenna. 'It's moments before kickoff and he's thinking about how he did on an exam. He's not worried about the game. He's worried about flunking out.'"[145]

As noted, Davis did flunk out but passed his math requirement and rejoined the team the following fall.

On this day, November 6, 1943, the field belonged unequivocally to the Irish. The 26–0 loss was one of the worst defeats for the Cadets in the history of the series. Army had not defeated the Irish since 1931. Two ties in 1935 and 1941, Blaik's first year, were hardly a consolation to the coach and his competitive team. Never one to accept any defeat well, Coach Blaik must have been particularly piqued by the lopsided score of the game.

With his impressive wins against Army and Navy, only two teams, both military, now stood in the way of Leahy's first undefeated season. Iowa Pre-Flight, the first of the two teams, made the trip to South Bend ranked number two nationally behind the Irish. The Seahawks were undefeated thus far in the season, riding an eight-game winning streak, having defeated teams such as Illinois, Ohio State, and Iowa. They had a roster loaded with talented college and professional players assigned to the Navy preflight program at Iowa.

For extra inspiration prior to the game, Coach Leahy took his team to Knute Rockne's gravesite. John Lujack described the visit. "As the team knelt around the grave, coach Leahy said, 'Lads, bow your heads and say a silent prayer to Rock that he will be with us tomorrow and help us defeat this great team.'

"After about a minute, I got off my knees and walked about ten yards away to the grave of the revered Notre Dame basketball coach, George Keogan, to pay my respects.

"Leahy raised his head and spotted me at Keogan's grave and said in that disapproving tone we all knew so well, 'John Lujack, this is not the time for that. You get back over here—this is the football season.'"[146]

The visit to the cemetery may have helped the team. They played inspired football against the tough Seahawks, managing to remain undefeated by the slim score of 14–13. The hero of the game was eighteen-year-old Fred Earley, who was perfect in kicking two conversions after missing three the week before in Notre Dame's 25–6 win over Northwestern.

Now only one more team, Great Lakes Navy, stood in the way of the Irish. Like Iowa Pre-Flight, the Blue Jackets had several former collegiate and professional players. There were several former Notre Dame players on the team, as well, including Emil "Red" Sitko who would return to Notre Dame after the war and become a College Football Hall of Fame running back for the Irish. When he faced his former team as a sailor at Great Lakes, Illinois, Sitko gained 114 yards on seventeen carries.

His effort and that of his teammates, plus a desperation pass in the last thirty seconds, was enough to upset the Irish 19–14, depriving them of the unbeaten season they had been working for all season. After the game, Sitko and several of the other former Notre Dame players went to the Notre Dame bus to see some of their former teammates. When they saw their former coach Sitko asked, "How are you doing coach?"

A downcast Leahy said, "Oh, Emil, my school lost today."

Sitko responded, "It's my school, too, coach."[147]

Despite the loss, the Irish were named National Collegiate Champions. That recognition, plus several individual awards, helped the team overcome their disappointment in not achieving a perfect record. Bertelli, who played only a partial season, was awarded the Heisman Trophy, and joined five other Notre Dame players named to an all-American team.

CHAPTER 14

1944

You can't believe the size of his legs. I know his thighs are better than twenty-eight inches... He'd have to split his uniform pants to get them over his legs, they were so big.
—Shorty McWilliams describing Doc Blanchard

IN 1944, THE allure of serving the country while being enrolled in the US Military Academy brought a key figure to the campus on the Hudson. Shortly before Glenn Davis returned to West Point for his second attempt to conquer the challenges of plebe math, another talented football player began his own rigorous odyssey with the plebe system. He was a well-regarded recruit who had already made a name for himself on the freshman team at North Carolina University. He was the son of Felix "Doc" Blanchard Sr., who had been an excellent football player at Tulane before he abandoned his sports aspirations to earn a medical degree and become a doctor in South Carolina.

The elder Blanchard encouraged his son to develop his football skills from an early age. Lest there be any doubts about his intentions, he placed a football in his son's crib shortly after his birth. Young Doc's sister, Dr. Mary Elizabeth Blanchard, remembered years later that Doc Sr. asked "Little Doc" to do two things for him. "My father asked him to play football and learn to dance. He would say that there was no use in being a football star on Friday night if you couldn't dance with girls on Saturday night. Well, my brother did learn to dance. And we would go to Denny's on Saturdays to dance."[148]

Raised in rural Bishopville, South Carolina, Young Doc was a humble and unassuming man of few words when discussing his own exploits. Even after he achieved considerable fame at West Point, he maintained those qualities. At the Heisman Trophy Award ceremony, which he received in 1945, his acceptance speech was a paragraph long reportedly written on looseleaf paper during the train ride to New York City.[149] However, in private and with his friends he was very gregarious and loved to tell stories.

Although the family lived in South Carolina, Doc enrolled in his father's prep school alma mater, Saint Stanislaus in Bay St. Louis, Mississippi. As he grew the *little* was dropped and he became just Doc.

In an ironic twist of fate that would be revealed years later, Frank Leahy was preparing his Boston College team for the 1940 Sugar Bowl at St. Stanislaus while Blanchard was a student there. While there, Leahy met Blanchard and remembered him when he became coach at Notre Dame. He later tried to recruit Blanchard to Notre Dame.

By his junior year at the prep school Doc had filled out to a stocky 180 pounds and was attracting attention from several major college football teams. He came to the notice of Coach Blaik, who had sent one of his assistants to interview the young man during his senior year in 1941. However, the senior Blanchard was not interested in having his son attend West Point. The young Blanchard chose instead to attend North Carolina University because it was close to his home, and head coach Jim Tatum was a close cousin of young Doc's mother. He was a standout on the freshman team leading the "Tar Babies" to the 1942 state title.

The rapid increase in military manpower requirements by the end of his freshman year at North Carolina in 1943 made it clear to both Blanchards that the youngster would soon be facing military service. College deferments were very rare then. Blanchard tried to get into a V-12 program but was rejected because he was by then a muscular 208 pounds, overweight by V-12 standards. He also had an eyesight problem from a childhood injury. Because the programs were designed primarily to produce Navy pilots, vision problems were a showstopper.

Blanchard settled on the Army. After basic training in Miami, he was assigned to a chemical warfare unit in Clovis, New Mexico. The elder Doc was not happy with the turn of events that had relegated his son to becoming a private at a remote Army base. He therefore rekindled the previously spurned West Point connection. He was able to quickly secure an appointment for his son. Young Blanchard passed the entrance exam and was soon on his way north. His pride and happiness in getting into West Point was sadly tempered by the sudden death of his father shortly before he reported to the academy. Doc and his dad had been very close, a relationship made closer by their mutual interest in football. He entered West Point on July 2, 1944 with the other 900 hopefuls of the class of 1947. He was soon undergoing the same trials and challenges of Beast Barracks that Glenn Davis had been subjected to a year earlier.

Like the other plebes in his class, Blanchard was required to participate in intense marching and military training and required to memorize a prodigious amount of plebe knowledge. When asked, he had to flawlessly respond to such questions as, "How is the cow?"

"Sir, she walks, she talks, she's full of chalk, the lacteal fluid extracted from the female of the bovine species is highly prolific to the nth degree."

"What is the definition of leather?"

"Sir, if the fresh skin of an animal, cleaned and divested of all hair, fat, and other extraneous matter be immersed in a dilute solution of tannic acid, a chemical combination ensues; the gelatinous tissue of the skin is converted into a non-putrescible substance, impervious to, and insoluble in water; this sir, is leather."

Despite these trivial rituals, Blanchard adapted to the West Point system with good cheer.

He was able to get some relief from the rigors of plebe year once the academic year started in late August. He would be free to eat on corps squad tables for intercollegiate athletes normally without bracing, unlike his less fortunate non-collegiate athlete classmates. Many of the plebe football players felt that practice was the easiest part of the day because they were out of reach of the harassing upperclassman. Years later, sportswriter John Feinstein would emphasize this same point in his excellent book on the Army-Navy rivalry, *A Civil War.* "These men are a special breed," Feinstein wrote. "Says one coach, 'At every other school in America, the hardest part of any football player's day is football practice. At the military academies, the easiest part of a football player's day is football practice.'"

Everyone who saw Blanchard marveled at his size, especially the girth of his legs. Teammate Thomas "Shorty" McWilliams recalled meeting Blanchard. "You can't believe the size of his legs. I know his thighs are better than twenty-eight inches. . . .. He'd have to split his uniform pants to get them over his legs they were so big."[150] A writer for the *Saturday Evening Post* claimed that Blanchard's thighs were larger than Scarlett O'Hara's corseted waist. Yet, he was surprisingly fast for a big man. Blanchard ran the first sixty yards of the hundred-yard dash faster than his teammate, speedster Glenn Davis.

Blanchard had not played football in 1943, so he and the Army coaching staff were anxious to see how quickly he could recover his prodigious skills on the field. The two key building blocks of a future national championship team, Blanchard and Davis, were now in place.

West Point provided a three-year refuge from the draft and the other uncertainties of military service. Even the Navy V programs could offer only slightly more than a one-year deferment for most enrollees during which they could play college football. Many talented football players already enrolled in other schools or like Glenn Davis right out of high school found the appeal of West Point and its sanctuary very attractive. There was such an abundance of these recruits that Coach Blaik was able to create two teams, each strong enough to compete effectively against their opponents.

In January 1943 another talented high school athlete started his collegiate career. Young (his real first name) Arnold Tucker had attracted the attention of Notre Dame Coach Leahy, who offered the youngster from Florida a scholarship. Tucker enrolled for the spring semester of 1943 but left Notre Dame several weeks later. Tucker intimated that it was the cold weather in January in South Bend that convinced him that the Notre Dame was not for him.

So, ironically, both Lujack and Tucker were on the same campus for several weeks. Each was unaware of the other, and each could not anticipate that they would ultimately meet each other on the gridiron in one of the most memorable college football games ever played.

Tucker was a graduate of Miami High School, where he won honors in both football and basketball. After his short stay at Notre Dame "Tuck" enrolled in the V-12 program at the University of Florida and then transferred to the University of Miami. He resigned from the V-12 program in July of 1944 after being recruited to play for Army. He joined the class of 1947 at West Point with Blanchard.

Tucker would become the regular Army quarterback in the '45 and '46 seasons and play a prominent role in the success of the Cadets during those years. However, because of the depth of the Army team in 1944, he played his first year as a backup on the plebe team.

"Tex" Coulter would be an especially valuable addition to the team. The six-four, 230-pound lineman was a fearsome competitor and key to opening huge holes for running backs. He had developed a smash-mouth brand of football at an orphanage, the Masonic Home in Fort Worth, Texas. The home was a small institute and could only field a limited number of boys for the football team, so they focused on hard-hitting rather than finesse.

"We played a certain kind of football," Coulter remembered. "We couldn't make what we call the city guys admire us for our situation, but we could make them fear us. You know, a good healthy fear. And the city boys at the Fort Worth high schools were frightened as hell of us. The goddamn guys would be bleeding all over the place. We played a very tough brand of football. The ball was snapped and you continued to hit people until the referee blew the whistle."[151]

While in high school at the Masonic home, Coulter earned all-state honors in Texas for three straight years and won the national high school championship in the shot put. He was given a scholarship to Texas A&M when he graduated, but was drafted by the Army before he could take advantage of the offer.

Following basic training, Coulter was stationed at Sheppard Air Base in Texas. He was not sure, but felt that word of his high school football prowess had come to the attention of an officer on the base who had played under Coach Blaik and helped the coach with recruiting.

Incredibly, after a year in the Army, the orphan from the Masonic Home found himself with an appointment to West Point. First, however, Coulter had to attend one semester at Cornell University preparing for the West Point entrance exam.

The war would create enormous turmoil in college recruiting. To a large degree that turmoil and dislocation of players had benefited the service academies. It wouldn't be until the year after the war that teams like Notre Dame would be able to overcome this recruiting disadvantage and compete for players on an equal basis.

Blaik had so much talent on the '44 team that he created two separate teams. Not only did he have an abundance of skilled players, but he had players with enormous versatility. Consequently, he structured his two platoons differently than most of the other coaches. He organized his squad into two complete teams that would play both ways. One team would be composed of returning lettermen under the leadership of quarterback Doug Kenna. The other team under quarterback Tom Lombardo would have a roster comprised of only plebes, except for the captain.

The veteran team would play the first and third quarters, and the plebe team would play in quarters two and four. Blaik only altered this arrangement during close games when he would choose individual players of one team to augment the other team to execute a needed strategy.

As the 1944 season unfolded, Blaik's unique two platoon system allowed the veteran team to dominate the play if needed while allowing the newcomers like Blanchard, Davis, Coulter, and Barney Poole to get significant playing time. Tucker got less time because he was playing behind team captain Tom Lombardo. However, even he got enough playing time to develop the skills that would propel the Army team to new heights.

Although the freshman team was comprised of newcomers to West Point, many were not new to college football. Blaik's scheme allowed them to play together from the very outset of their arrival at the Military Academy without depriving the senior players of the playing time they had earned.

It was obvious even before the season that Army finally had the offensive power and depth it had lacked in previous seasons. The preseason intra-squad varsity scrimmage between the teams led by team captain Tom Lombardo and Doug Kenna proved to be closer and more exciting than many of the games Army played that season. Each of those teams had an abundance of talent. The recognition bestowed upon them in Army's three undefeated seasons ('44, '45, '46) was unprecedented. Over those years, seventeen Army players from these teams were named all-Americans.

All American honors in '44, '45, or '46 are designated with an *AA*.

LOMBARDO'S TEAM		KENNA'S TEAM
George (Barney) Poole AA	LE	Dick Pitzer AA
Tom Hayes		
DeWitt (Tex) Coulter AA	LT	Archie Arnold
Bill LaMar		
Shelton Biles	LG	Jack Green AA
Herschel (Ug) Fuson AA	C	Bob St. Once AA
Jim Enos		
Art Geometta	RG	Joe Stanowicz AA
Harold Tavel	RT	Al Nemetz AA
Bill Webb		
Henry (Hank) Foldberg AA	RE	Ed Rafalko AA
Tom Lombardo	QB	Doug Kenna AA
Young Arnold Tucker AA		
Glenn Davis AA	LH	Dale Hall AA
Johnny Sauer		
Dean Senanbaugher	RH	Max Minor AA
Dick Walterhouse AA		
Felix (Doc) Blanchard AA	FB	Bobby Dobbs
Bill West		

Blaik knew he had a very strong team. Not given to flamboyant statements, even he couldn't restrain himself when addressing his team at the first practice in August. "I expect you to be the greatest football team in the history of West Point."[152]

Blaik was confident but not cocky. He knew his traditional rivals Navy and Notre Dame would be able to field strong teams as well. Navy, like Army, had been able to recruit several outstanding players from other colleges. These recruits, when added to the returning players from the strong 1943 Navy team, made the Midshipmen the top pick to win the National Championship in the 1944 preseason polls.

Army played its first four games at Michie Stadium. The 1944 season would be the first season in which Blanchard and Davis played together. The first team to encounter the duo was North Carolina. Blanchard and Poole had both played for the Tar Heels, so they had a chance to renew some old friendships before and after the game.

The cordiality of the two Army stars did not extend to the playing field, however. North Carolina was able to gain only fourteen yards rushing and twenty-one yards through the air. They were crushed 46–0. Because of Blaik's two-team strategy, Blanchard and Davis only played seventeen minutes in the game. Davis scored three touchdowns and Blanchard scored one. The *New York Daily News* described the start of Army's 1944 season by declaring, "Football exploded out of its yearlong slumber at West Point yesterday afternoon and sprayed touchdowns all over North Carolina."[153]

The North Carolina game was followed by strong wins against Brown 59–7, Pitt 69–7, and the US Coast Guard Academy 76–0. The new Army juggernaut outscored these first four opponents by a combined score of 250–14.

As the season unfolded, much attention was focused on

Blanchard and Davis. However, it soon became apparent that several other players acquired by Coach Blaik provided exceptional experience and maturity as well as talent. Recruits that had transferred and entered West Point that July provided probably the most outstanding plebe class in West Point football history. Many of them had played a year at other colleges: Barney Poole (North Carolina), Herschel "Ug" Fuson (Tennessee and Navy), Jim Enos (Santa Clara), Art Gerometta (Illinois), Dean Sensanbaugher (Ohio State), Tom Hayes (Nebraska), Harold Tavzel (Miami, Ohio), Tom Hayes (Colorado), John Green (Tulane), Al Nemetz and Bill Webb (Wake Forest), Max Minor (Texas), Shelton Biles (Vanderbilt), and Bill West (Dartmouth). Hank Foldberg, Joe Starnes, and "Tex" Coulter had gone directly into the Army from high school and from there to the Military Academy.[154] They would join returning lettermen Doug Kenna and Tom Lombardo at quarterback and backs Glenn Davis, Dale Hall, Bob Chabot, Max Minor, Bobby Dobbs, Dick Waterhouse, and Johnny Sauer. Returning linemen included Dick Pitzer, Roland Catarinella, Bob Wayne, Bill LaMar, Jack Green, Bob St. Onge, Joe Stanowicz, Bill Webb, and Ed Rafalko.

Significantly, it was Blaik's request to General Eichelberger in 1941 asking for a waiver from the surgeon general to change the weight and height requirements of cadets that allowed Blanchard, Poole, Coulter, Fuson, and other big, husky players to play for Army.

On the same day that Army unveiled its prowess and power against North Carolina, their two major rivals were also in action. Notre Dame, national champion from the preceding year, easily defeated Pitt 58–0 in their first start without Coach Leahy, who had enlisted in the Navy earlier in the year. Bob Kelly, the son of the congressman and an almost Army recruit, scored four touchdowns and kicked two extra points. Navy was upset by North Carolina Pre-flight whose V-12 players included future Cleveland Browns superstar Otto Graham. The pre-flight program known as the Cloud Busters was coached by Jim Crowley, former coach at Fordham and one of Notre Dame's famous Four Horsemen from the 1920s. He was assisted by a young assistant coach, Bear Bryant.

The strong start to the season confirmed Blaik's high assessment of his team. North Carolina, Brown, Pitt, and the US Coast Guard Academy quickly fell to the new Army juggernaut by a combined score of 250–14. Still, the press and the public were not ready to concede that this Amy team had the stuff of national champions. Sports writers with lengthy memories recalled the long winless droughts against Navy and Notre Dame.

On October 28, two weeks before the Notre Dame game, Army met Duke in the Polo Grounds, its first game of the season away from Michie Stadium at West Point. The Polo Grounds was a storied venue for the Cadets. They had played several memorable games there against both Navy and Notre Dame.

Duke would be the first real test for the Cadets. The Blue Devils came into the game as one of the strongest teams in the South, well known for its defensive toughness. They led at halftime 7–6 before the Army offense got going. In the second half, Army scored three touchdowns to win 27–7. It was enough to convince the sports writers that the Cadets should be ranked number one for the first time in many years.

The following week before the all-important Notre Dame game, Villanova made the short trip north from Pennsylvania to Michie Stadium. Blaik, Herman Hickman, and several other scouts traveled south to Baltimore to watch Notre Dame play Navy, a *twofer* for the scouts and Army's coaching staff.

Assistant Coach Andy Gustafson was left behind to coach the Villanova game. He tried to restrain his exuberant team, which increasingly had its thoughts on the looming showdown with Notre Dame. Blanchard was nursing a knee injury and did not play. Despite the heavy use of third- and fourth-string players, Army pummeled

Villanova 83–0. The game was so one-sided that Army punted on first down throughout much of the fourth quarter. By "mutual consent of both teams and the American Humane Society, the third quarter was cut to nine minutes." [155] Another armistice was declared in the fourth quarter when the quarter was mercifully shortened to eight minutes by both coaches anxious to end the embarrassing exhibition.

While Army was enjoying its easy romp against Villanova, Notre Dame and Navy were locked in a bruising battle 200 miles south. What could be better for the salivating West Point team than to have their two key rivals beat each other up. The Irish were only able to gain ninety-six yards rushing, forcing them to use their passing attack more heavily than they had planned. They threw the ball thirty-two times for a total of 164 yards against Navy's forty-seven yards, the only measurement that favored the visitors from South Bend. In a hard-fought battle, the Middies handed the Irish their first loss of the season and the worst defeat ever administered by a Navy team, 32–13. It was the first time that Navy had defeated Notre Dame since 1936.

Fate had not been on Notre Dame's side. Before the matchup with Navy, Notre Dame had lost several players because of the mandated transfer of some V-12 trainees on November 1, one of the key dates in the program that moved students to new assignments. Even so, sports pollsters were unforgiving, dropping Notre Dame to number two in the college rankings. Army replaced them as the number one. Coach McKeever tried to comfort his outclassed team. "Navy had a well-drilled, well-organized, hustling team, and would be hard for anyone to beat today," McKeever said, adding, "and our great bunch did the best they could, and I'm as proud of them as if they had won."[156]

The only thing these early games showed was that 1944 would be an unpredictable year for college football. Although Army was clearly a talented team, it had finished eleventh in the 1943 rankings, well below Notre Dame and Navy. They hadn't defeated Notre Dame since 1931 or Navy since 1938. The Army coaches and players knew that the real test of their abilities would be revealed in the games against these two key rivals.

In mid-April 1944, Coach Leahy could no longer stand by watching as his boys went off to war. He had joined the Navy and was awarded the rank of lieutenant, equal to a captain in the Army. He was encouraged by Assistant Coach Krause, who understood that Leahy's relationship with his players would be enhanced if he had a shared experience as a returning veteran. Leahy's health was not great, so he could probably have avoided the service if he had chosen to. The coach served under the popular and highly regarded Pacific submarine commander Admiral Charles Lockwood. Leahy's official job was to organize and supervise the athletic programs for the submariners in the Pacific theater. He operated out of forward bases at Midway, Guam, and Saipan after they had been recaptured from the Japanese.

To assist him in his duties, Leahy was given access to military aircraft that enabled him to visit troops and bases throughout the theater. Never one to waste an opportunity, the coach used this assignment to scout athletes at Marine and Naval bases throughout the Pacific.

Two veterans who would be key to the rebuilding of the Irish football team, George Connor and Jim Martin, were both recruited during Leahy's Navy service. Connor, a future Notre Dame great, related his initial meeting with Coach Leahy. "I was stationed at Pearl Harbor and one day a command car pulled up and the guy said, 'Ensign Connor, Commander (he had already been promoted) Leahy would like to see you at the Royal Hawaiian.' He talked me into coming to Notre Dame. He said we'd win the national championship and I'd make all-American. It all came true."[157]

Leahy met Martin on Iwo Jima in 1945 after it had been secured. The tough, six foot two, 204-pound, square jawed, fearless

Marine was just the type of recruit Leahy was looking for. A tattoo on one of his powerful arms depicted a sword cutting through a dragon beneath the words *Death Before Dishonor*. His wartime accomplishments proved that the words were not simply a slogan to the young Marine. Martin and Connor would join fifty-one other former service members in South Bend after the war ended.

The Irish, like other civilian schools, were constrained by trying to cope with the constant turnover and personnel turmoil brought on by the war. They faced numerous destabilizing factors that made this Notre Dame team different from the 1943 National Championship team. The team would now be guided by young Assistant Coach Ed McKeever, whose job would be difficult because twenty-four letterman had been lost through graduation, the draft, and enlistment.

In September, only five returning lettermen from the previous year returned to the campus, which by then had fewer than 700 civilians in attendance. In addition to Leahy's departure, the Irish's promising new quarterback, John Lujack, had been called to active duty, also with the Navy. Frank Dancewicz, a junior with limited playing time, became the quarterback. Although they had lost several V-12 players forced to transfer, McKeever and the Irish team looked very strong. They were bolstered by the return of Bob Kelly at halfback, an unpleasant reminder to Coach Blaik of his failed recruiting effort several years earlier.

Strong wins over Pitt (55–0), Tulane (26–0), and Dartmouth (64–0) thrust Notre Dame into the top spot for the first three weeks of the season. A close win against Illinois (13–7) and the loss to Navy dropped them to second place, setting up a one-versus-two showdown with Army.

All eyes now would be on Yankee Stadium and the reckoning between Army and Notre Dame. All Blaik's hard work was about to be tested in one of the contests he cared about the most. The Notre

Dame coaching staff had also been following Army's exploits during the season thus far. Jack Lavelle, the Notre Dame scout who observed Army play more often than any other scout, gave Ed McKeever, the interim Irish coach, a pessimistic assessment of the upcoming game. When asked how they should get ready for the Cadets, Lavelle consulted his notes briefly and then said forcefully, "Cancel the game." [158]

Lavelle knew the Cadets had scored an incredible 360 points in their first six games while allowing their opponents only twenty-one points. Glenn Davis had thus far in the season achieved the extraordinary record of scoring every other time he carried the ball. In twenty-six running plays he had scored thirteen touchdowns. The other plebe phenom, Doc Blanchard, was also making his presence felt in a big way. In the Pitt game earlier in the season, the big back had shown his power and versatility. As Army's kicker, he kicked off four times into the end zone, he punted once for forty-four yards, he caught three passes in three attempts for one hundred eight yards, and ran four times from scrimmage for forty-five yards. He scored two touchdowns, one on a twenty-one-yard pass play, and another on a twenty-one-yard interception. He did all this while playing only twenty-two minutes in the game.

Creighton Miller, now a graduate assistant, had also scouted the Army for the Irish and knew the strength of the Army team. He had a slightly more realistic strategy for his team than Lavelle. He told McKeever to "play close, pass, and hope."[159] Nonetheless, almost everyone expected Notre Dame to play its normal strong game against its archrival. After all, the South Benders were the defending national champions.

Notre Dame had an excellent passing quarterback in Frank Dancewicz, who later played three years in the NFL with the Boston Yanks. In 1946 he was the first overall pick for the NFL draft. Coupled with running back Kelly, several talented freshmen, and a few returning players who had been discharged from the service, Notre Dame would be no pushover. McKeever knew that he would face a difficult task if he tried to match up against the power of Army's line or their running game. So, he elected to utilize his quarterback's passing ability and try a wide-open offense that might take the Cadets by surprise.

"We," he asserted grimly, "are going to New York with a punt, a pass, and a prayer—and the only thing we're really sure of is the prayer."[160]

Traveling to an away game highlighted the constraints under which Notre Dame labored during the war. Coach McKeever brought his team in two echelons east to meet Army. The first was a contingent of the twenty-four civilian players. They were followed the next day by the eleven Navy V-12 members who were allowed only a forty-eight-hour pass from their duty station and so had to delay their departure. It might have been one of the biggest football games of the season, but it was clear that the regulations of the military remained paramount.

For the service academies, on the other hand, the only disruptions they had to contend with were graduation, academic proficiency, and the fact that some young men had opted out of football to participate in flight training. The rigorous academic load combined with the long hours of flight training made it difficult for many cadets and midshipmen to commit to football.

These factors made the dynamics of the 1944 game substantially different from 1943, when Army had lost to Notre Dame 26–0. Still, all bets were off going into the game; when Army played Notre Dame, anything could happen.

The game was played on November 11, 1944, at Yankee Stadium before 76,000 fans.

It rained the day before the game. Cadet players already in New York were unable to work out because the field at Yankee Stadium was covered by a tarpaulin. The Notre Dame squad, staying at the Bear Mountain Inn, bussed to nearby West Point for a light workout in the field house.

The much-anticipated contest quickly became lopsided. Notre Dame was unable to answer West Point's strength, speed, and depth. It was the worst defeat in Irish history. Notre Dame trailed 26–0 after the first quarter.

Both coaches were stunned, McKeever by the ineffective play of his team, and Blaik by the explosive power of his squad against one of his key rivals who had previously been so miserly in allowing touchdowns. There was disbelief around the world. The game was being broadcast via shortwave from New York and San Francisco to servicemen across the globe. Frank Leahy on Midway Island was speechless. Lieutenant Colonel Gus Farwick was sure that he was listening to a misleading enemy propaganda broadcast.[161]

The thumping only whet the appetite of the Corps of Cadets, who cheered lustily and demanded that the team, "Roll that score—way up." And roll the score way up is what they did. After each touchdown they yelled, "More yet! More yet! More yet!" finally getting a chance to vent their frustration at the many defeats suffered at the hands of the South Benders. The Cadets responded by scoring two more touchdowns in the third quarter.

In the fourth quarter, Davis scored his third touchdown on a sixty-four-yard romp to make the score 52–0. With four minutes to go Coach Blaik put in his subs. Another interception resulted in the final cadet touchdown. When the final gun sounded, the Cadets had handed the Irish their worst defeat ever at 59–0, surpassing the 58–0 loss to Wisconsin in 1904.

The run-up of the score would be remembered vividly by Irish fans and players once Notre Dame reestablished its dominance after the war.

Blaik had finally gotten the revenge he sought for the losses he had suffered at the hands of the Irish in 1942 and 1943. However, he did it in such a way that only intensified the rivalry between the two teams going forward.

Blaik, in his low-key manner and perhaps with a hint of

embarrassment, attributed the lopsided score to a bad Notre Dame strategy. He felt that had the Irish played more conservatively, the score would not have been as high as it was. "After the first touchdown by Kenna, they went for broke with a passing attack that boomeranged to hand us one touchdown after another," he said.[162]

Sportswriters were effusive in their praise of Blaik's team, recognizing the abundance of talent on the 1944 team by naming fourteen of Army's players to an all-American team that year.[163] It was only the second loss for the South Benders in fifteen games, but it was enough to drop Notre Dame to number five in the AP college rankings, their lowest ranking since 1942.

Next up for Army was Penn. Blaik and his players felt they also had a score to settle with the Quakers. In the Army coach's three games against Penn, Blaik and his teams had lost twice and managed one tie, the preceding year. It was at the 1940 Penn game that Blaik had been offered the coaching job after watching Penn hand the Army football team its worst defeat ever.

Blaik was concerned that the Penn game, sandwiched between Notre Dame and Navy, would cause the Cadets to lose focus as they keyed from one important rival to the next. In addition, he fretted that the enormous press coverage of his team after the Notre Dame game might turn their heads and cause them to be further distracted.

Before 70,000 fans at Franklin Field on the Penn campus, Blaik's fears were heightened by his team's poor play in the first quarter; the score was 7–7. Then, Army's strength and depth took its toll on the home team. Before it was over, Blanchard scored two touchdowns and Davis three. The final score of 62–7 allayed Coach Blaik's fears and allowed the team to concentrate fully on their last and most important game against Navy.

Even though Army entered the game undefeated, a few skeptics remained who felt that only a win over Navy could finally confirm the crowning of the Cadets as national champions. True, Navy had lost earlier in the season to North Carolina Pre-Flight and Georgia Tech by slim margins, (14–21) and (14–17). They had rebounded and won their last four games, shutting out three of their opponents. Yet, Coach Blaik and the Army players knew not to take anything for granted in this game. They were still smarting from the 13–0 loss the year before and were very aware that the Cadets hadn't defeated the Middies in five years. They also knew that Navy wanted more than anything to spoil their rival's perfect season.

Facing Army would be a true test between the two service academy teams that had been unmolested by wartime personnel turmoil and had the same advantages of recruiting star players from other schools. As several sportswriters noted, "Sure Army's got a ball club. But they've been running against civilian college competition that's sub-normal on account of the war. Only Navy's got wartime football players like Army. Let's see what they do against Navy."[164]

Other sportswriters were quick to point out that Navy had defeated Army the last five times they played. In those five contests the Cadets had managed to score only a single touchdown. Of course, stats didn't matter when these two teams met. Neither the last five years nor the current season record would matter to the cadets and middies who would meet on the field and who knew their play would be followed closely by servicemen around the globe. One hundred and forty-three stations of the Columbia Broadcasting System as well as several shortwave facilities would carry the game. It seemed fitting that the two academies representing the sixteen million American servicemen then locked in battle across the globe should be playing to determine the national championship.

The top ranking of the two service academies was testimony to the impact that the war had on college football. Five of the six top teams in the college rankings at the end of the season were associated with the military: Army, Navy, Randolph Field, Bainbridge Naval Training Station, and Iowa Pre Flight. Only number two Ohio State was not affiliated with the military.

President Roosevelt had once again decreed that the annual Army-Navy game would be the scaled-back affair it had been for the preceding two years. Both chief of staff George Marshal and secretary of the army Henry Stimson were not enthusiastic about allowing the game to be played at all. They felt that the game negatively distracted the public from the deadly business being prosecuted by the country's armed forces. Newly appointed secretary of the Navy James Forrestal was ambivalent about the game. Enthusiasm for a greatly expanded meeting of the country's two top teams came instead from a groundswell of war-weary American football fans who were seeking relief from the grim war news.

Fortunately for these fans, there were other members of the president's cabinet who were more creative and imaginative than the military leaders. They suggested a way that would allow the game to have a bigger stage and yet keep a focus on the war effort. Secretary of the treasury Henry Morgenthau, Jr. and his assistant in the War Finance Division came up with a unique scheme to use the game as a vehicle to raise money that would help to finance the war.

As the fervor surrounding the pending contest continued to build, Washington officials saw an opportunity to showcase the game for morale purposes and parlay the keen interest into a war-bond event. Fifteen days prior to the game, the Treasury Department plan was adopted. A decision was made to move the game from Annapolis' Thompson Stadium, which could hold only 20,000, to Baltimore's Municipal Stadium, where 70,000 fans could view the game.

Attendees were strongly encouraged to buy war bonds. Three quarters of the eager fans purchased a series EE $25 bond that enabled them to purchase a ticket for $4.80. Those desiring better seats were required to purchase more expensive bonds. Six box seats sold for one million dollars each. Over 1,400 other prime seats sold for between $100,000 and a million dollars. As the crowd settled into their seats, a banner was unfolded on the field indicating that $58,637,000 had been raised. It was the single most successful bond event of the war.[165]

To add to the pageantry and drama it was decided that both the full Corps of Cadets and Brigade of Midshipmen would attend. Enthusiasm at both schools was raised to a fever pitch by the announcement. It would be relatively easy for the Middies to get to the game since they were only thirty miles away. However, getting the 2,400 cadets to Baltimore, which was over 230 miles from West Point, would be daunting, given the wartime travel restrictions. There was little to nothing said publicly about how that travel was arranged.

An article written in 1994 by John Steadman and published in the *Richmond Times Dispatch* to commemorate the fiftieth anniversary of the 1944 game touched on the topic. The story stated that the blackout of information was a military secret in 1944. The Corps of Cadets was to be moved by troop transport ship from West Point to Baltimore. Nazi U-boats off the East Coast of the US were still a threat. It would've been a devastating loss to the US and a significant propaganda coup for the Germans if they had been able to sink an American troopship loaded with 2,400 future officers.

The trip turned out to be an unusual odyssey for the cadets, never before or since duplicated. The troopship, the USS *Uruguay*, a converted passenger liner, docked at West Point's South Dock on the Thursday before the game. The ocean-going vessel required some minor alterations to enable it to get up the Hudson River. Its mast had been shortened to allow it to pass under the Bear Mountain Bridge, and much of the ballast had been removed so it could negotiate the shallower areas of the river. The land-loving cadets might have been distressed to learn that the *Uruguay* had been involved in a collision at sea in January 1943 that killed twenty men and injured many others. As part of a convoy headed to North Africa, the ship had been rammed by a Navy tanker and had to be rerouted to Bermuda for repairs.

After an uneventful voyage, the ship docked in Baltimore at 9 p.m. on Friday evening. The following morning the cadets had a five-mile march to the stadium in the bitterly cold December morning. When they finally were settled in the stands at the stadium, they were able to see a terrific football game.

The first quarter was a defensive struggle. Each team made only one first down. Finally, in the second quarter Army managed to score by moving the ball sixty-six yards in six plays. It was only the second touchdown the Cadets had scored against the Middies in five years. More importantly to the outcome of the game was the loss due to injuries of Navy's star halfback Bob Jenkins and all-American tackle Don Whitmire.

Nonetheless, Navy as expected, put up a good fight. However, when the gun was fired at the end of the game, Army prevailed 23–7, its first victory over the Naval Academy in five years. In defeating Navy, Army had finished with a perfect 9–0, its first undefeated season since 1916.

When the game was over the Corps of Cadets had hoped for some time to enjoy Baltimore before returning to the academy. That was not to be; the soldiers retraced their steps back to the ship and reboarded. They were at least looking forward to a promised victory dinner aboard ship once it got underway. Even that was denied them. A freak storm hit Chesapeake Bay as the vessel began its return trip to West Point. Hardly any of the cadets were interested in food as the storm violently tossed the ship and its passengers.

From his headquarters in the Pacific, General Douglas MacArthur cabled Coach Blaik with his congratulations. "The greatest of all Army teams stop We have stopped the war to celebrate your magnificent success. MacArthur." [166] Honors continued to be heaped on the undisputed national championship team and its players.

Perhaps the praise that meant the most to the team members came in a postseason message from their coach, a man from whom praise did not flow easily. "Seldom in a lifetime's experience is one permitted the complete satisfaction of being part of a perfect performance. To the coaches, the 23–7 is enough. To the squad members: by hard work and sacrifice, you superbly combined ability, ambition, and the desire to win, thereby leaving a rich athletic heritage for future Academy squads. From her sons West Point expects the best—you were the best. In truth, you were a storybook team."[167]

Feelings were not as satisfying in South Bend. "Losing to Army by such a big score put a stigma on this team that has lasted through the years."[168] Yet, six days after the season ended the university announced that McKeever would remain as coach and would return for the 1945 season. The announcement was met with enthusiasm on the Notre Dame campus. However, events transpired soon after the announcement that changed the plan.

Father Hugh O'Donnell spoke at the annual football banquet. The focus of his comments was the tradition of excellence of football at Notre Dame. He spoke in glowing terms of the success of Frank Leahy's tenure thus far at the university, which had culminated in the national championship of 1943. He then went on to speak about the resumption of those great years once Leahy returned from the Navy.

Many of those who attended the dinner reported that the president never congratulated the team nor acknowledged their efforts during the 1944 season. After the dinner, Coach McKeever invited several players to his home. He was particularly close to Bob Kelly and Frank Szymanski and wanted to vent his anger at the president's affront. "McKeever told Kelly and Szymanski how angry he was at Father O'Donnell for not mentioning the team. According to Kelly, 'This infuriated McKeever, not because O'Donnell didn't talk about him, but that Father O'Donnell did not give any credit to the 1944 team and their accomplishments—he never mentioned the team once during his talk.'"[169]

Shortly after these events McKeever accepted an offer from Cornell to be their head coach.

CHAPTER 15

1945

"Listen fat boy, if you don't behave you're going to get killed." I looked up at him and replied, "Okay Tex."
—Bill Fischer Notre Dame lineman during his first Army game.

AS 1945 BEGAN, the country's mood was somber. The Battle of the Bulge and the final assault into Germany accounted for almost 75 percent of all US casualties in the European war. The slow but steady attrition of US forces slogging through the muddy mountains of Italy and the bloody campaigns of Iwo Jima and Okinawa signaled much more bloodshed ahead in the Pacific.

Then suddenly and incredibly it was over. The dropping of two new and mysterious weapons had, unbelievably, forced the Japanese to sue for peace. The first reaction of the population was one of disbelief, followed quickly by relief, and then an explosion of jubilation throughout the world. An estimated one million American casualties were avoided by Japan's surrender. It would have been difficult in August 1945 to find anyone, especially in the US, who would have condemned the use of the new, powerful atomic weapons.

The end of the war was the first truly happy moment the country had enjoyed in sixteen years since the stock market crash in October 1929. The grinding poverty of the Depression had affected almost all of the country's population. Countless government programs seemed unable to significantly impact or improve the daily lives of most Americans. This pervasive cloud of unemployment and hard scrabble living darkened the country's mood for over ten years. And, just as the Depression ended, America's involvement in WWII began.

American citizens were now free at last to pursue the dreams and aspirations that had been denied to most of them since the beginning of the Depression in 1929. The United States had emerged from the war as the most powerful country in the world and the sole possessor of a terrible new weapon. It was hard not to believe that peace and stability would reign for many years into the future.

The cornerstone of that rosy outlook of the future rested on a solid national foundation of unity and confidence, a direct result of the difficult but triumphant war years. Four years of pervasive governmental and media exhortations to work and sacrifice together for a noble cause had planted itself deep within the country's psyche. This vast reservoir of national unity and pride was deep and robust.

As the war entered its final stages, both Coach Leahy and Coach Blaik looked ahead to a return to normalcy on the gridiron and resumption of the Army-Notre Dame rivalry unencumbered by wartime constrictions.

At the start of 1945, Coach Blaik had reason to be pleased about the upcoming football season. His national championship team of 1944 had scored an amazing total of 504 points against their opponents thirty-five. The undefeated Army team had averaged a spectacular fifty-six points per game. Davis averaged almost twelve yards per carry in fifty-eight rushing attempts and scored twenty touchdowns. Blanchard averaged five-and-a-half yards per carry and scored nine touchdowns. Despite these impressive stats, together the dynamic duo, who only played about thirty minutes per game, accounted for only 174 of the team's total offensive production of 504 points, revealing the depth of the Army squad and Blaik's use of his two-unit system.

Blaik would be able to build his team again around Blanchard and Davis, who were returning for their second year. The coach also was optimistic about the talent of some of his newer players. He was especially bullish on sophomore Arnold Tucker, a gifted athlete who would strengthen the Cadets passing game and therefore the overall potency of Army's T-formation, which was now in its third year. The team had primarily been a running team. With the addition of Tucker, the 1945 team became much more balanced. In addition, Glenn Davis had improved as a passer, making him, and by extension, the entire team a far more versatile offensive threat.

Despite the depth of talent, Coach Blaik had some key holes to fill in the 1945 team. He had lost several standouts called into service, including all-Americans Doug Kenna, Joe Stanowicz, Bob St. Onge, and team captain and quarterback Tom Lombardo.

After reviewing films of players in colleges and universities around the country, Blaik dispatched his coaches to seek out the most promising. The Army coaches succeeded in recruiting top-notch athletes from other schools during these visits. Some of these recruits played key roles in Blaik's efforts to rebuild his team. "Shorty" McWilliams from Mississippi State, Joe Steffy, a guard from the University of Tennessee, Gobel Bryant, a tackle from Texas A&M, Bobbie Jack Stuart, a halfback from Tulsa, Elwin "Rip" Rowan, a fullback from LSU, and Clyde Grimenstein all joined the plebe class in July of 1945.

Years later when discussing his teams he said, "The greatest squad was 1944 and the greatest team was 1945." [170] Proof of that assessment was borne out by the fact that by the end of the 1945 season, Army would have twelve players named to an all-American team.

It was in 1945 that the Army team took on the nickname they still retain in shortened form, *The Black Knights*. Will Wedge of the *New York Sun*, using clever alliteration, was the first to call the Army football team *Blaik's Black Knights*. His colorful and descriptive label captured both the importance of the coach and the noble cause of representing the Army during wartime. The black stripe on the helmet and black arm bands of the uniform aided in the graphic description of the original nickname that Wedge had bestowed on the Army team.

By the time the 1945 college football season started, civilian colleges and universities were looking forward to welcoming war veterans back to their campuses. Coaches were especially anxious to greet their former players who would now be more mature and probably even physically in better shape. The trickle of returning veterans initially would turn into a torrent in 1946, but it would be too late to significantly impact the 1945 football season.

The sports world anxiously awaited the debut of the 1945 Army team to see if would be as good as the championship team. The first contest on the schedule was against Personal Distribution Command, an Air Force team that have been put together to play other military teams for the benefit of boosting morale among the troops of the newly named US Army Air Forces (formerly known as the Army Air Corps). The team had several former NFL players, and was no pushover. They were able to prevent the 1944 national champions from scoring in the first quarter. But, by the game's end glimpses of the versatility of the 1945 version of Army football became evident. Although Davis had injured his back in practice prior to the first game, he scored two touchdowns, and newly recruited Shorty McWilliams scored two touchdowns. Davis also connected on a pass to Blanchard for the final touchdown on the last play of the game. However, the full array of the Cadets's offensive power was not on display because newly minted quarterback Arnold Tucker was injured and did not play. Even with an injured Davis and Tucker unable to play, the Black Knights prevailed 32–0.

Wins over Wake Forest and Michigan quickly followed. Another military team, The Motor Torpedo Boat School, was next on the schedule. The Melville, Rhode Island Navy team had several excellent former college players. They led the Cadets 13–0 at the end of the first quarter before Army rolled to a 55–13 win.

The Cadets next met Duke in New York City, where they defeated the Blue Devils 48–13. The following week, Blaik, Hickman, and others on the coaching staff went to Cleveland to watch undefeated Notre Dame battle a very tough Navy team. While the Middies and the Irish were beating each other up, Army was coasting to an easy 54–0 dismantling of Villanova.

Although elated at the war's end, there was more than a little anxiety among Notre Dame administrators worried about the effect the loss of the Navy midshipmen programs would have on the financial health of the school. Since 1942, these programs had been sustaining the university as civilian enrollment plunged. Some of the fiscal anxiety was relieved when the Navy approved retaining the midshipmen program on the campus until June of 1946.

The football program had much the same problem as the administrators. The football staff was charged with producing a top-notch football team with the Navy and other students on hand while awaiting the return of their coach and many of the veteran players who had helped the team win the national championship in 1943. Those returning players would now also be augmented by the recruits Coach Leahy had signed up during his Navy service. However, the return of the coach and these excellent players would not occur until after the 1945 football season.

Meanwhile, the Fighting Irish would be coached by popular Hugh DeVore, a former Notre Dame player and assistant coach. DeVore had been recruited by Knute Rockne in 1930, the year before his death. After graduation, DeVore became an assistant coach at Fordham where he helped to develop the *Seven Blocks of Granite*. He then moved on to coaching positions at Providence College and Holy Cross before returning to Notre Dame.

DeVore's 1945 team was mostly comprised of players from the 1944 team. Notre Dame's schedule for 1945 would be virtually the same, too, replacing only Iowa with Wisconsin. The abrupt end of the war had almost no impact on the strong military teams of the previous year. Discharges would not affect these teams until after the season ended. Several of the servicemen of the Great Lakes Naval team delayed their discharges until after the Notre Dame game so that they could get one more chance at the Irish.

DeVore's team squeaked by a tough Illinois team at home, 7–0 in its opening game. Easy wins over Dartmouth (34–0), Iowa (56–0), Georgia Tech (40–7), and Pitt (39–9) followed. After five games the undefeated Irish were ranked second behind the previous year's national champions, Army.

The Irish then traveled to Cleveland, a neutral venue that had hosted the game five times in the past and could seat more fans than the 60,000 Notre Dame Stadium. They would face third-ranked and undefeated Navy before a huge crowd of 82,000 fans that was on hand to watch a fired-up Notre Dame team intent on avenging the previous year's embarrassing loss.

The game proved to be a bruising defensive struggle. Irish quarterback Frank Dancewicz was able to complete only four passes out of fourteen with four interceptions while Navy was able to gain only sixty yards rushing. The two teams played to a 6–6 tie, both suffering many injuries. Irish fullback Frank Ruggiero needed thirteen stitches to close the wound on his jaw. Halfback Elmer "Bud" Angsman lost eleven teeth during the game and two more the following week when he visited the dentist. "Pep" Panelli had a shoulder separation that eliminated him for the rest of the season. Hardly a player on either team escaped unscathed, a fact that did not go unnoticed by the observing Army coaches in the stands. Even though the game ended in a tie, Notre Dame's tough play against the Middies was strong enough to topple the sailors from third place in the college rankings.

Coach Blaik and several members of his staff no doubt left the game with confidence that the wide-open offensive play of Tucker, Blanchard, and Davis would prove to be an effective antidote against both Navy and Notre Dame.

The two teams met in Yankee Stadium on November 10. The Irish were shorthanded and still banged up from the physical beating they had taken against Navy the previous week. In contrast, Coach Blaik was happy to announce that all his players were in top condition.

It took the cadets only sixty-six seconds to score after Bud Angsman, still nursing injuries from the Navy game, fumbled. A run from Blanchard was followed by Davis's scamper for a touchdown. The first quarter ended with the cadets leading 7–0. However, the Irish still had plenty of fire. They had led the Black Knights in first downs in the opening quarter.

In the second quarter, however, the power and depth of the cadets began to again assert itself. A touchdown pass to Davis and a short run by Doc Blanchard gave the Army a 21–0 lead at halftime. As the Irish began to wear down, they turned to some of their freshmen players. Bill Fischer who became an all-American lineman at Notre Dame in 1947 and 1948 recalled his introduction to Army Notre-Dame football in that game.

"Jack Fallon and I were freshman tackles. Ed Mieszkowski was the first-string tackle and I was his substitute. After we were down about twenty-one points, Devore told Fallon and me to warm up and get ready to go in. As we were about to go in the game, Fallon turned to me and said, 'We may not win, but let's go in and kick the hell out of them.'

"The Army had the ball. The quarterback went back to pass. I was trying to get around my guy. I was hitting him in the face (no face masks) and everything else I could possibly do. The guy grabbed me and almost picked me off my feet and said, 'Listen fat boy, if you don't behave you're going to get killed.' I looked up at him and replied, 'Okay Tex.' The player was Dewitt Coulter, the all-American Army tackle who was about six-feet-six, weighed about

260, and was the heavyweight boxing champion of both military academies."[171]

By the end of the game Army prevailed by the lop-sided score of 48-0. There was little doubt about Army's strength nor its ability to again carry the mantle of national champion. Only Penn and Navy stood between them and a second consecutive top ranking.

Prior to the Penn game, Coach Blaik was worried that his team had lost some of its intensity after the Notre Dame game, which had been the focus of their attention for so long. "We never have played well against Penn." Blaik obviously had forgotten, or had chosen to forget, that the Black Knights had crushed Penn 62–7 the year before.[172]

But this Penn team looked to be better than the previous year's version. About a third of the football team were recently returned veterans. They were led by their captain, tailback Bob Evans, who had been decorated for heroism in the Army Air Corps in Europe. George Savitsky, another veteran and a 245-pound tackle, was a former Marine who would be named an all-American in 1945 and go on to play for the Philadelphia Eagles. Returning Army veteran and future NFL player Chuck Bednarik also helped the 1945 Quakers to become more formidable.

Coach Blaik worried that his team might underestimate Penn. The Quakers were ranked sixth with only one loss by a single touchdown against Navy.

As it turned out Blaik didn't have much to worry about. The Black Knights breezed by the Quakers, 61–0, Penn's worst defeat since losing to Princeton 63–0 in 1888.

There was only one more hurdle for the Cadets to overcome to achieve a significant milestone in the storied history of Army football. If they could beat the Middies they were likely to be declared national champions for a second straight year. In addition, no Army team had ever beaten Notre Dame and Navy in two consecutive years.

Of course, the sailors would have liked nothing better than to prevent the Army from achieving those goals. The only blemish to their record had been the 6–6 tie with Notre Dame. So, for the second season in a row, the two service academies faced off, both undefeated. The annual clash of the academies once again captured the interest of much of the country.

Mingled with the sense that life was slowly returning to normal was the realization that the football dominance of the service academies might be coming to an end. Service members were streaming back from their overseas posts ready to resume their academic and athletic careers in America's civilian colleges and universities. Newspapers carried daily notices of the progress of the monumental task of bringing home American service men and women.

On the day of the game, the Headquarters of the Western Sea Frontier in San Francisco happily announced that 313,889 soldiers, sailors, marines, coast guardsmen, and civilians had arrived at West Coast ports in November. *The Des Moines Register* on December 2, 1945, featured a photo of the aircraft carrier USS *Enterprise* entering New York harbor with four thousand returning veterans alongside a column that listed by town every Iowan recently discharged by the Navy.

The pageantry of the Army-Navy game was heightened by the attendance of President Truman and senior military leaders. General Dwight Eisenhower addressed the Corps of Cadets at a pep rally by telephone. "After saying that Army and Navy had a close relationship during the rest of the year, Eisenhower added, "But on this one half-day next Saturday afternoon, we reserve the right, the sweet privilege, of rocking them and socking them into respectful recognition of West Point's superiority."[173] At the same time the Middies were treated to a rousing speech by one of the heroic figures of the naval battles in the Pacific, Admiral William "Bull" Halsey.

One hundred and two thousand fans eagerly filed into Philadelphia's Municipal Stadium to witness the showdown. A new technology, television, broadcast the game in Philadelphia, New

York City, and Schenectady to those few Americans who owned TV receivers. Radio was still the primary means of reaching the millions of fans anxiously awaiting the contest. Red Barber, the voice of Dodger baseball, described the game to millions of listeners in the US and countless more at military bases around the world via short-wave radio.

Navy, like Army, had a strong team bolstered by transfers from other schools. Bob Jenkins had starred at Alabama and became an all-American at Navy in 1944. Skip Minisi had been a standout running back at Penn the year before. Bob Hoernschemeyer had played two seasons at Indiana University, while Clyde "Smackover" Scott from Smackover, Arkansas had played two years at the University of Arkansas.

Blaik had reason to be concerned going into the game. His quarterback, Arnold Tucker, had spent the last few days before the game in the West Point hospital because of a severe cold. Although not 100 percent, by Saturday the scrappy signal caller was ready to play.

Army got off to a quick start, scoring three touchdowns in the first quarter. The Navy defense stiffened in the second quarter holding the Black Knights scoreless. Navy offense scored a touchdown. By the time Truman left the Army side where he had spent the first half, and was escorted to the Navy side, the score was still in Army's favor 20–7.

Early in the third-quarter Blanchard picked off a Navy pass at midfield and returned it for a touchdown. The Middies scored once more but it would not be enough to overcome the Cadets, who won 32–13 for their eighteenth consecutive victory and second undefeated season.

Honors were heaped on the repeating national champions. Blanchard won the coveted Heisman Trophy as well as the Sullivan award as the best amateur athlete in the country. Davis finished second in the Heisman voting. In addition to Blanchard and Davis, Army players, Coulter, Jack Green, Al Nemetz, and Hank Foldberg were consensus all-Americans. This was an astounding accomplishment in 1945 since only eleven players were named as first-team all-Americans because they played both offense and defense.

CHAPTER 16

1946

I don't reckon West Point was made to be liked.
—Army lineman Tex Coulter after flunking out of West Point

IT HAD TAKEN almost four years to get US troops to their foreign destinations. Now, in 1946, there was enormous pressure to bring them home much faster. It was the equivalent of having a 100,000-ton aircraft carrier doing thirty knots reverse its course immediately while the impatient passengers yelled out their displeasure to the struggling crew.

President Truman, a veteran of WWI, anticipated the dissatisfaction that he knew would quickly follow the end of hostilities. On August 23, 1945, he correctly and bluntly asserted that whatever demobilization plan the government had wouldn't make any difference because somebody wouldn't like it.

To prioritize the return of the millions of Army personnel overseas, the US Army established what many considered at the time to be a fair way to determine who should come home first. It was based on the general principle that "those who had fought longest and hardest should be returned first." A point system was developed that rewarded soldiers in accordance with that principle.

1. A soldier was awarded one point for each month of service.
2. A soldier was awarded an additional point for every month served overseas.
3. A soldier was awarded five points for every combat award such as the Distinguished Service Cross, Silver Star, Bronze Star . . . etc.

4. Soldiers with dependent children were awarded twelve points for each child under eighteen.

An enlisted man needed eighty-five points to be considered for demobilization.

Initially, this system seemed to be accepted by the service members as well as their families. A public opinion poll of people with a relative in the service conducted by Gallup in late September 1945 showed that 55 percent of those surveyed thought that the release rate of soldiers was satisfactory while only 29 percent thought the release rate should be faster. Sixteen percent had no opinion.[174]

However, by early 1946 the mood of the soldiers awaiting discharge had changed dramatically. Soldiers in Guam, Manila, London, Paris, Frankfurt, and at a number of other bases marched openly to show their displeasure with the delay. In London, 500 US troops marched on the hotel where Eleanor Roosevelt was staying. She met with a delegation of the group and wrote to General Dwight Eisenhower the next day outlining the soldiers"grievances. There was some evidence that soldiers with communist leanings were fomenting and organizing the protests.[175]

By mid–1946 the crisis had passed. Thanks to a Herculean effort most service members were transitioning back to civilian life. Now, however, the enormous task of assimilating the returning vets back into civilian society began.

The country was anxious to avoid the problems of earlier demobilizations such as the 1932 Bonus March, which pitted WWI veterans against a government beset by Depression financial problems. Planning for demobilization actually began in 1942, long before any realistic end of the war could be envisioned.

The federal government gave a huge impetus to this hopeful outlook by implementing the GI Bill of Rights. This legislation had been signed by President Roosevelt on June 22, 1944, even as the war was reaching its most intense period. Under this legislation,

The Servicemen's Readjustment Act of 1944, service members were entitled to federal aid, which provided vets with assistance for hospitalization, purchase of homes and businesses, and especially education. The act provided tuition, subsistence, books and supplies, equipment, and counseling services for veterans to continue their education in a trade school or college. Returning servicemen and women were also eligible for government-backed loans, unemployment allowances, and help with finding a job. In 1947, World War II veterans accounted for nearly half of all college admissions. Half of all World War II veterans participated in some form of education or job-training with benefits.

The GI Bill was the largest and most generous legislation of the twentieth century. Its positive impact would be felt for years to come. The legislation, when finally introduced had almost unanimous support from federal lawmakers. When the proposal reached both the floor of the House and the Senate, not a single negative vote was cast. However, like all issues in Washington, even this popular measure was challenged when it was first proposed. John A. Rankin, a Democrat from Mississippi, initially opposed the bill, saying that taxpayer dollars should not be used to assist able-bodied men who should be able to take care of themselves.[176]

Rankin specifically objected to the bill's proposal for unemployment compensation, which provided $15 per week to single veterans and $25 per week for veterans with three or more children. In 2021 dollars the $25 stipend for a family of five would amount to $21,000 per year. The 2021 poverty line for US families was $26,500. Rankin felt that such largess "might be encouragement through the liberal unemployment compensation provision of idleness."[177] Army Lt. Bert Bertine, writing a column for the *Frederick Leader* in Oklahoma, referenced a popular Army newspaper to highlight soldier displeasure with the Mississippi congressman. "*Army Times* pointed out to Rep. Rankin that the idleness of servicemen is not likely to exceed that of certain members of Congress, and that his criticism of soldiers at this time was both in bad taste and ill-timed."

The congressman's opposition to the proposed bill was certainly ill-timed, coming a few months before the D-Day invasion. As casualties mounted with the invasion of France and offensive campaigns in the Pacific, support for those fighting the war became even more intense. Rankin and the other critics of the bill were soon overwhelmingly silenced by the vast majority of Americans.

Once implemented, the law's provisions impacted almost all aspects of the American economy. Homeownership grew rapidly during the postwar years as veterans received a loan guarantee from the government. The guarantee made veterans safer investments for banks since the government would pay back either 50 percent of the loan or $2,000 if the recipient failed to pay for the loan. These loans could be used for the purchase, construction, or improvement of property. Additionally, a veteran could purchase a farm or farm equipment with the loan. This program proved especially popular. The Veterans Administration guaranteed over two million home loans by 1950.[178]

Largely because of the GI Bill, housing starts exploded as entire neighborhoods were built to accommodate young vets and their growing families. William Levitt, a Navy veteran who had served in the Seabees, capitalized on this almost insatiable demand by developing a technique of building houses that mimicked the production lines of automobiles. He and his brother bought twenty square miles of land near Hempstead, Long Island, where they implemented their system. Levitt identified twenty-seven tasks necessary to build a house. He organized teams that would move from home to home preparing the foundation, framing, and drywall. To further streamline the system, he built identical 750-square-foot, Cape Cod-style, two-bedroom houses. During the Depression, builders built two houses per year. Levitt built thirty per day. His first community had 17,000 homes which sold for $7,990 each.

The appetites of returning veterans for homes, autos,

appliances, and other consumer goods were insatiable. American industry, which had been untouched by the war, quickly converted from wartime production to the manufacture of the consumer products that were in strong demand. Manufacturing in the US soon accounted for half of all the world's manufacturing.

Birthrates soared after the war, but so did divorces. During 1945, the US had the highest divorce rate in the world—502,000. Even Bill Mauldin, the popular GI cartoonist who had been perhaps the most celebrated champion of the ordinary soldier was one of them. It was ironic that the originator of the two most famous fictional GIs of the war, Joe and Willie, who had shared so many hardships with typical grunts during the war, would share the heartache of a divorce when he returned home. Long separations from spouses and veterans' difficulty coping with civilian life stressed a lot of unions. Those with psychological and physical injuries had an especially difficult time.

The Best Years of Our Lives, a movie released in 1946, won nine Academy Awards. The film showed the return of several veterans and the difficulties they faced in adjusting to civilian life. It also heralded Hollywood's turn away from the production of action, spy, and war movies that had been the mainstay of the industry for the preceding four years. In 1947, *Tales of the South Pacific* by James Michener became a bestseller and in 1949 a very successful Broadway musical. The movie and the original musical were indicators that the country was eager to forget about the war. South Pacific tales had changed in a few years from the grim reporting on Guadalcanal, Tarawa, and Iwo Jima to a love story centered on a lovely tropical island filled with homesick sailors.

Despite the tolls war had taken, and those struggling to cope, America was ready to move on to brighter times. And much of that transition was occurring on college campuses.

The GI Bill enabled many of the returnees to consider a college education for the first time. Many came from families who had never previously had a member attend college. In 1930 12.4 percent of the population attended college. By 1950 that number increased to almost 30 percent. During the period from 1930 to 1950 the population increased from 122 million to 151 million, which meant that the number of college students rose from 1.5 million to 4.5 million. Colleges and universities welcomed the flood of new students after facing lower enrollments during the war years. Notre Dame's student body increased from 2,800 to 4,500 from 1946 to 1947.[179] Notre Dame announced at the beginning of 1947 that new enrollments for the upcoming fall semester had been closed to all but those former students who had left the campus to join the armed forces.[180]

The addition of so many returning veterans to college campuses greatly impacted college football across the board. Nowhere was that change more visible than in the upcoming 1946 Army-Notre Dame game.

While many civilian schools were now awash with young men, many of whom had served in the war, the opposite was happening at the Military Academy. With the war's end the allure of West Point as a three-year haven was lost. From July 1945 until March 1946, 173 cadets resigned. This number did not include those who were expelled for academic or other deficiencies. And, unlike civilian educational institutions, West Point had a fixed enrollment. Once a cadet left, he could not be replaced. New additions to the Corps of Cadets could only be made with the arrival of the new plebe class in July of each year.

The Navy was bleeding students as well. At the Naval Academy, 142 midshipmen or 4.74 percent of the Brigade of Midshipmen, quit, while 173 cadets, or 6.9 percent, of the Corps of Cadets left West Point. The bulk of the departing West Pointers, 75 percent, were veterans who had recently entered the academy with the new plebe class. Many of these young men quit to take advantage of their educational benefits under the newly instituted GI Bill of Rights, which they could pursue without a military commitment after graduation.

Some of Blaik's star wartime recruits were in danger of being ousted from West Point involuntarily. Tex Coulter was found deficient in mathematics in June 1946 and dismissed from the academy. When he was asked, after leaving, how he had liked West Point he said, "I don't reckon West Point was made to be liked."[181]

Glenn Davis, who had his own problems with the math department, had left the academy for a year and was strong testimony that football players at West Point were cut little slack. He continued to struggle with math for his entire three years as a cadet after he returned.

The additional loss to graduation of All-Americans, team captain Jack Green and Al Nemetz greatly weakened the Army line. Of course, Blaik still had Mr. Inside and Mr. Outside, but the loss of these key lineman from 1945 would make their jobs more difficult. Recognizing this deficiency in the 1946 team, the coach gave an indication about a change to his strategy going into the new season. "We're going to have to throw the ball more than we have in the last two years . . . and even then it will be tough going."[182]

The public was sensitive to learning that cadets who had been sheltered from the draft while at West Point might be seeking to leave their posts now that the war had ended. That was one reason why the case of Army star halfback Shorty McWilliams evoked such strong emotions when he announced his desire to resign from the Military Academy in the summer of 1946.

His departure was covered extensively by the national media. McWilliams had been aggressively recruited by Army in 1944 after his freshman year at Mississippi State. Bulldog fans and Coach McKeen specifically were not happy about losing their star player. But, with the war still on-going with no short-term end in sight, the Military Academy had a significant recruiting advantage over its civilian counterparts. West Point would be a much better option than having the uncertain future of an enlisted man.

McWilliams became a starter in the backfield with Blanchard, Davis, and Tucker after scoring two touchdowns against Wake Forest early in the 1945 season. It was therefore somewhat of a surprise when McWilliams announced his intention to resign from the Military Academy in the summer of 1946. The optics for West Point were terrible. A star football player, recruited during the war, was leaving now that the war had ended.

The events surrounding the McWilliams affair carried by newspapers around the country was not a discussion that either side wished to have. Now that the war had ended, a closer scrutiny of service academy recruiting during the war seemed to be more acceptable. Herman Hickman and other Army coaches had traveled around the country in pursuit of top-notch football players complete with congressional appointments already arranged. This all appeared to be unseemlier in the immediate post-war.

On the other side, it appeared that the sudden availability of large numbers of excellent football players encouraged many colleges to provide suspicious incentives in their recruiting efforts. A *Time* magazine article in September 1946 outlined what it called a black market in college football. The great Grantland Rice also lamented the payments that some colleges and alumni provided to secure top-notch athletes. "It is my belief that college paychecks are going to lead to a national scandal unless there is a sudden check. The fight for young stars, plus inducements offered, have already broken all past records. Athletic scholarships and jobs that can take a young fellow through college are okay. But not a substantial paycheck on the side, usually handled by the keyed-up alumni."[183]

McWilliams' stated plan to leave West Point infuriated the academy superintendent General Maxwell Taylor. The famed airborne commander of World War II was outspoken about his opposition to the proposed resignation. He accused some unnamed colleges of trying to lure star football players with fantastic financial offers.

Coach Allyn McKeen of Mississippi State felt that the general was referring to him with his thinly veiled charge. He challenged Taylor to produce evidence of the alleged recruiting malpractice. Many coaches, especially those in the Southeast, weighed in on the controversy, accusing Army of being a case of the pot calling the kettle black. The Cadets' recruiting of top-notch players during the war was still a sore spot among many coaches.

As late as August, it appeared that Taylor's obstinance over the issue would prevail. An *Atlanta Constitution* article noted on August 29 that McWilliams had drawn new shoes in preparation for football practice, which was scheduled to start the next day. It was a surprise to almost everyone, therefore, when on September 11, the superintendent reversed himself and allowed McWilliams to resign. An Academy spokesman stated that, "The action of this recommendation was based on considerations peculiar to this case. It is recognized that there is an unfulfilled obligation to the military service owed by a cadet who has received a year's education and who in addition, has signed an agreement to serve in the Army for eight years, as is required of all entering cadets.

"Nevertheless, a careful consideration of the case of Cadet McWilliams led the superintendent to the conclusion that the effect of this recently publicized circumstance had so weakened McWilliams' will to succeed at West Point as to render questionable his value as a cadet and his promise as a future army officer. In general, it was felt that promising upperclass cadets should not be allowed to resign during the current shortage of officers except when such action is in the interest of the military service."[184]

The McWilliams case had struck a nerve on many levels, as did the resignation of 173 other cadets. The country had provided them with a haven while tens of thousands of others were killed or wounded. The Black Knights merely played football.

The dilution of Blaik's team was front and center. His team was no longer two-squads deep. His young stars would now have to play sixty minutes instead of just thirty. Sports writers who had followed Army closely knew that the Black Knights who sallied forth from their bastion on the Hudson to do battle in 1946 were very talented but could not afford any injuries to its first team players. The loss of McWilliams and back-up halfback Bobby Jack Stuart due to a hernia made the Cadet backfield even more dependent on Blanchard, Davis, and Tucker.

"Chances are that the Cadets will have only the best backfield in the country this year, instead of the two best backfields and the two best lines. Their forward wall will be only good, instead of wonderful, and their shortage of reserves might catch them where it hurts before the season is over."[185]

Almost complete turnover of rosters at universities across the country made it difficult to accurately assess the other major teams going into the start of the 1946 season. At the end of week one, Texas was ranked number one in the college football national rankings. By week nine they were not even in the top ten.

The Black Knights began the season proud of their streak of eighteen straight wins. Their last loss had been against Navy at the end of 1943. Their opening game of the 1946 season was against Villanova at West Point and drew the largest opening game crowd in the academy's history. Rain had made the turf in Michie stadium soggy and treacherous for the slashing running game of the Cadets.

Led by Blanchard and Davis, each who scored early touchdowns, Army looked as if they had picked up right where they left off at the end of 1945. When Army got the ball again late in the first quarter, Blanchard broke through the left side of the Villanova line. As he approached the Villanova fifteen-yard line headed for the goal line, he was slowed by the Wildcat 200-pound center Silvio Yanelli. This glancing blow was just enough to allow Francis Kane, the Villanova end, to catch Blanchard and tackle him at the twelve-yard line. Just as Kane hit him, Blanchard's right heel sunk into the soggy turf forcing his knee to hyper extend backward. He slowly raised himself to his knees and knelt on the ground in obvious pain.

He slowly limped off the field where he was examined by the Army team physician, Dr. Herman Bearzy. Even though he didn't return to the game, Army went on to win 35–0. However, the big story coming out of the game was the extent of the injury to Mr. Inside. After the game Coach Blaik tried to minimize the severity of the injury by saying that his big fullback had strained a ligament in practice and was kept on the bench to prevent further injury.

Dr. Bearzy knew after examining Blanchard that the injury was significantly more serious than the coach had described. Blanchard had a torn anterior cruciate, as well as torn internal-lateral and external-lateral ligaments and a torn membrane. These injuries would have been enough to put most players out for the season. However, because of Blanchard's strong leg muscles, he was able to resume playing in three weeks. The immense size of his legs was readily apparent to anyone who saw him up close. But those who had closely followed the football exploits of the powerful Army running back could see a difference in his performance after the injury. He was no longer able to punt or kick off. His ability to generate quick starting speed and power was diminished. He was still an extraordinary player, but some felt he possessed only 60 percent of the ability he had before the injury. But a 60 percent Doc Blanchard teamed with Glenn Davis and Arnold Tucker still made Army formidable.

By the end of the weekend a more sobering assessment of Blanchard's injury was announced by line coach Colonel Harvey Jablonski, who disclosed only that Blanchard had a leg muscle bruise, with, for the first time, the ominous hint that the star Army fullback might not play against Oklahoma in the upcoming game.

The uncertainty of Blanchard's status continued right up to game time to deceive the Sooners. The home crowd, including President

Harry Truman, the first president to watch a football game at Michie Stadium, was surprised to see Blanchard suited up. He joined Davis as a co-captain at midfield for the coin toss. However, he did not play. Early in the game, Oklahoma, not worried about Blanchard inside contained the Cadets by concentrating on Davis.

It was Tucker, the under recognized third member of the national championship backfield, that saved the day for the Cadets. With Army trailing 7–0 just before the half ended, Tucker orchestrated a sixty-one yard, six-play drive that ended with the scoring pass to end Hank Foldberg.

In the second half, the talented quarterback completed a fourteen-yard pass, which set up a touchdown by substitute fullback Fuson. Tucker then intercepted a pass on the Army three that stopped a key Sooner drive. On Oklahoma's next possession he snatched a fumble in midair on his own fourteen-yard line and raced for a touchdown, giving the Black Knights their nineteenth consecutive win, 21–7.

Against Cornell the following week Davis scored four touchdowns while Tucker set up two more with punt returns as the Cadets rolled up their twentieth straight victory 46–21. Blanchard sat out for a second week.

Next up was a very tough Michigan team in a game played at the *Big House*, then a stadium that held 88,000 fans. To counter the strong Michigan presence, West Point sent all 800 members of the first class at the academy. The Michigan team was led by Bob Chappius, a recently returned veteran. Like many of the young men who donned football uniforms that fall, Chappius had a dramatic story of survival from his service days. After being shot down over German occupied Italy, Chappius was hidden by an Italian family for several weeks until he could safely return to the American lines.

Now he was back at his Michigan alma mater and hoping to end the Army winning streak. The Wolverines were optimistic that they could be the team to topple the Black Knights helped by the injury to Blanchard.

"We're playing not only to win for ourselves," said one Army player, "but also to justify the 1944 and '45 teams. Sure, I know how great they were. But lots of folks say they beat mostly below-par, wartime competition. Well, we've still got Blanchard and Davis and Tucker, but Doc's condition is doubtful and we're not as strong up in that line from tackle as we were in the last two years. If we can keep winning now against stronger teams, it will give an idea what those 1944 and '45 teams would be doing."[186]

For the first time since the Villanova game Blanchard tried his injured leg in full competition. The Michigan players had no regard for the injury and tried their best to remind the West Point star that this was his first tentative return since he had been sidelined three weeks earlier. When Blaik took him out for a breather, he came to the sideline and hugged the Army trainer. "Beaver," he exuberated, "it's all right. It'll carry me. I can play on it."[187]

However, the good news of Blanchard's return was offset by an injury to Tucker early in the game. The Black Knights quarterback fielded a punt and was driven out of bounds. He sprained his wrist and elbow and separated his shoulder, all in his passing arm. The Army trainer shifted his attention from Blanchard to Tucker and patched him up well enough so that he was able to continue. He was limited to short passes and handoffs, but it would be enough to keep the Cadets in the game. To cope with the situation, Blaik switched to Glenn Davis to throw the long passes.

With the score tied at 7–7 late in the second quarter, Davis completed a forty-four-yard pass to Blanchard, who out jumped two Michigan players. After a few more plays the Cadets found themselves on the Michigan thirty-one, with fourth down and eighteen yards to go.

Tucker called for a handoff to Davis, who would then pass to substitute end Bob Folsom. The Michigan line was ready and broke through the Army defense, causing the handoff to be bobbled. The ball got away from Davis, who finally recovered it and in one quick motion fired a long pass into the end zone where it was caught by Folsom with a leaping grab.

With this spectacular play the Cadets were able to go into the locker room at halftime leading 13–7. The Army trainer put a brace on Tucker's right shoulder, working on his elbow and taping his wrist. The Army team knew they were lucky to be ahead. Blanchard and Davis especially knew it would take a better effort in the second half to win the game. "Heck," Glenn said, "we've got to get going out there."

"I'll be better this half," Blanchard muttered.[188]

Michigan wasn't going to make it easy. They took the second-half kickoff and drove for a touchdown. A missed point after touchdown made the score even. While Blanchard, Davis, and Tucker began to work their magic, the Army defense dug in, preventing any more Wolverine scoring.

At the end of the game the Black Knights had their twenty-second victory, squeaking by the Wolverines 20–13. Fittingly, it was Blanchard who scored the winning touchdown, serving notice to future rivals that the "Doc" was still a formidable threat. He would still be one of the finalists for that year's Heisman Trophy.

The Army coaches were overjoyed with their victory. On the train back east, the staff enjoyed a celebration with the accompanying sports writers well into the evening. Even Blaik showed his relief at achieving the victory by having a glass of sherry.

On October 14, undefeated Army was ranked number one with Notre Dame right behind them at number two. It would stay that way right up to the end of the season when the national championship would be decided. Although the cadets had three more games before they would face the Irish, they could already feel the hot breath of the South Benders on their neck.

By the end of the spring semester of 1946, 3,000 students

were enrolled at Notre Dame. The student body comprised 1,000 returning and new students, 800 midshipmen, and 600 veterans enrolled under the GI Bill. Many of those GI Bill students already on campus plus those soon to arrive were married. The university administrators, led by young priest Theodore Hesburgh scrambled to find accommodations for these young families.

The solution was found in Weingarten, Missouri, 418 miles from South Bend. The government had built barracks there in 1943 to house thousands of Italian POWs. The thirty-nine barracks buildings were broken down and shipped to a thirteen-acre site near the main campus. The federal government subsidized the $400,000 relocation project while Notre Dame contributed $36,000 for new roads, sewers, and water mains. When the barracks were reassembled, each unit was sub-divided into three units with a tiny kitchen, bathroom, living room, and two bedrooms.[189]

The return of GIs to Notre Dame soon became a flood. By 1946 that number had risen to 74 percent of the much larger 4,532 student body. The generous allowances of the GI Bill helped both the veteran and the university. At the time, tuition, room, and board at Notre Dame cost $1,100. Veterans could receive up to $500 a year paid directly to the university, and $65 per month paid directly to the individual student for living expenses, which amounted to total annual benefits of $1,280. Over two million veterans were able to attend American colleges and universities under the GI Bill with 15,000 of those choosing Notre Dame.[190]

The football team also was flooded with potential recruits. However, not everyone was thrilled to see the enormous pool of talent that Leahy was amassing. Phil Colella, a Navy vet who had been on two ships sunk by Japanese torpedoes, had been the second leading Irish ball carrier in 1945. When he came out to preseason practice in the spring of 1946, he took one look at the backs Leahy had stockpiled, and transferred to St. Bonaventure.[191]

This unusual blend of players gave Leahy and the Irish some

unique benefits, and challenges. The maturity and toughness of the vets were sure to give the Notre Dame team some strong qualities on the gridiron. However, the fact that most of the squad had not played together would test the coaching staff's ability to mold the players into a cohesive unit by the start of the football season a short six months away. Although many post-war college teams faced the same issues after the end of the war, Leahy seemed to have planned more thoroughly for the changes then underway. His two-year sabbatical in the Navy had freed him from the day-to-day concerns of coaching and allowed him to focus on recruiting and building his post-war team.

Notre Dame started the season with convincing wins over Illinois (26–6), Pitt (33–0) and Purdue (49–6). In the two weeks before the Army game, Notre Dame defeated Iowa (41–6) and Navy, their other wartime nemesis, (28–0). Meanwhile, Army continued its win streak without much difficulty by defeating Columbia (48–14), Duke (19–0), and West Virginia (19–0).

This match-up between the two archrivals was shaping up to be much different than the meetings of the two previous years. The 1946 Notre Dame team was significantly stronger than the teams Army had faced in 1944 and 1945. Coach Leahy was back from the Navy along with several new players recently released from the service, among them Jim Martin and George Connor. Quarterback John Lujack was rejoining the team after a two-year stint in the Navy. He would be joined by halfback Bob Kelly who had spurned Blaik, and returning veterans like Kelly and Emil Sitko. There were also young talented freshmen like Terry Brennan and Leon Hart who would help to sustain the strength of the Irish for years to come.

CHAPTER 17

THE GAME

The students rallied around a cheer that even the team began yelling at practices, "Fifty-nine and forty-eight, this is the year we retaliate."

REQUESTS FOR TICKETS overwhelmed both schools. "If Yankee stadium had one million seats we would still fill it for this game. I have never seen anything like it,"[192] said West Point athletic director Colonel Biff Jones.

Sales to the public didn't begin until August 1, although almost all the seats had already been sold despite the hefty five-dollar price for most seats. Two days later, ticket sales were officially closed and both schools began the task of returning money to those who had missed out.

The Notre Dame student body was understandably among the most ardent in its anticipation of the game. For several months prior, Coach Blaik received daily postcards from South Bend with predictions of the upcoming Irish triumph. Most were signed SPATNC, which the Army staff, familiar with acronyms, quickly deciphered to mean "The Society for the Prevention of Army's Third National Championship."

"When he became West Point superintendent in 1945, General Maxwell Taylor was shocked by the volume and tone of letters from Fighting Irish 'zealots' complaining about Army's 1944 and 1945 routs of Notre Dame. In a private note to General Dwight Eisenhower, he described how 'our coaches and players are now being flooded with threatening and often scurrilous letters and postcards.' Another West Point insider stated that 'officers of this post have received 5,000 vicious letters' from Notre Dame fans 'in the past few years,' many accusing the academy of anti-Catholicism."[193]

Notre Dame President Cavanaugh abhorred this behavioral aspect of the so-called subway alumni, and he sympathized with General Taylor. The Golden Dome received its full portion of hate mail from anti-Notre Dame fans, many of them Army supporters. Often these fanatics denounced Catholics in general, seeing Notre Dame football as an especially evil manifestation of the Papacy; others simply attacked Frank Leahy and his current Fighting Irish.

In his letter to Eisenhower, Taylor summed up the fan situation. "In the eyes of a large portion of the public, it (the Army-Notre Dame game) pits West Point against the Catholic Church The Academy had worked hard during the war to convince the public that "it belongs to everyone in the United States," but the rivalry with Notre Dame threatens to turn a portion of the population against West Point."[194]

Coach Leahy may not have approved of fan antics, but he surely wanted his team to remember the two most recent humiliating games against Army. He posted a sign in the locker room at Notre Dame that reminded them in bold print of the scores of those two games, 59–0 and 48–0. Leahy was looking for payback and carefully monitored his West Point foe.

The Notre Dame Scholastic, the prolific student magazine of the university, weighed in on the status of Army's two stars several weeks before the big game. "Rumors are drifting out of West Point that 'Doc' Blanchard is seriously hurt, and (brace yourselves for this one) Davis is in need of an appendectomy, but the Army big guns are trying to stall an operation until the end of the football season." The article then went on to wish (not too sincerely) that the rumors were not true. "All of us here at N.D. hope these rumors aren't true; we all want Army to be at top strength when they meet the Fightin' Irish; the fruits of victory will be that much sweeter."[195]

The students rallied around a cheer that even the team began yelling at practices, "Fifty-nine and forty-eight, this is the year we retaliate."[196] It was an obvious reference to the scores West Point had amassed in their two previous matchups with the Irish.

On the day of the game, the mood of the crowd was more than enthusiastic. The attitude of the people filing into the stadium reflected more than just anticipation of a hard-fought college football battle between two great teams. The country's mood was buoyant believing that America's strength had prevailed and that its unselfishness would be rewarded by bright days ahead. West Point and Notre Dame personified that strength and commitment.

Yankee Stadium was supposedly a neutral venue. But for Coach Blaik it was anything but. "What Army did find sharply distasteful was that segment of Notre Dame's 'subway alumni,' neither small not (sic) quiet, which had in the early thirties and early forties come to regard the game in Yankee Stadium as a sporting event only so long as Notre Dame continued to win it," Blaik said. "With the healthy and unhealthy segments of the subway alumni added together, we appeared to have 90 percent of the Yankee Stadium crowd against us. To these people, apparently, our winning two years in a row by big scores after a twelve-year drought constituted an unpardonable sin."[197]

The coach was particularly offended on behalf of his players because some among the Notre Dame faithful accused the Army team of being slackers and draft dodgers, having spent much of the war at West Point. The accusation, although directed at the team, by association impugned the entire Corps of Cadets. In fact, many of the Army football players as well as the majority of the 2,400 other cadets present that day would see combat in America's future wars. Several had served in the war that had just concluded. But none of that mattered to the jeering subway alumni. Instead of taunting the Cadets, Notre Dame alum and students should have celebrated the forty-six members of its team who had served during the war.

Among the 74,000 fans in the stadium were several West Point graduates who had served so effectively in the recent war. Generals Dwight Eisenhower and Omar Bradley, who had played football at the Military Academy were present, along with Hap Arnold, the commanding general of the Army Air Corps. Old airborne comrades, Maxwell Taylor, now the superintendent at West Point, and tough Major General Anthony McAuliffe of Bastogne fame were also there to cheer on their alma mater.

By the time Army co-captains Blanchard and Davis met their Notre Dame counterparts, Lujack and Cowhig, at the fifty-yard line for the coin toss, the crowd was at a fever pitch. From the outset, however, it was evident that the game between these two high-scoring teams would instead be a defensive struggle. Early in the first quarter Notre Dame halfback Emil Sitko fumbled on the Irish twenty-four-yard line. A short pass from Tucker to Davis moved the ball to the Notre Dame eighteen. Three successive tries by Blanchard moved the ball closer to the fourteen before the Irish stopped the Cadets one foot shy of the first-down marker. It was an early indicator that Mr. Inside was going to have trouble with the big aggressive Irish line.

Neither team threatened again until midway through the second quarter. Lujack engineered an eighty-eight-yard drive to the Army four. Using a series of laterals, bootlegs, hard-hitting plunges, and a pass, Lujack took the Irish to within inches of a first down deep inside Army territory. Leahy considered a field goal a failure, so he elected to go for the first down and was turned back by the staunch Army defense.

After an exchange of punts, Army recovered a fumble by Irish halfback Terry Brennan on the Notre Dame thirty-five. With time running out in the half, Tucker tried three short passes, all batted down by Irish defenders. Shortly after Notre Dame got the ball, Tucker intercepted a Lujack pass, the first of three that day.

With Army in possession just before the half ended, Tucker kept the ball and ran for thirty yards before Lujack made a touchdown saving tackle. It would be one of many fine Lujack defensive plays by the versatile quarterback. The half ended in a 0–0 tie, surprising both coaches and disappointing millions of fans following the game worldwide.

Early in the third quarter Notre Dame threatened again when they recovered the first of three Army fumbles on the Black Knight's thirty-four. Hard-hitting defensive play was evident by the number of fumbles in the game, three for Army and five for Notre Dame.

Notre Dame quickly turned over the ball when Tucker intercepted the second Lujack pass on Army's ten and ran it back to the cadet's thirty-two yard.

Finally, Blanchard was able to break through the line and elude the Irish backs. He raced down the left side line with only Lujack to beat. The Notre Dame quarterback streaked across the field from his safety position and made a perfect tackle on the Army star at the Irish thirty-seven, spoiling the big Army back's best chance at a TD that day.

Years later Blanchard and Lujack met again at a Heisman Award dinner. They greeted each other warmly then recalled the most memorable play of that memorable 1946 game. "Blanchard said, 'Remember the tackle you made on me in the '46 game? You scared the hell out of me.'

Lujack knew he had hit Blanchard hard, but was surprised at this comment from the indestructible Army ace. He could only reply 'Really?'

'Yes,' said Blanchard, 'I thought I'd killed you.'"[198]

Blanchard's run energized the Army fans. Following more rushes by Blanchard and Davis, a Tucker pass gave the Black Knights a first down on the Irish twenty. By now the Army fans were in a frenzy, sensing a score at last. It turned out to be short-lived as Tucker's next pass was intercepted. The emotions of the fans were being whipsawed as elation turned to despair and then quickly reversed throughout the sixty-minute battle.

Early in the fourth quarter the Cadets threatened again by moving the ball to the Notre Dame thirty-three. This drive ended with yet another intercepted Tucker pass. A booming fifty-five-yard punt by Lujack removed the threat to the Irish by moving the ball well away from their end zone.

Notre Dame had one final chance at a score late in the fourth quarter. They drove the ball to the Army thirty-four before being stopped by Tucker's third interception of the afternoon. With forty-eight seconds remaining in the game, Davis connected with Blanchard on a short pass. Blanchard had been harried all afternoon by Pete Ashbaugh, a former B-29 pilot. When Blanchard caught that pass in the closing minute, Ashbaugh was right on him. "Get it, Doc. Get it!" Ashbaugh taunted. When Blanchard caught it Ashbaugh said, "Nice catch, Doc. Too bad you were out of bounds." Blanchard looked down at his feet and laughed.[199]

A final short Blanchard gain of one foot over the midfield stripe seemed to be the perfect ending to the afternoon struggle. The game had started on the fifty-yard line with the coin toss and ended at almost the same spot after four hours of clashing by some of the best athletes ever to play college football.

★ ★ ★

No one was happy with the outcome. Fans and sports writers had been sure it was going to be a high-scoring game. In the five games prior to the Army game, Notre Dame had scored 177 points against opponents while Army had scored 208 points against its opponents in its seven contests.

So what happened? Lots of turnovers, which ended strong drives by each team. Army fumbled the ball three times and the Irish five times. Army intercepted Notre Dame passes four times while the Irish snagged two Cadet passes.

Army quarterback Arnold Tucker intercepted three of the four Notre Dame miscues. In a rare moment of humor after the game Coach Leahy asked Irish quarterback John Lujack about the interceptions. "Tell me John," Leahy said to his quarterback, "how did you happen to throw so many of them to Tucker?"

"Well it was this way, Coach," Johnny answered, "he was the only man I could find open."[200]

Unquestionably, the conservative play of both teams had a huge influence on the 0–0 tie. It appeared that both coaches played not to lose and were not as willing to take offensive risks. Both Leahy and Blaik stayed primarily with their starting players. The cadets used only ten substitutes while the Irish used thirteen even though most of the players that saw action on both teams played on both offense and defense.

Both quarterbacks, Tucker, and Lujack, bristled under the tight play calling from their coaches. With ten minutes remaining, Tucker was taken out of the game to get instructions from Army assistant coaches on how to conduct the final minutes of the contest. By then the scrappy signal caller had had enough of the restrictions placed on him. Before the coaches could say anything Tucker said, "Don't worry Coach, I know just what I'll call."[201]

Tucker flatly said after the game, "I think it's safe to say that we may have been too conservative."[202] In later years after the emotions had subsided, Blaik apparently agreed. "While having lunch with Red Blaik and columnist Red Smith years later, we talked about the game, and Red said, 'Leahy and I both choked,'" Terry Brennan recalled in 2014."[203]

On the other side of the field, Lujack felt that the Irish should've tried for an early field goal that might've given his team an edge in the first quarter. With the ball on the Army four and with fourth and two, Coach Leahy chose not to try for a field goal. "I think that when we neared their goal in the first quarter, maybe we should've gone for a field goal," the junior quarterback said.[204] However, Lujack knew that his coach considered a field goal a defeat and an unacceptable admission that his team was incapable of out-toughing the Cadets.

Army also rejected a few field goal chances. Blaik and Leahy wanted to show that they could dominate the other team. Both coaches thought that field goals showed weakness. Blaik hadn't tried a field goal since 1943.

The touchdown twins, Blanchard and Davis, were bottled up for most of the afternoon by the fierce Irish defense. Davis gained only thirty yards on seventeen rushes, a disappointing average of less than two yards per carry compared to the eight-plus yards per carry he had achieved during his entire football career at Army. Blanchard, still affected by his injured knee, gained only fifty yards on eighteen rushing attempts. The best performing Army back was Tucker, who ran for thirty-seven yards on nine carries, most of them impromptu runs set up by busted plays caused by the strong Irish defensive play.

The standout for the Irish was also their quarterback. John Lujack was key on both offense and defense, vexing the Cadets with his passing, punting, and sure tackles. His game tackle of Blanchard in the third quarter had saved Notre Dame from defeat.

Despite the disappointment of the millions of fans, the scoreless game featured some of the best athletes ever to play the game. Five of the eleven first-team all-Americans named that year had competed: Blanchard, Davis, and Hank Foldberg from Army, and Lujack and George Connor of Notre Dame. Davis won the prestigious Heisman Trophy, succeeding his teammate Blanchard who had won it the year before.

Ultimately, four players from that game would be recipients of the Heisman Trophy: Blanchard, Davis, Lujack, and Leon Hart. Both Leahy and Blaik would be named as Hall of Fame coaches in the future. Blaik was named Coach of the Year in a poll of coaches conducted by the *New York World Telegram* and Scripps Howard newspapers. Blaik received 112 first place votes out of 397 ballots cast. Frank Leahy finished fourth with thirty votes.[205] However, as with all else concerning the Black Knights and the Irish that year, nothing was conclusive. The *New York Daily News* conducted its own poll and named Leahy Coach of the Year, undoubtedly with a nod to the large number of Irish subway alumni among its readers.

Following the game, Blaik made a startling prediction to the assembled reporters in the Army dressing room. "We will never have another chance to beat Notre Dame again."[206] No one other than Blaik knows for sure whether it was disappointment at the results of the game or the stark realization that he was about to lose the key members of his championship team. Certainly, a realistic assessment that Army would lose its recruiting advantage must have influenced the coach's comment. Blaik would continue to be the head coach at Army for twelve more years, and his prediction about future victories over Notre Dame turned out to be amazingly accurate. Army would beat Notre Dame only once (1958) in the next seventy-five years in which they played a total of eighteen times.

PART III

THE SUNSET

CHAPTER 18

THE BEGINNING OF THE END

I think it was very smart on the part of Army to drop Notre Dame. The Army's only natural rival is Navy and as a national institution the Military Academy should play a varying schedule and not tie itself down to any one school.
—Stanley Woodward New York Herald Tribune

THE ANALYSIS AND conjecture of how "The Game of the Century" with so many talented athletes could end in a 0–0 tie provided fodder for sports writers for some time. As rehashing of the game finally faded from the sports pages, two unexpected events thrust the Army-Notre Dame rivalry back into the limelight.

The first surprise occurred on December 3, when the nation's sports writers named Notre Dame as national champions. Both teams were undefeated with only the tie between them to mar their records. However, Notre Dame had followed the Army game with convincing wins against Northwestern (27–0), Tulane (41–0) and USC (26–6). The Cadets, on the other hand, after a 34–7 win over Penn, struggled mightily against a Navy team that had won only one game all year. The clock ran out on the Midshipmen when they were on Army's three-yard line. The last-minute stand by the Cadets was enough to give them a slim 21–18 victory over their archrivals, but not enough to convince the sports writers that they were the best team in the land. Of the 184 ballots cast, an even 100 selected the Irish as national champions with only 48 naming the Cadets as the top team.

Losing the national championship was a considerable shock to the Cadets. They had been ranked in the top spot every week except three over the course of 1944, 1945, and 1946. Some newspapers continued to call the Army team the co-national champions, but it was clear that West Point's dominance of college football was at an end.

The second unanticipated shock occurred in late December when both schools made a startling joint announcement which verified that a significant era was ending. Both West Point and Notre Dame decided to suspend the popular series after one more game to be played at Notre Dame in 1947. A decision about any revival of the contest would be determined sometime in the future.

The announcement had been scheduled to be released between 7 p.m. and midnight on January 1, 1947, to avoid shifting the attention away from other teams playing in the bowl games on New Year's Eve and New Year's Day. However, sportswriter Harry Wismer, in New Orleans for the Sugar Bowl, was tipped off and he preempted the announcement in a radio broadcast on December 29. Both schools had no choice but to make a joint announcement on December 30.

The carefully worded statement was issued by Major General Maxwell D. Taylor, superintendent of the United States Military Academy, and the Reverend John J. Cavanaugh, C.S.C., president of the University of Notre Dame. It did little to explain the true motivation of both teams in cancelling the popular series.

There were, in fact, two reasons which led to the decision. The first was the conviction of the authorities of both schools that the Army-Notre Dame game had grown to such proportions that it escaped the control of the two colleges, some of which were not conducive to wholesome intercollegiate sport. The second reason was the desire of West Point as a national institution to achieve greater flexibility in the scheduling of intersectional opponents throughout the country.

"In coming to the decision to interrupt the series both Army and Notre Dame avow the intention of renewing the traditional rivalry from time to time when the reception will serve the interests of both institutions and intercollegiate athletics.

"Out of consideration for the cordial relationships which have always existed between West Point and Notre Dame, the Army team will travel to South Bend in 1947 for the game on November 8."[207]

The following day, Father Cavanaugh sought to further soften the blow and dispel any rumors of hostility between the two schools by issuing a personal statement. "General Maxwell D. Taylor and I, in amicable discussions, have, with the advice of the athletic boards of both institutions, come to the decision just announced. Notre Dame's long-standing respect and friendship for the United States Military Academy and my personal esteem and warm regard for General Taylor remain, of course, unchanged. Both the general and I feel that our decisions will be good for both institutions and for intercollegiate athletics as a whole. While Notre Dame deeply regrets that our team will not appear in New York next fall, we also recognize gratefully Army's gracious tribute of friendship in coming out to Notre Dame in 1947."[208]

Sports writers weighed in on the surprising announcement with opinions that varied from support to cynicism. Dan Parker, sports editor of the *New York Daily Mirror*, wrote, "What a relief! It takes a thousand pass hounds off my back immediately." Stanley Woodward of the *New York Herald Tribune* opined, "I think it was very smart on the part of Army to drop Notre Dame. The Army's only natural rival is Navy and as a national institution the Military Academy should play a varying schedule and not tie itself down to any one school. Notre Dame, unfortunately, has become the victim of one of the lowest mobs in all sports history. That mob has made the game and its attendant trappings disgusting."

Oscar Fraley of the United Press was less sympathetic. He pointed out some inconsistencies in Army's stated reasons for ending the series. "Subsequently, Army emissaries stated that the ticket situation was too much to handle and took too much time of the Cadet athletic staff. It can be nothing but a weak supporting excuse for the fear of retribution when you consider that the game attracted some 74,000. Meanwhile there is no talk of canceling the Army-Navy game where the crowd hits 103,000."

Both General Taylor and Father Cavanaugh were relatively new at their positions as chief executives of their institutions. They were similar in that they both brought high ideals and aspirations to their jobs. The spectacle before and during the game dismayed both men who felt the rivalry was out of control.

The clamor and demand for tickets had overwhelmed both schools and intruded on all aspects of their school's activities. A key Notre Dame administrator noted that even the clergy at the university had been impacted. "Even some of the priests around here last (football) year received long-distance calls from places as far off as Texas. These calls were placed by persons the priests did not know at all and inquired about the state of a player's health etc."[209]

Nor was West Point immune from unsolicited questions during the football season. "Similarly, at West Point in 1946 frequent telephone inquiries about player injuries burden the officers on the post."[210]

Both Taylor and Cavanaugh were especially repelled by the betting and gambling surrounding the game, and the enormous sums being offered by scalpers to students for their tickets. The conservative estimate was that over $5 million had been bet on the game, equal to almost $70 million today. The clear winners after the contest were the bookies. They had offered a half a point on each team and were delighted by the outcome, which allowed them to keep all the money.

The concern of both leaders was accentuated by an event that came to light in mid-December. Hours before the kickoff of the 1946 NFL championship between the New York Giants and the Chicago Bears, two key players of the Giants confessed that gamblers had offered them money to throw the game. Quarterback Frank Filchok and fullback Merle Hapes revealed the plot. Hapes was kept out of the game, but Filchok played. The tainted Giant quarterback threw six interceptions certainly aiding the Bears's win and confirming for many fans that the game was rigged. Filchok claimed that he had played to win. However, the league suspended him indefinitely. He was allowed to return after sitting out for a few years.

Taking the highroad for Notre Dame would be costly. It was easier for General Taylor to come to the decision to suspend the series. The US Military Academy was a government-funded school, so foregoing the revenue of the Notre Dame game was not much of a sacrifice. For Notre Dame, however, the loss of revenue was a major blow. The endowment of the university in 1946 was four million dollars, so the loss of $200,000 per year from the Army game was a significant financial sacrifice. Father Cavanaugh clearly understood the ramifications of this decision. He was a businessman by training and had managed Notre Dame's books for six years as the university's vice president.

Army's stated desire to become a more national team also figured heavily into its decision to suspend playing Notre Dame. The Military Academy sought to recruit cadets from across the entire country, hoping to raise its profile as "America's Team" to help with recruiting. To do so, it wanted to play notable teams throughout the country, particularly West Coast universities. However, that's not what happened. In the nine years following the decision, Army played only seven times against teams from west of the Mississippi.

Some of the more obscure reasons that Army may have wanted a temporary suspension of the series were hinted at by Blaik's earlier comment after the 1946 game that Army would not beat Notre Dame again. Over the thirty-five years of the rivalry, Notre Dame had won twenty-three times against Army's seven, with four games tied. Prior to the arrival of Blanchard and Davis in 1944, Army hadn't defeated Notre Dame since 1931. And, after the Blanchard and Davis years, which ended with the 1946 game, Army would defeat Notre Dame only once in eighteen attempts. With the end of the war, it was clear to Blaik and others that the pendulum of recruiting talented players would swing back again strongly in Notre Dame's favor. The wild, freewheeling recruiting practices of the war years also had a bearing on the decision with both schools claiming the high ground.

Internal documents of the Military Academy, which were made public years after the event, shed greater light on some of the elements that went into Army's decision to suspend the series. A memo to the academy superintendent General Maxwell Taylor from the Army Athletic Council unanimously recommended the suspension. Surprisingly, one of the major sources of friction identified between the two schools was the so-called kidnapping of John Lujack, Notre Dame's star quarterback. As mentioned earlier, Lujack had an appointment to West Point and had visited the academy. He did not meet Blaik, nor did there seem to be much interest in Lujack by the coaching staff when he was there. He subsequently had a tryout at Notre Dame and was offered a scholarship, which he quickly accepted. It's been suggested by a family member and others that Notre Dame was always Lujack's first choice.

In my interview with Lujack it was obvious to me that his first choice had always been Notre Dame. In July of 2022 I subsequently asked his grandson, Grant Pohlman, to specifically ask his grandfather about the Army claim that he had been stolen away. His response was, "West Point did offer him a scholarship but when Henry Operhman (sic) from his hometown of Connellsville called the ND Scout out of Pittsburgh, and subsequently had a tryout with Coach Leahy, it was Notre Dame all the way."[211]

The West Point version as outlined in the memo to the superintendent from the academy's Athletic Council in the fall of 1946 stated, "In 1942 Congressman Schneider of Pennsylvania appointed to the Military Academy one Johnny Lujack, an outstanding young man from Connellsville, Pennsylvania, and a star football player. There was quite a ceremony when Mr. Schneider visited the town and presented the letter of appointment to Lujack, who proudly accepted it and at once began preparing for the West Point examination. Mr. Leahy ... enticed the boy away. He was given a summer job in Chicago ... with the usual football scholarship to Notre Dame to follow. Even the boy's mother, who was more than indignant at the turn of events, did not know where he was for some time. When the matter was called to Father Cavanaugh's (then president of Notre Dame) attention, he brought Mr. Leahy to West Point. The latter at first denied all knowledge of what had taken place, but when faced with evidence provided by the boy's mother, he had to admit he was lying. Father Cavanaugh was deeply distressed, but the harm had already been done, and Notre Dame kept the boy. Today he is their greatest star."[212]

The bad blood over the Lujack affair had been simmering since 1942. Murray Sperber cites a confidential report about a little-known visit to West Point by Father John Cavanaugh and Coach Leahy. (Author's Note: At my request, the West Point library conducted a search for this document and was unable to locate it.)

Sperber writes in *Onward to Victory*, "After the rendition of the facts by Mr. Leahy, frank discussions took place. Both Colonel Counts and Colonel Fenton (of the West Point Athletic Board), and also (football) Coach Blaik, felt that since the Army offered an outstanding opportunity to a boy to get a commission to follow the military profession and in consideration of the fact that Army, because of the difficulty of getting suitable (football) material, had in the past been beaten frequently by Notre Dame, Notre Dame in this case (the recruiting of Johnny Lujack) acted in an unsportsmanlike way. Both of these colonels, together with Colonel Jones (Army AD) and Coach Blaik, felt that when a boy is offered an appointment to the United States Military Academy, no persuasion should be used to keep him from accepting such an appointment. On the contrary, they felt that an institution such as Notre Dame and all the persons representing it, should do their utmost to encourage such a boy to accept such an appointment."

The affair in which Blaik was rebuked by Congressman Kelly on behalf of his son was unmentioned in the superintendent's 1946 memo. Perhaps the fact that Kelly's father was still a powerful congressman might have led to more discretion in not citing that Kelly also got away.

The bright beginning of the partnership became sullied by the end. For a time, the contest between the two schools burned brightly and innocently, capturing the attention and hearts of their followers and the nation. However, two world wars and the Great Depression had hardened the country and by association the environment in which the two teams competed. Cynicism and the overriding need to prevail on the national stage ultimately replaced the innocent motives of the series' humble regional beginning.

CHAPTER 19

1947

Competitive sports keeps alive in all of us a spirit of vitality and enterprise. It teaches the strong to know when they are weak and the brave to face themselves when they are afraid. To be proud and unbending in defeat, yet humble and gentle in victory. To master ourselves before we attempt to master others. To learn to laugh, yet never forget how to weep, and it gives a predominance of courage over timidity.
—Former Army Coach Vince Lombardi

THE INTEREST IN the post-Blanchard/Davis 1947 Army team was enormous. The two backfield stars, in addition to quarterback Arnold Tucker, had been instrumental in the Cadets's string of twenty-eight consecutive wins. The first two games of the season played at Michie Stadium gave the Army faithful hope that perhaps the team had retained some of the old magic. Villanova fell 13–0, followed by a 47–0 romp over Colorado.

A trip to Yankee Stadium, the venue of so many Notre Dame games, pitted number five Army against number six Illinois. In a tough defensive game, the Cadets managed a 0–0 tie against the Illini extending their unbeaten string to thirty. A 40–0 win over VPI (now Virginia Tech) took the winning streak to thirty-one and preceded a game against unranked Columbia at Baker Field in New York. The Cadets had not lost a game since facing the Navy in 1943.

On October 25, 1947, at Baker Field at Columbia University, Army's unprecedented string of victories ended. Columbia unleashed a surprising and powerful passing attack that proved just good enough to defeat the Cadets 21–20. No one was more disappointed by the loss than the Notre Dame team and fans who felt that it was their right to shatter the record. Two weeks later the Cadets travelled to South Bend to play the final game before the suspension of the series.

The environment in South Bend for the final game was very friendly, recalling the cordiality of the Corps of Cadets who had welcomed the little-known Notre Dame team to the Military Academy in 1913. Father Cavanaugh met General Taylor at the train station to welcome him personally. The simmering hostility of the fans, which had played an important role in the cancellation of the series, was very muted and cordial.

The 1947 game itself was anticlimactic and seemed to confirm Army's pessimistic outlook about the future of the rivalry. On the opening play, Notre Dame halfback Terry Brennan ran back the kickoff for a ninety-seven-yard touchdown, the longest kick return in Army-Notre Dame history. Eight minutes later the Irish scored again. The Cadets dug in, but the South Bend squad was just too strong for the visiting Black Knights. When the final gun sounded Notre Dame had won by a score of 27–7. The Army team took some small consolation in the fact that they finally had scored a touchdown against a Leahy team. However, it was clearly a convincing win for the South Benders. Notre Dame had gained almost two hundred more rushing yards than Army. Games in the future for the two schools and many other premier football programs would face new pressures as the game grew in popularity.

Changing the landscape was expanding TV coverage and other revenues from games. Having a winning program produced financial windfalls, placing pressure on athletic departments to recruit the very best players, prioritizing athleticism over academics. For Notre Dame, the tension between academic excellence and football prominence was palpable.

"Notre Dame has long valued the mind as well as the body. Since the Greeks defined the dichotomy between the two, no institution has systematically achieved excellence in both. But the University of Notre Dame has engaged this conundrum more seriously than has any other school in the world, and Notre Dame's struggle with its athletic culture and its academic aspirations will likely continue well into the next century."[213]

West Point's football fortunes had ebbed and flowed since Dennis Mahan Michie first organized the Army football team at the turn of the nineteenth century. During that time, West Point's mission to produce leaders of character who can lead our soldiers to victory during war, has remained focused and constant. The nation's support of the Military Academy has also ebbed and flowed during and after our country's wars. However, from the universal popular support during WWII to the divided national attitude during the Vietnam conflict, West Point graduates have heeded the call to follow their time-honored values of Duty, Honor, Country.

Football at West Point has always been secondary to its mission. However, football and the other sports, collegiate or intramural, mandatory for all cadets, have provided valuable lessons and experience for the young leaders there. Vince Lombardi, a former assistant football coach at West Point spoke eloquently about the importance of sports in developing future Army officers at the academy. "I need no greater authority than the great General Douglas MacArthur, and I would like to quote some of the things he said to me. Namely: 'Competitive sports keeps alive in all of us a spirit of vitality and enterprise. It teaches the strong to know when they are weak and the brave to face themselves when they are afraid. To be proud and unbending in defeat, yet humble and gentle in victory. To master ourselves before we attempt to master others. To learn to laugh, yet never forget how to weep, and it gives a predominance of courage over timidity.'"[214]

Both Notre Dame and West Point would continue to adhere to their timeless values. For Notre Dame, *God, Country, Notre Dame* would continue to provide a beacon for their sons and daughters in the face of a rapidly changing world. But for the famed coaches of the rivalry, fate would take a darker turn.

CHAPTER 20

WHAT HAPPENED TO THEM

On the lake, with the sun a screaming red in the west, a lonely mallard lifted out of the water with a piece of food in his mouth. He headed toward a copse of pines burning bright in color, silhouetted against the sun. At the last minute, he dropped the food. For a while he circled frantically, looking for what he had lost. Then he streaked off into the sunset, and was seen no more. "Just like a football coach," said Leahy. "Just like a football coach."

AFTER DEFEATING ARMY in the 1947 game at South Bend, Coach Leahy and the Irish continued their winning streak by overcoming Northwestern, Tulane, and USC. The undefeated season gave Leahy his third national championship, and John Lujack the Heisman Trophy following Blanchard and Davis, the winners in the two preceding years.

Army finished eleventh in the college rankings with a 5–2–2 record. The awards heaped on the Irish and Lujack could have only confirmed to Coach Blaik and General Taylor that they had made the right decision to suspend the series between the two schools. Army's once dominant recruiting advantage had now waned.

Meanwhile, 1948 was a continuation of the dominance of the Leahy teams. Only a tie with USC late in the season allowed undefeated Michigan to claim the national title. The last time that Notre Dame had lost had been to Great Lakes Naval during the final game of the 1945 season, having won twenty-six games with two ties. Leahy was now at the peak of his career rivaling the success of even his mentor, the great Knute Rockne. However, in 1949 he would face a challenge to his position from an unexpected source, the administrators of the university he loved so much.

Some of the newer and younger administrators at the university feared that the school was becoming known more for its athletic achievements than its academic excellence. In 1949 Father John Cavanaugh reorganized the upper levels of the Notre Dame administration to address this issue. He appointed a young priest, Father Ted Hesburgh, to the newly created post of executive vice president. Part of Hesburgh's responsibility was to oversee the football program. Under his predecessor, Father John Murphy, Leahy had a free hand to do whatever he wanted in the program. In addition, the men in the Athletic Business Affairs Office had been in place for many years, and they were also used to running their departments without interference. Cavanaugh was probably aware of the stories circulating at the university about "how the business offices of the athletic department were transformed at Christmas time into virtual department stores by a near obscene deluge of gifts from favored ticket holders and from those wanting to be favored."[215]

Cavanaugh asked Hesburgh to begin a complete review and reform of the athletic department. One of the first changes he made to gain control was to relieve Leahy as athletic director. Leahy had served as AD and head football coach since his arrival back at Notre Dame eight years earlier. Hesburgh appointed "Moose" Krause, a former Notre Dame football player and basketball coach as the new AD reporting directly to him. Krause was the perfect choice to manage the important liaison role between the coach and the new executive.

The press release announcing the change to Leahy's role was benign, even though the impact was rather significant. Leahy was quoted as saying, "he believed it was prudent for the university to have the football coaching and directorship handled by separate persons."[216] Father Cavanaugh was effusive in complimenting the coach. "We at Notre Dame have always felt privileged in having the services of Frank Leahy. As a result of performing the duties associated with both positions as football coach and athletic director, he has more often than not had to put in sixteen to eighteen hours. We have now come to the realization that too much has been demanded of Frank Leahy." It wouldn't be the last time that Leahy's health would be cited in relation to his football duties at Notre Dame.

Despite these amicable descriptions of the change, a conflict soon erupted between the two strong-willed adversaries, Hesburgh and Leahy. One of the first clashes occurred shortly before the first away game of the 1949 season against the University of Washington in Seattle. Hesburgh had decided that Notre Dame would comply with a Big Ten Conference rule limiting the number of players to thirty-eight on the traveling squad. Hesburgh specified that the coach would submit the names of the players to him prior to traveling so that their academic standing could be checked, and to verify that no more than thirty-eight would be traveling.

Years later Hesburgh recalled the confrontation with Leahy. "By Tuesday, when I had not yet received the list of players who were going, I telephoned Herb Jones, the business manager of the athletic department. 'How many players,' I asked, 'were on the list?' Forty-four. I told him forty-four players were not going to Seattle. Only thirty-eight were going and that he had better go and find Leahy, wherever he was, and tell him.

"Leahy was out on the practice field, he told me. That was another thing I was against, but I would handle that later. The players were going to miss a week of school as it was, and I did not think they should be out practicing when they were supposed to be in classes. But at the moment, all I wanted was the travel list from Leahy. That was crucial. Jones said he'd go find him. 'He's too busy to get you the list. He's getting ready for a big game,' Jones reported back.

"'I'll give you a shorter message for him,' I shot back. 'Just tell him to give me the names of the six players who are going to reduce that number to thirty-eight. Because if he does take all forty-four, the six extra players are going to be out of school for good because they will have missed classes without excused cuts. I'm approving only thirty-eight for excuses.'

"Before I left to catch the train out of Chicago, I stopped by (university president Fr. John) Cavanaugh's office to warn of the showdown I had predicted in June. 'If he takes forty-four players, you're going to have a nice choice to make,' I said. 'You're either going to get a new coach or a new executive vice president.'

Cavanaugh grinned at me. 'Oh, that's easy,' he said. 'We'll get a new coach.'

"Boarding the Chicago, Milwaukee, St. Paul & Pacific Railroad, I ran into Jones and asked him how many players were making the trip. He said, 'Thirty-eight, but Frank is very angry. He's ready to explode.'"[217]

It was clear from the beginning of his tenure as a senior leader of Notre Dame and later its president that Hesburgh's focus would be on enhancing the university's academic credentials. At his first press conference after becoming president in 1952 he emphasized that point. When asked by a group of sports writers to pose with a football, Hesburgh denied the request and replied, "Would you ask the president of Yale to do that?"[218] In later years after an eight-year dry spell for Notre Dame football, Hesburgh took a more balanced view of the importance of football to the university. "Texas has oil. Notre Dame has football. Neither should apologize."[219]

Leahy settled in under the new regime and produced another national championship team in 1949, his fourth and last. The strain of the new restrictions imposed by Father Hesburgh on the football program and the increasing competition in the wide open post-war collegiate environment began to take its toll on Leahy.

His 1950 team, was the worst of his coaching career, achieving just four wins. He lost four games in that season, more than his eight previous years going all the way back to his Boston College days. Although the team improved in 1951 to 7–2–1 Notre Dame was ranked thirteenth in the country. The following year for the Irish was again lackluster (for Notre Dame), as they finished again with a record of 7–2–1.

The 1953 team improved substantially with a record of 9–0–1 led by Irish halfback and Heisman Trophy winner John Lattner and quarterback Ralph Guglielmi. However, two events marred the almost perfect season. The Irish had a strong start to the 1953 season beating number six Oklahoma followed by wins over Purdue and Pitt. The fourth game on the schedule, however, would not be so easy. Georgia Tech, ranked fourth in the country, would be coming to South Bend on the strength of a thirty-one-game winning streak. However, this was a strong Irish team every bit a match for the Yellow Jackets. Notre Dame took the opening kickoff and marched relentlessly down the field for eighty yards and a 7–0 early lead.

While most of the crowd was focused on the action on the field, a different struggle was taking place on the Notre Dame bench. Early in the game Coach Leahy was seen gasping for breath, trying to cope with pains in his chest. At halftime, one of his assistants, Bill Earley, had to help him into the locker room.

Once inside, Leahy sat on a trunk and scribbled some notes about what he intended to say to his team during halftime. Suddenly, his notebook and pencil fell from his grasp on to the floor. When he reached down to pick them up, he fainted. His assistants placed him on a training table while Earley left to page Leahy's private physician, who was in the stands.

Several of the priests of the university had witnessed the coach's unsteady departure from the field and when they heard the page for his doctor they raced to the locker room, Father Edmund Joyce, the vice president of the university among them. When Joyce arrived, he saw the coach on the training table in obvious distress. Fearing the worst, he immediately administered the last rites to Leahy.

However, after he received a shot from his doctor that put him into a deep sleep, the coach recovered. His team returned to the field worried and anxious about their leader but determined to give him a victory. After overcoming a 7–7 tie, the Irish went on to beat the undefeated Yellow Jackets 27–14, undoubtedly inspired by the distress of their coach.

All of those around Leahy feared a heart attack. It turned out to be acute pancreatitis no doubt brought on by stress and Leahy's poor diet. During the long hours of work, his meals would often consist of Campbell tomato soup heated on a hot plate, or a sandwich washed down by a soft drink or milk which he drank from the carton. He also most often slept on a cot in his office during the football season.

In later years, Leahy reflected on the enormous pressures he felt as head coach of the Irish. Many of those pressures were self-induced, and several others transcended the normal responsibilities of a football coach. "The pressure at Notre Dame was probably the heaviest in the country at the time. They kept saying in the administration that they did not mind if our team lost a few games. But Notre Dame had millions of followers all over the country. Our football team was a source of immense pride to Catholics everywhere. Most of them were second generation Americans who were just moving out of the slums and into positions of importance. There was still much anti-Catholic prejudice in America. That is why it always made me very pleased to run into a man who was obviously from an old-line Protestant family who told me that he was a Notre Dame rooter. We were helping to break down barriers by our successes. I was always conscious of that fact. And there was a tradition of excellence. And . . . I hated to lose. It destroyed me a little inside to lose. I even hated tie scores. Oooh, football was a means to an end."[220]

The second event that altered Leahy's career and the trajectory of his reputation occurred on November 21, 1953. The Irish were within reach of another undefeated season, facing a tough Iowa team in South Bend. Late in the half, the Irish trailed 7–0 and had no timeouts left. With only seconds remaining and Notre Dame in possession of the ball on the Hawkeyes twelve, Frank Verrichione fell to the turf seemingly in apparent pain, stopping the clock and giving the Irish one more play. With the extra time, quarterback Ralph Guglielmi fired a pass to wide receiver Dan Shannon for a touchdown, tying the score at 7–7.

As if to further emphasize the dramatic and questionable first half touchdown, the Irish second touchdown came with six seconds remaining in the game on another Guglielmi-to-Shannon pass, tying the game for the final score of 14–14.

Sports writers and fans around the country felt that Verrichione's fake injury deprived Iowa of a victory. Although many other college teams at the time used similar tactics, many of them were appalled at the lapse of integrity from Notre Dame. The scorn heaped upon the Irish was relentless.

The student body back in Iowa City was, of course, outraged. One of its students gave new life to the episode by mocking the South Benders with a clever new nickname that soon spread to newspapers around the country. He dubbed the Notre Dame football team the "Fainting Irish."

Iowa Coach Forest Evasheski also added to the tumult by penning a witty verse for the student newspaper. "When the One Great Scorer comes to write against your name, it's not whether you win or loss, but how you got gypped at Notre Dame."[221] It was a cruel parody of a couplet from Grantland Rice, a great admirer of Notre Dame, who had earlier defined a high standard for athletic behavior. "When the One Great Scorer comes to write against your name—He marks—not that you won or lost—but how you played the game."[222] The criticism could hardly have been more cutting to the university that prided itself on its high ideals.

The story remained on the sports pages for an embarrassingly long time. Letters from friends and foe alike poured into newspapers as well as to the good fathers at the school of Our Lady. Because of the uproar, the administration did not allow Leahy to accompany the team to California for the USC game. However, it made little difference as the Irish crushed the Trojans 48–14. The following week Notre Dame dispatched SMU 40–14 in South Bend for another undefeated season.

When the national championship was announced, Notre Dame, which had been ranked number one for almost the entire season, was dropped to number two. The championship was awarded to Maryland, probably to punish Notre Dame for its indiscretion in the Iowa game.

One of the people most dismayed by the negative publicity heaped upon the university was Leahy. His love of the school and his dedication to his faith were unquestioned. This event seemed to bring shame to both. In early January 1954, he went to Cincinnati for a dinner honoring Jim Tatum, the coach of Maryland. Once there, Leahy asked host Joe Williams if he could be on his nationally broadcasted sports show to give his side of the Iowa story. When Father Joyce heard of the coach's intentions, he strongly advised Leahy to cancel his appearance. The good Fathers wanted the story to die as quickly as possible.

The end of Leahy's extraordinary football coaching career ended shortly after. His resignation was announced on January 31, 1954. Both Father Hesburgh and Coach Leahy issued friendly statements citing the coach's health problems as the primary reason for the departure. However, there is ample evidence that shows he was at the very least strongly encouraged to resign by the new administration at Notre Dame.

His wife raised the issue of Leahy's heath while he was hospitalized. "Frank," said Florence Reilly Leahy the first time he could have visitors at St. Joseph's hospital in South Bend, "you're going to have to get into a more relaxing form of work."

"Don't tell me what I already know, Floss," he snapped. "Don't tell me. You've wanted this for a long time and now you've got it. I'm through and I guess I know it. You don't have to tell me."[223]

Coach Leahy's record of 87–11–9, with a winning percentage of .887, was fittingly, a respectful one hundredth of a percentage point below his mentor, Knute Rockne's win record of .897. His replacement, twenty-five-year-old, Terry Brennan, was announced almost simultaneously with Leahy's resignation, perhaps to ensure that Leahy knew that there could be no backtracking on his decision. He was gracious in the transition that passed the baton to one of his former players.

The Iowa Fainting Irish scandal continued to eat at him even into retirement. In March of 1954 he wrote an article for *Look* magazine attempting to explain his side of the story. Feigned injuries were used by almost all college teams, Leahy said. It was not what was done, he wrote, but who did it. Many sports writers agreed with him. While criticizing Notre Dame they complimented the Irish in a backhanded way. New York columnist Joe Williams offered an explanation as to why the incident seemed to resonate so long in the press.

"Actually the criticism of Notre Dame is a major tribute to the position it holds in the heart of the average football fan, and having earned this position, Notre Dame has a responsibility the like of which exists in no other college. The Irish must play it impeccably clean and straight at all times."[224]

Leahy never again coached. In 1958 he came close to accepting the job of head coach at Texas A&M. On a tour of the school, Leahy verbally accepted the position with the caveat that he would take the job only after a thorough physical checkup at the Mayo Clinic. While there, his blood pressure rose significantly. After reviewing the results of the physical, the doctors advised him not to coach, advice which he reluctantly accepted.

Leahy was still a relatively young man at age fifty when he turned down the Aggies job in 1958. He was too intense and restless to sit at home. He had numerous friends and contacts in the business world who were anxious to partner with him in various ventures.

Early on he was offered a chance to become a partner in a local insurance agency. It would have been a perfect stress-free job for Frank, just meeting and greeting clients. But unlike Ara Parshegian, who held a similar job after his retirement, Leahy was not willing to be a front man. He had to have a job where his hands were firmly on the steering wheel.

He tried several occupations and ventures, most of which turned out to be failures, some because of Leahy and some because of poor advice and unscrupulous partners. He did return to football in 1960 for one year as the general manager of the Los Angeles Chargers of the American Football League. It turns out that his intensity and desire to master every detail of the coaching trade was not transferable to his business ventures.

Leahy died in Portland, Oregon on June 22, 1973, of congestive heart failure. Shortly before he died Father Hesburgh visited him. "There was not even the mildest hint of animosity or rancor. Whatever had gone before was totally obscured by the mists of time. It was like a visit from the Holy Father himself. Few men get to be head football coach at Notre Dame. Few men get to be president of the school. They spoke of many things, even social conditions, archliberal cohabitating with ultraconservative. It had been an extremely warm meeting, a tying-up of long forgotten loose ends. As Father Hesburgh left, he and Leahy embraced. It was a thoroughly unexpected gesture on the part of two undemonstrative men."[225]

Toward the end of his life Leahy provided a poignant insight into the regrets he had about his coaching career. He was being interviewed by author Wells Twombley for Leahy's official biography. The two of them were sitting in Frank's lakeside home speaking quietly and observing the serenity of the lake. "On the lake, with the sun a screaming red in the west, a lonely mallard lifted out of the water with a piece of food in his mouth. He headed toward a copse of pines burning bright in color, silhouetted against the sun. At the last minute, he dropped the food. For a while he circled frantically, looking for what he had lost. Then he streaked off into the sunset, and was seen no more.

"Just like a football coach," said Leahy. "Just like a football coach."[226]

The graduation of Blanchard, Davis, and Tucker had reduced interest in Army football. Still, Blaik was able to put an impressive squad on the gridiron. He was aided by the addition to his staff of a young man relatively new to college football coaching. Vince Lombardi, who would go on to legendary greatness, had been a high school coach only two years prior to joining the Black Knights. Lombardi would attribute much of his success as a professional NFL coach to Blaik and the years he spent on the Army coaching staff. "As integral as religion was to his sense of self, it was not until he reached West Point and combined his spiritual discipline with Blaik's military discipline that his coaching persona began to take its mature form. Everything he knew about organizing a team and preparing it to play its best, Lombardi said later, he learned at West Point. 'It all came from 'Red' Blaik.'"[227]

The 1950 Army team was ranked number two nationally with a respectable record of 8–1, which included the important win over Navy. The Black Knights were led that year by quarterback Bob Blaik, the coach's son. The satisfaction over the success of the team was dampened by word that two former Army players, Tom Lombardo, captain of the 1944 team, and Johnny Trent, captain of the 1949 team, had both been killed in action in Korea. More devastating news of an entirely different nature from an unexpected source lay just over the horizon as the 1950 football season came to an end.

In April 1951 Coach Blaik's tidy world began to unravel. First, his idol and mentor, General Douglas MacArthur, was relieved of his command in Korea by President Harry S. Truman. The dismissal had been in the making for some time, as the general had openly challenged the president by his words and deeds.

Shortly after MacArthur's ceremonious return to the US, Blaik visited his old benefactor at his new headquarters in the Waldorf Astoria hotel. While there he encouraged MacArthur to consider a run for the White House. In a follow up letter to the general, Blaik used a sports metaphor that he knew MacArthur would appreciate. "The best hope for the future lives in fielding a new team in Washington." He added his own criticism to the administration's Korean war policy. He wrote that the policy, "was comparable to a football team with a strong ground game and air game always punting on first down and through fear presenting the initiative to the opponent."[228]

Blaik would soon face a crisis of his own leadership. In late April of 1951 information about a massive cheating scandal among cadets, many of them football players, began to emerge at West Point. Ultimately, ninety cadets would be dismissed from the Military Academy for violating the cadet honor code. The code is simple and uncompromising; a cadet will not lie, cheat, or steal or tolerate those who do. The code requires that those that learn of an honor violation must report the offender or be guilty of a violation themselves.

It was this part of the code that was most difficult for some cadets, especially those that were members of an athletic team or other close-knit group. Of those discharged, sixty were members of an athletic team, including thirty-seven football players. Most of the remaining thirty non-athletes were tutors for the athletes. Those athletes caught up in the scandal either cheated themselves or refused to turn in a teammate whom they knew had cheated.

The country was appalled by the scandal. It was front-page news for many newspapers and the subject of many magazine articles. Like the Notre Dame faked-injury episode, who did it amplified the recrimination. The cheating scandal was a flagrant violation of West Point's exalted honor code of Duty, Honor, Country. How could it have happened at the institution that had produced many of the leaders who led the country to victory in World War II and were now fighting in Korea? Several factors were involved. Increased pressure to produce winning football teams and lax oversight of the testing procedures were two key elements of the scandal.

Testing at the Military Academy occurs frequently. Every cadet recites or is tested every day and is graded daily. In addition, periodic exams are administered to all cadets. In 1951 (and during my time there in 1958 to 1962) the same exam was given to the entire class of cadets. Because the Corps of Cadets was large meant that exams might be given over a two-day period. The test would be administered to two cadets of the same class and the same unit (company, battalion, regiment) to which they were assigned, which dictated where they lived.

That was not a problem for most cadets because they would not encounter cadets from another battalion or regiment who may have already taken the exam. However, athletic team members were mixed without regard to their unit assignment. Therefore, those that had already taken an exam could be at a practice or at meals with those who had yet to take the same exam. Under the honor code, a cadet can only say if there was or was not a test. Anything beyond that is an honor violation. For instance, telling someone that there were questions about World War II would be an honor violation.

The violations among the ninety dismissed cadets ranged from cheating, to passing on any information beyond whether there was a test or not, to refusing to turn in a classmate or teammate under violation. The dismissals devastated the football team and included the coach's son, team quarterback Bob Blaik. It's difficult to believe that Coach Blaik wasn't aware of at least some aspects of the violations. He was aware of and sanctioned a tutoring system for some members of the football team which facilitated the illicit transfer of test information.

Jim Beach, an AP reporter who followed Army football closely, indicted the coach. "Blaik knew all about the cribbing—it was total bullshit then and it still is, that he knew nothing about it. He called his tutors 'coaches' and he worked with them like he worked with his football coaches. Blaik introduced me to some of them, and it was obvious that he was totally on top of their work . . . Earl Blaik was on top of every single thing at the Point that had to do with his football players, including the cribbing . . . Of course, the AP would never let me work on the story."[229]

On August 3, the West Point's public information office issued a news release detailing the scandal and the dismissal of the cadets. By 3 p.m. that day, many members of the press arrived at West Point seeking more information. There was no further information coming from school officials or students, so the attention shifted to Coach Blaik.

Somewhat shaken by the events, the coach and his wife went to New York City the next day to visit his old mentor, General Douglas MacArthur. The general listened for two hours to Blaik's description of what happened. When the coach finished MacArthur urged him not to resign. "Earl you must stay on. Don't leave under fire."[230]

He did stay on. Blaik neither criticized the actions taken by the academy authorities nor condoned the actions of the dismissed cadets. He did express admiration for the character of those caught up in the scandal. "I believe in the youngsters with whom I've been dealing," Blaik said. "I know their families. I know them, and I know they were men of character . . . My entire endeavor from now on shall be to see that these boys leave West Point with the same reputations they had when they came in."[231]

Blaik and his coaches helped many of the dismissed cadets to enroll in other schools. And, an anonymous donor offered to provide financial aid to any of the expelled cadets who wanted to transfer to Notre Dame and met the requirements of the school. Based on existing Notre Dame rules, they would not be able to play football for the Irish. Thirteen cadets ultimately transferred to Notre Dame with the help of the donor who turned out to be Joseph P. Kennedy, father of the future president.[232]

After the cheating scandal, the Black Knights had a dismal 2–7 record. They were ranked 100 out of 116 teams in the country. Blaik continued to rebuild his program, culminating in an undefeated season, 8–0–1 in 1958, his last year. The team was ranked third nationally and included the important victories over Notre Dame (14–2) and Navy (22–6). It was the perfect time for him to exit.

Earl Blaik died at the age of ninety-two in 1989 in Colorado Springs. His outstanding record at Army of 121–33–10 was highlighted in most of the articles reporting his death. The cheating scandal of 1951 was also mentioned in the descriptions of Blaik's career as coach. Like Leahy and the Fainting Irish episode, Blaik was unable to shake the stigmatizing asterisk associated with the cheating scandal.

The scandal lived on even beyond Coach Blaik's death. Bob Blaik, the coach's son, commissioned a statue of his father, which he intended to have placed at the Military Academy. His stipulation was that the statue would have a plaque listing all the letterman who played under his father at West Point, including those that had been dismissed in the 1951 cheating scandal. Opposition from Academy graduates to listing the expelled cadets soon derailed the younger Blaik's plans. The statue instead was installed in the College Football Hall of Fame, then located in South Bend, Indiana. For a short time in 2004 during the dedication, the controversy again was in the news. Bill Yeoman, a Hall of Fame Coach at the University of Houston and a center for Army under Blaik from 1946 to 1948, tried again fifty-three years after the event to explain the scandal. "What you have to understand is many of them did not take part in it at all other than conceivably being aware of it. I know for certain many of them were not involved." [233] It was clear, however, that at the academy over half a century had elapsed but still had not softened the emotions of graduates who could not forgive the lapse of those who failed to measure up to its ideals.

On June 4, 1947, Blanchard and Davis graduated from West Point. General Dwight Eisenhower was the guest speaker. The 310 members of the graduating class filed up the ramp to receive their diplomas from the academy superintendent General Maxwell Taylor. The cadets received their diplomas in the order of their class standing. The applause grew noticeably louder toward the end of the ceremony when Blanchard, fifteenth from the bottom, and Davis sixth from the bottom received their diplomas. Special applause also greeted cadet Robert Ehrlich, the last man in the class who received his diploma and a pat on the back from a smiling General Eisenhower.

The graduation ceremony marked the end of a star-studded period in the lives of Mr. Outside and Mr. Inside. The momentum of their fame at West Point kept them in the limelight for a short time after they graduated. During their two-month graduation leave they were given permission to star in a movie, *The Spirit of West Point*. They were each paid $20,000 for portraying themselves in the movie, a sum equal to almost four years of their Army pay.

They appealed for a two-month extension to their graduation leave hoping to play for a short time with the professional San Francisco 49ers. They also asked for additional four-month leaves during the next four years to play professional football. In return, Blanchard and Davis were willing to make a twenty-year commitment to stay in the Army, far exceeding their initial three-year commitment.

General Taylor had granted their requests. However, after an outcry from others in the Army and the media, the general rescinded his approval. Blanchard then began a career in the Air Force. Davis, after attending a Los Angeles training camp, became an infantry officer and was sent to Korea, by then at peace. West Point graduates were allowed to choose their branch assignments based on their class standing, as long as there were openings available. It's very possible that Davis was assigned to the infantry because of his low ranking in the class.

It was at this point that the closely linked dynamic duo chose different paths that separated them for the remainder of their lives. Davis chose a more-high profile lifestyle than his partner. Upon his return to the US after his tour of duty in Korea, Davis was met at the airport by a young starlet named Elizabeth Taylor. *Life* magazine was there to snap a picture of the handsome young lieutenant wiping lipstick from his face after a kiss from Miss Taylor. Taylor and Davis carried on a highly visible romantic relationship for about a year before it ended. Davis did not become one of Taylor's several husbands. He ultimately married another young actress, Terry Moore, a marriage that lasted for two years.

After resigning his commission in early 1950 just prior to the Korean War, Davis joined the Los Angeles Rams, where he played two years before reinjuring his knee forcing him to retire from football. Ironically, the original injury to his knee had occurred during the filming of *The Spirit of West Point*.

After a few years in Texas where he worked in the oil industry, Davis returned to California, where he joined the *Los Angeles Times* as special events director in charge of organizing and directing the newspaper's charity fund-raising activities. In 1996 he married Yvonne Ameche, widow of football great Alan Ameche. Davis died of prostate cancer in 2005 at the age of eighty in La Quinta, California. He is buried at West Point.

Blanchard chose a different path from his football partner. The word most commonly used to describe Blanchard by those who knew him was humble. After being denied his request by the Army to play professional football, Blanchard settled in to a long and distinguished military career. In the autumn of 1948, he earned his pilot's wings and became a fighter pilot. He was commended for his bravery when in 1959, while with the 77th Tactical Fighter Squadron and flying back to his base at RAF Wethersfield near London, Blanchard's F-100 Super Sabre developed a fuel leak, causing his plane to catch on fire. Rather than escaping and parachuting out safely, he decided to stay with the plane and land it because of a village on the ground that would have been damaged.

In the Vietnam war, Blanchard flew 113 missions from Thailand, eighty-four of them over North Vietnam, in the F-105 Thunderchief fighter-bomber during a one-year tour of duty that ended in January 1969. He retired from the Air Force in 1971 as a colonel, then spent several more years as the commandant of cadets at the New Mexico Military Institute, a junior college that prepares students to enter the service academies.

Blanchard died of pneumonia at the age of 84 in 2009 in Bulverde, Texas, where he was living with his daughter. He is interred at Fort Sam Houston National Cemetery in San Antonio, Texas.

Like teammates Blanchard and Davis, Arnold Tucker graduated from West Point in June of 1947 after three years at the academy. During his time there his considerable athletic prowess was overshadowed by his more famous teammates. On any other team at any other college Tucker would have been exalted. He was named an all-American in 1946 and was ranked fifth in the Heisman Trophy balloting behind teammates Davis and Blanchard. He was captain of the Army basketball team and received the prestigious Sullivan Award given to the best United States amateur athlete for 1946.

He served as a B-29 pilot and flew with the Military Airlift Command in Tokyo, Japan. He returned to West Point as a tactical officer and assistant coach to Vince Lombardi, who was Army's line coach at the time.

He retired from the Air Force after thirty-one years with the rank of lieutenant colonel. His awards included the Distinguished Flying Cross, the Bronze Star Medal, and the Meritorious Service

Medal. In civilian life he was assistant director of athletics for sales and promotions at the University of Miami. Arnold Tucker died in Palmetto Bay, Florida in 2019 at the age of ninety-five.

John Lujack was one of the most talented athletes ever to attend Notre Dame. While there he earned varsity letters in four sports: baseball, football, basketball, and track. He was a two-time unanimous all-American in 1946 and 1947 and led the Irish to national football titles in 1943, 1946, and 1947. He was awarded the Heisman Trophy in 1947 and named the AP Athlete of the Year one year after Glenn Davis had received the same awards.

In 1948, Lujack joined the Chicago Bears as a defensive back and kicker. He kicked forty-four out of forty-six extra points and hauled in eight interceptions. In 1949 Lujack hosted a radio show, "The Adventures of Johnny Lujack," a summertime replacement for the popular boys' show, "Jack Armstrong, the All-American Boy."

In the final game of the 1949 season against the Chicago Cardinals Lujack threw six touchdown passes and set an NFL record of 468 passing yards. In 1950 he set another NFL record by scoring eleven rushing touchdowns, the most of any quarterback.

After four years with the Bears, Lujack joined Notre Dame as an assistant coach to Frank Leahy for 1952 and 1953. There was some talk that Leahy wanted Lujack to succeed him as the head coach, but Terry Brennan was chosen instead by Theodore Hesburgh, the university president.

In 1954 Lujack became partners with his father-in-law in a Chevrolet Dealership in Davenport, Iowa. He retained ownership in the dealership until 1988. John teamed up with announcer Chris Schenkel to broadcast New York Giants games on CBS from 1958 to 1961. When in 1962 Ford became a major sponsor and found out that Lujack was a Chevrolet dealer he was replaced by Pat Summerall.

At this writing, Lujack is retired and lives in Florida where he remains as of this date the oldest living Heisman Trophy winner.

EPILOGUE

EXTRAORDINARY MEN

Many brave men lived before Agamemnon; but all are overwhelmed in eternal night, unwept, unknown, because they lack a sacred poet.
—Horace Odes, IV, ix, l. 25

WHEN I FIRST started writing this book, my intention was to include only the war stories of those participants who played in the 1946 Army-Notre Dame game. However, as I began my research, I discovered a number of fascinating and heroic stories of former football players who had served in war. These are the stories of some of them.

The Mosquito Bowl

Even in the bases close to the war, athletics and especially football were alive and well. Wherever young Americans gathered, American sports were on display. Guadalcanal, the island in the South Pacific, which had been the location of America's first offensive land victory over the Japanese, became the scene of a football game played by several college and professional gridiron standouts who were serving in the armed forces.

In late 1944 the 6th Marine Division was training on Guadalcanal in preparation for the upcoming invasion of Okinawa, a stronghold close to the Japanese mainland. A touch-football game between two of the division's regiments was organized for Christmas Eve 1944.

The game was a microcosm of the war that interspersed brief

interludes of normalcy with the somber and dangerous tasks that awaited these young men. The roster of players for this impromptu contest read like a program for a football All-Star game. George Murphy had been captain of the Notre Dame team in 1942. Walter "Bus" Bergman was a star halfback who had earned ten letters at Colorado A&M. Dave Mears had been a solid lineman at Boston University. The backfield of the 29th Marine Regiment featured Wisconsin halfback Bud Seelinger and fullback Tony Butkovich, who was the nation's leading rusher at Purdue and the number-one draft choice of the Cleveland Browns in 1944. Chuck Behan, formerly of the Detroit Lions, coached the team and also played end. The Fourth Marine Regiment's assistant coach was John McLaughry, a Brown University standout, and an ex-New York Giant.

The game was played on a parade ground strewn with coral rocks. Estimates of the crowd ranged between 2,500 to 10,000. It was supposed to be a touch football game but trying to control the exuberance of these young Marines proved difficult. McLaughry, the player coach, wrote home to his parents describing the game. "It was really a lulu, and as rough hitting and hard playing as I've ever seen. As you may guess, our knees and elbows took an awful beating due to the rough field with coral stones here and there, even though the 29th did its best to clean them all up. My dungarees were torn to hell in no time, and by the game's end my knees and elbows were a bloody mess." [234] The hard-fought game ended in a 0–0 tie.

The pleasant respite from the war ended all too quickly and intense training resumed for the battle ahead. On 1 April 1945, the 6th Marine Division landed on Okinawa with Army units as part of the 10th Army Expedition Force. By the time the campaign ended, 2,938 Marines were killed or missing. Army killed and missing were another 4,675. Both team captains from the Christmas Eve game, Behan the ex-Detroit Lion, and Wisconsin all-American Dave Schreiner, were among those killed.

The list of the other players killed was a grim reminder of the widespread and painful sacrifices that touched homes, communities, and colleges across the country:

> George Murphy Notre Dame end
> Tony Butkovich, Purdue fullback
> Bob Baumann, Wisconsin tackle
> Bob Fowler, Michigan center,
> John Hebrank, Lehigh tackle
> Hubbard Hinde, Southern Methodist tackle
> Rusty Johnston, Marquette halfback
> John Perry, Wake Forest and Duke halfback
> Jim Quinn, Amherst end
> Ed Van Order, Cornell tackle

For a more detailed narrative of the Mosquito Bowl and its participants read *The Mosquito Bowl: A Game of Life and Death in World War II.*

There were other former football players who had put their playing days behind them and were now engaged in a deadly game of trying to overcome a dangerous enemy and survive. As the war reached its conclusion, the stories of the valor and sacrifice of many young men became more widely known. Like many other colleges and universities, graduates of Notre Dame and West Point made considerable and costly contributions to the war effort. By war's end, over 10,000 Notre Dame graduates had served in the war; 310 were killed and 1,200 were wounded.[235] Of the over 9,000 West Point graduates who served in World War II, over 500 were killed. In addition, most of the major commanders of the Army and Army Air Force and many of the junior leaders were West Point graduates.

Motts Tonelli

One of the most interesting and harrowing stories I came across concerned Mario "Motts" Tonelli, a 1939 Notre Dame graduate and fullback on the football team. His most remembered exploit on the gridiron took place on November 27, 1937. The Fighting Irish and USC were tied 6–6 late in the fourth quarter. The five-eleven, 195-pound Tonelli took a handoff deep in Irish territory and raced seventy yards down the field before being tackled just short of the goal line. On the next play he scored the game-winning touchdown.

At his graduation in 1939, Tonelli proudly received his gold class ring inscribed with his initials, M.G.T. and his graduation date. After graduation, he spent a short time as an assistant coach at Providence College, and then one season of professional football with the Chicago Cardinals. In early 1940, Tonelli joined the Army intending to fulfill his one-year military obligation. He chose to spend his brief military commitment in Manilla, the exotic Pearl of the Orient. Motts felt that this assignment would allow him to quickly complete his service while seeing a different part of the world.

The Japanese attack on Pearl Harbor and the subsequent invasion of the Philippines upset Tonelli's' carefully planned timetable and unalterably changed his life. After several months of intensive combat against the much better armed and experienced Japanese army, Tonelli and his 15,000 fellow American surrendered in April of 1942.

Tonelli and the other captured Americans, plus 90,000 Filipino prisoners were forced to undertake a brutal sixty-five-mile march that infamously became known as the Bataan Death March. During the march, the Japanese were quick to execute anyone who could not keep up or who tried to leave the column of struggling prisoners to seek drinking water.

Tonelli and the other prisoners were constantly harassed by guards seeking to steal the possessions of the weary captives. A guard approached Tonelli and demanded his Notre Dame ring. He refused. The guard threatened him, brandishing his bayonet, making it clear that Tonelli had no choice but to comply.

"Give it to him," yelled a nearby prisoner. "It's not worth dying for."

Reluctantly, Tonelli gave his ring to the guard.

A nearby Japanese officer who observed the theft approached Tonelli and asked him in perfect English, "Did one of my men take something from you?"

Surprised Tonelli replied, "Yes he took my school ring."

The officer then took the ring back from the guard and returned it. "Here," he said. "Hide it somewhere. You may not get it back next time."

After witnessing so many brutal acts by Japanese soldiers during the march, Tonelli was speechless. "I was educated in America," the Japanese officer explained. "At the University of Southern California. I know a little about the famous Notre Dame football team. In fact, I watched you beat USC in 1937. I know how much this ring means to you, so I wanted to get it back to you."

Although nearly 700 Americans and 10,000 Filipinos died on the march, it was only the beginning of a harsh and gruesome three years of captivity for the prisoners. Throughout those years, Tonelli hid his ring. He was able to conceal the ring from the Japanese even though he was transferred to several different camps and shipped to Japan to perform slave labor.

After the dropping of the atomic bombs and the surrender of the Japanese, Tonelli was freed. After forty-two months as a prisoner, Tonelli weighed only ninety-eight pounds. When he returned home, he was suffering from malaria and other tropical diseases that would plague him for the rest of his life. Despite his greatly weakened state, Tonelli signed with the Chicago Cardinals during the 1945 season and played in one game against the Green Bay Packers. He later followed a career as a local politician in the Chicago area.[236]

Bob McBride

Thousands of miles separate the small Ohio town of Logan

from the village of Saint Vith in the mountains of Belgium. For Bob McBride, the contrast between his peaceful upbringing in the gently rolling hills of southeast Ohio and the violent challenges he would face in the rugged terrain along the Belgian-German border could not have been greater.

McBride grew up in Logan, thirty miles southeast of Columbus. In high school he was an outstanding athlete, earning recognition as an all-state fullback his senior year. His football skills were recognized by several colleges, including nearby Ohio State that offered him scholarships. He chose instead to attend Notre Dame to play for Coach Elmer Layden.

As everyone knew he would, he excelled at football, earning letters playing for the Irish in both the 1941 and 1942 seasons. As America's role in World War II deepened so too did its need for young men to fill the ranks of its rapidly growing Armed Forces. McBride enlisted after the conclusion of the 1942 football season, signing up for an Army officer training program, which he was told he would attend after he completed his thirteen-week basic training. As happens so frequently in the armed forces, especially in wartime, the needs of the service trump all earlier promises or commitments made to service members.

Upon completing basic training, McBride was told that the officer training program wasn't accepting new applicants. Shortly thereafter, he was put on a train and sent to Fort Benning, Georgia, where he joined the 176th Infantry Regiment.

When he arrived, the regimental commander put him in touch with the coach of the unit's football team. McBride soon met the other members of the team, which included other collegiate players from Georgia, Clemson, Missouri, UCLA, Texas A&M, Indiana, and LSU to name a few.

The team played several other service teams. After completion of the ten-game schedule, McBride asked to be transferred to the Army Air Forces because he wanted to fly. He was granted the transfer and passed all his tests only to be told that he was being transferred back to the infantry due to a need for young blood. Fate and the needs of the service derailed Bob's plans a second time.

It was then, in the late summer of 1944 that McBride was assigned to the ill-fated 106th infantry division. The division had been activated in the spring of 1943 at Fort Jackson, South Carolina.

The unit was initially allotted 16,000 soldiers, which was an over-strength of 10 percent in anticipation of future losses. Morale was high and cohesiveness was strong as the division began its advanced training in August of 1943. However, that soon changed. The division was ordered to send 3,000 of its trained infantrymen to other units earmarked for deployments before the 106th was scheduled to depart for Europe. This was followed by a continuous drain of more officers and men who had been trained in infantry, artillery, and signal skills.

McBride's division spent much of November through March in field training in South Carolina and Tennessee in deep mud and freezing rain. These conditions duplicated those that the soldiers of the 106th division were to find a year later in the Ardennes.[237] After this field training, the division was ordered to Camp Atterbury fifty miles south of Indianapolis and 150 miles south of Notre Dame, where McBride had spent two pleasant years only a short time before.

They expected to get new equipment and be on their way to Europe immediately. But the need to once again provide replacements to overseas units stripped the 106th of soldiers who had trained with the division. In the first week of April, another 2,800 infantrymen and 800 artillerymen were sent to replacement centers prior to overseas deployment.

Once on the continent, McBride's division traveled 300 miles by truck to Saint Vith in Belgium to relieve the veteran 2nd Infantry Division. When they arrived, the troops were "numb, soaked and frozen."[238] They were now responsible for a sector in excess of twenty-seven miles, far greater than a division could reasonably defend.

The dark and foreboding woods to their front concealed a massive buildup of German troops. The enemy forces facing the 106th and the other US units of this front had roughly a five-to-one advantage in artillery and a three-to-one advantage in armor.

McBride and the other unsuspecting soldiers of his unit were still trying to familiarize themselves with their new surroundings when the German attack began at 5:30 a.m. on December 16. The Germans sent four divisions, two infantry and two panzer divisions against the overextended 106th. The enemy forces quickly penetrated the wooded hills just north of the division sector and swung south into its undefended rear area. This area to the north had been assigned to the 14th Cavalry Group, which was quickly overwhelmed by the attacking Germans, who ripped a huge gap in the American lines.

McBride's unit, the 106th Infantry Division, was now extremely vulnerable, and he was about to face the most challenging and trying time of his life. He would become a participant in what later would be called the Battle of the Bulge. More than 75,000 US soldiers were killed, wounded, or captured in the battle, almost 8 percent of all US World War II casualties. The 106th Infantry Division had the highest casualties at over 8,500, many of them POWs.[239]

Two of the division's regiments, the 422nd, and the 423rd, which was McBride's unit, were quickly surrounded. McBride took refuge in a church with other soldiers and a captured German officer. He and two other soldiers left the church and made their way back to American lines. Once reunited with US troops they were told to stay in the American camp. Instead, McBride persuaded his superior officers to let him and several other men return to the church to lead his fellow soldiers still at the church back to friendly lines. The entire group was just leaving the church when they were captured by the Germans.

The fact that they had earlier treated a captured German officer humanely ended up saving their lives. McBride was knocked to the ground, hit in the back with the butt of a rifle (something that gave him problems for the remainder of his life) and had the business end of a weapon trained a couple of inches from his head. The wounded German officer screamed at the soldier to put the gun down and ordered all the guards not to shoot any prisoners.

After being captured, McBride was forced to walk thirteen days on frozen feet. He was then placed in two different POW camps before a fifty-day march during the German retreat. A starvation diet of one-seventh of a loaf of bread per day resulted in his weight dropping from 212 pounds to ninety-three pounds by the end of the ordeal. After 122 days of captivity, McBride was liberated. For his service, he received three battle stars, a Purple Heart, and a Presidential Unit Citation.

After a short recovery period after returning home, he took a construction job to rebuild his body before returning to Notre Dame in the fall of 1946 to finish his senior year. He was elected honorary captain by his teammates for the Army-Notre Dame game that season. After coaching football at a high school in Chicago he returned to Notre Dame as an assistant to Coach Frank Leahy from 1949 to 1953.

Jim Martin

"Jungle Jim" Martin was another key addition to Leahy's post-war dream team. Martin played a number of positions on the Notre Dame teams of 1946, 1947, 1948, and 1949. During the years the Irish did not lose a game. He was co-captain in 1949, and was named a first-team all-American that year by the Associated Press. He also was a boxer and won Notre Dame's heavyweight title in 1949. Before his stardom, he was a combat Marine.

By the summer of 1944, US forces in the Pacific had made significant progress in the island-hopping strategy. The costly capture of Tarawa in 1943, followed by the capture of Kwajalein in early 1944, gave the US forces bases 2,200 miles from Tokyo. The capture of Saipan in July 1944 reduced the distance to Tokyo another 1,000 miles. The new B-29 bomber then rolling off American assembly lines, had a maximum range of 5,600 miles, which meant each leg of a bombing mission could not exceed 2,800 miles.

The island of Tinian lay only three miles from Saipan. Its relatively flat terrain made it ideal for the construction of airfields that could be used for the upcoming bombing campaign against Japan, including the two atomic missions over Hiroshima and Nagasaki.

As part of the Marianas chain of islands, both Tinian and Saipan had been secretly fortified by the Japanese after taking possession of these islands from Germany after World War I. That meant that the islands would be costly to conquer.

Having accurate information on the potential landing sites for US troops was crucial to the success of the invasions. Knowledge of the beaches on Tinian was especially important since the landing areas were limited. Photos of the island were not sufficient. The task of scouting Tinian's beaches prior to the invasion would fall to Marine volunteers and Navy Underwater Demolition Teams, forerunners of today's SEALs. Reconnoitering the beaches of the island occupied by 9,000 Japanese troops would be a difficult and dangerous job.

On the evening of July 10, 1944, several Navy and Marine teams boarded the destroyer transport Gilmer. The teams debarked the Gilmer and paddled their rubber boats to within 500 yards of the shore. They then swam the rest of the way to the beaches.

Martin, and a Marine named Ollie Kelson, and Donald Neff, a second lieutenant, reached the shoreline under cover of darkness. Neff left the two Marines just offshore, and worked his way inland to assess possible exit routes for vehicles. While ashore, he saw three Japanese guards and heard other Japanese work crews talking.

When Neff returned, the three swimmers silently left the shore and swam back to their rafts undetected. The information they had gathered was extremely important to the success of the invasion of Tinian, which took place several weeks later.

After his service and years playing for Notre Dame, Martin was drafted by the Cleveland Browns in 1950 and played defensive end. In his first season with the Browns they won the NFL Championship. The Browns finished the 1950 season with a 10–2 record. In a playoff game against the New York Giants, Martin sacked Giants quarterback Charlie Conerly in his own end zone for a safety, a play that was key to the 8–3 victory for the Browns.

Martin was traded to the Detroit Lions in 1951. In 1952 and 1953 with his help and led by quarterback Bobby Layne and halfback Doak Walker, the Lions defeated the Browns to win the NFL Championships both years. Eventually, Martin even became the team's kicker. He is the team's fifth-leading scorer with 259 points. In a game against Baltimore in 1960 he kicked two field goals of more than fifty yards. Martin left the Lions In 1961 to become assistant coach with the Denver Broncos. After a series of other coaching jobs with high school, college, and professional teams, Martin retired from football in 1975. He passed away of throat cancer at the age of seventy-eight.

Jack Chevigny

Although World War II was primarily fought by young men, there are many stories of sacrifice and loss among older service members. As the war dragged on and casualties mounted, age restrictions were greatly relaxed. Jack Chevigny (pronounced "shev-knee") is an excellent example of the patriotism of some older citizens who could have avoided combat duty. Instead, the thirty-eight-year-old Notre Dame football standout during the late 1920s asked to be transferred from coaching Marine football teams at Camp Lejeune, North Carolina. In February 1944, at his request, he was transferred to the Fifth Marine division at Camp Pendleton, California then preparing for an offensive action in the Pacific theater.

Chevigny was a native of Hammond, Indiana. At Hammond High School, the five-seven, 170-pound Chevigny starred in football, baseball, and track. He also had roles in several school plays and was elected president of his class. When it came time to choose a college, he chose Notre Dame, just eighty miles away. He joined the football team in the fall of 1924, the same year that Grantland Rice immortalized the Notre Dame varsity backfield as The Four Horsemen of the Apocalypse.

Chevigny played halfback for the Irish for three years. He is most remembered for the part he played in the Army-Notre Dame game of 1928 where the "Win one for the Gipper" legend began.

After graduation, Chevigny was an assistant coach under Knute Rockne. After Rockne's death in early 1931, he shared head coaching duties with Hunk Anderson. In 1932 after one year of sharing coaching duties at Notre Dame he spent one season coaching the Chicago Cardinals in the new National Football League. He then moved to Austin, Texas where he became the head coach of Saint Edward's College, which had also been founded by Father Edward Sorin, the founder of Notre Dame. The Texas Longhorns took note of the young coach's success at Saint Ed's and hired Chevigny the next year. Part of the attraction of the Texas job for Chevigny was the fact that Notre Dame was the second team the Longhorns would play in the coming season.

Against all odds, Texas defeated Notre Dame 7–6. For a short time, Chevigny was the toast of Austin. As the expectations of the Longhorn fans rose and the schedule got tougher Chevigny's tenure got shorter. He left Texas after three seasons and took a job as a deputy attorney general in the Lone Star State and later a job as attorney for an oil company.

When World War II broke out, Chevigny tried to enlist but was rejected because of an old football knee injury. However, as the war progressed and casualties mounted, physical requirements were relaxed. Chevigny at first enlisted in the Army but soon transferred to the Marine Corps Reserve, where he was appointed a first lieutenant.

He was sent to Camp Lejeune for officer training. While there, he was recruited to coach the camp's football team. However, Chevigny became restless, wanting to transfer to combat duty. Chevigny was by then thirty-six years old. He could easily have stayed at Camp Lejeune and continued to coach football and train other Marines for combat. Instead, he pushed for a combat assignment. His actions surprised no one. From his earliest days he had always sought out the toughest assignments, both on and off the football field.

In February 1944, Chevigny was transferred to Camp Pendleton to train with the Fifth Marine Division then preparing for amphibious operations in the Pacific Theater. After a year of training, he and thousands of other Marines landed on Iwo Jima on February 19, 1945, where they engaged in some of the toughest and costliest fighting of the war. In one of his last letters to a friend, Chevigny wrote, "Right now we're checking over our final signals. I wanted to be here because I felt that to have the information correct you had to get in the position of the first team quarterback. Colonel Wornham has given me the opportunity of being on his first team and now I'm hoping I can perform to his expectations."[240]

Humble, noble, and courageous to the end, Jack Chevigny was killed in the early days of the invasion. As Admiral Chester W Nimitz said of the Marines engaged in combat on Iwo Jima, "Among the men who fought on Iwo Jima, uncommon valor was a common virtue."

Joe Savoldi

After leaving Notre Dame, Joe Savoldi played one year of professional football with the Chicago Bears. In 1931 he became a professional wrestler, where he was famous for his finishing move, the flying dropkick. The athletic Savoldi would accomplish this crowd-pleasing move by leaping in the air and disposing of his opponent by kicking him in the chest. Savoldi continued his wrestling career for most of the 1930s. He wrestled in venues around the world. With the advent of WWII, his global appearances came to an end.

In 1942, members of the Office of Strategic Services (OSS), the forerunner of the CIA, approached Savoldi to aid their espionage efforts in fascist Italy. Savoldi's fluent Italian and obvious hand-to-hand combat skills made him an excellent recruit for the agency.

As a member of the OSS, Savoldi took part in several missions behind enemy lines from 1943 to 1945. One of those missions involved locating and extricating an Italian admiral and scientist from Rome, which was then occupied by the Germans. Savoldi helped to move the duo to the Amalfi coast, where they were evacuated by US forces. The scientist had developed a highly successful magnetic torpedo, which the Germans used in their submarine warfare against the Allies. The scientist, Carlo Calosi, was sent to the US, where he helped to develop countermeasures for the torpedo.

After the war, Savoldi tried to revive his professional wrestling career. His age and the onset of arthritis limited his ability to regain his prewar fame. He returned to college and earned a degree in education, which enabled him to take a job teaching science at Henderson County High School in Henderson, Kentucky.

Joe Savoldi died in 1974 at the age of sixty-five, a proud Notre Dame football player, a successful professional wrestler, and American hero.

Moe Daly

Maurice Francis Daly played varsity football at West Point for three years, 1924–1926. He was known at West Point and throughout his Army career as Moe. He was the starting center on the 1925 Army football team that beat Notre Dame 27–0, the largest loss ever inflicted on a Rockne-coached team by an Army team. During Daly's junior year at West Point, he was named an all-American. At five-eleven and 185 pounds, Daly wasn't the biggest on the Army team, but he was one of the toughest. He also played hockey and lacrosse at the academy, seeking out the toughest sports in which he could participate. Tom Trapnell, a classmate of Daly's, was also a halfback on the football team during those same years.

They would be reunited under tragic circumstances in 1942.

Daly was commissioned in the Army Air Corps at his graduation in 1927. After flight training and several other assignments, Captain Daly arrived at Clark Field in the Philippines in 1940, a flashpoint for Japanese ambitions in the Pacific.

After Pearl Harbor, Daly was promoted to major followed quickly by another promotion to lieutenant colonel. Although he was an Air Corps officer, he soon found himself as a ground commander. Japanese air superiority had quickly overwhelmed the US aircraft and drove them from the skies.

Daly and his men fought as ground troops for a short time before they became prisoners of the Japanese. In mid-April 1942, Daly and the other American and Philippine captives were forced to march from the tip of the Bataan peninsula to a POW camp in northern Luzon—the Bataan Death March.

After a few months in Camp O'Donnell, Daly and many of his fellow prisoners were then moved to another camp at Cabanatuan on Luzon in June of 1942. At Cabanatuan, Daly was reunited with two of his classmates, Tom Trapnell and Joe Granahl, both also lieutenant colonels.

In December 1944 as American forces drew closer to the POW camps, the Japanese decided to move the prisoners to Japan. Daly and 1,700 other POWs were loaded on a ship in Manila. By that time, the US had almost complete control of the skies. Unfortunately, the ship was not marked as a POW ship and was attacked by American planes on December 15.

The attack killed 300 of the prisoners. The Japanese ordered the 1,300 survivors, including any of the wounded who could make it, to swim to the shore one quarter of a mile away. When the survivors reached shore they were crowded onto a tennis court, where there was only room enough for the prisoners to stand. They were given very little water and only a handful of rice.

After five days of scorching heat during the day and freezing temperatures at night on the concrete enclosure, the prisoners were moved to a camp farther inland. On Christmas morning, they were moved back to the coast, where they were loaded onto another Japanese freighter.

On January 2, the ship reached Formosa. Two days later it was attacked again by American planes while still in the harbor. A bomb from the attacking planes landed squarely in the crowded hold where the prisoners were held. The bomb killed 300 of the prisoners and injured many others.

The Japanese offered no medical assistance to those in the chaotic prisoner hold. Daly and the other uninjured Americans worked tirelessly to aid their wounded comrades. They tore up their own clothing and that of the dead to make bandages.

On January 11, all surviving prisoners were transferred once again to another ship that left for Japan four days later. Once again, the Japanese provided little water or food for the freezing prisoners in the unheated hold. Of the 1,700 Americans who had left Manila a month earlier, only about 900 survivors remained.

Three classmates, Daly, Granahl, and Trapnell, from the West Point class of 1927, tried to organize aid to the weakest of the group. They even traded their West Point class rings to the Japanese for additional water for the injured.

As the freighter moved slowly up the coast of Japan in the freezing winter weather, Daly's body could take no more. "Moe Daly had exhausted the last vestiges of strength in his once stalwart, tireless body. Now he lay weakly in the hold, too ill to eat any of the meager rice, able to take only a few drops of water from Trapnell. There was a long time to think. Or to fall off into a sleep and dream. Dream perhaps of a day twenty years before, when he had gone in his strength and his youth, the warmth of the roaring crowd around him, against Rockne's team, and the Navy, under the brightness of the skies at home.

"Early in the morning of January 21, Moe fell off to sleep again in

Tom Trapnell's arms. He stirred slightly and smiled as if he had just got a package in the mail. And he slept on, duty well performed."[241]

ACKNOWLEDGMENTS

IT TOOK THREE years to complete this tribute to the giants of Army and Notre Dame football, and the two institutions they represented. My work was supported throughout by several people who encouraged and gently prodded me to continue my journey to its conclusion. Some of those with whom I discussed this project encouraged me without realizing the impact their kind words had on my efforts.

I am especially grateful to John Lujack and his grandson Grant Pohlman, who graciously shared their time with me at their beautiful country club. Being in the presence of someone who played such a key role in my story was especially meaningful. Lujack's enthusiasm for those long-ago days was inspirational for me.

Tony Blanchard provided me with valuable insights about his dad, "Doc" Blanchard.

My friend Pat McBride provided the harrowing details about his dad, Bob McBride, and his ordeal as a POW.

My classmate Russ Broshous was helpful in providing information about his dad, BG Russ Broshous, who played an important role in the 1930 Army-Notre Dame game.

Doug Litts in the Archives and Special Collections Department at the USMA Library was very patient and helpful in providing additional information and confirmation of my research.

Craig Ethier is more knowledgeable about all things Notre Dame than anyone else I know. He was a constant source of encouragement and patiently helped me with the early revisions of this book. He also helped me with the Lujack connection.

My golf buddies listened with rapt attention (real and feigned) to my many revelations each time I discovered some interesting fact about the Army-Notre Dame rivalry. Yes, Ron Tinney the book is finished.

And finally, to my G-1 classmates at West Point, Dave Armstrong, Fred Bothwell, Wayne Willis, Paul Wertz, Jim Krause, and Bernie Skown, who listened patiently and offered encouragement to me during our many Zoom calls.

PHOTOS

Photos provided by US Army Photo.

Army - Notre Dame postgame.

Blanchard takes pitch from Davis.

Davis in action.

ENDNOTES

1 Army battle casualties in World War II—Comptroller of the Army Washington, D C.
2 ibid p. 948
3 West Point The First 200 Years John Grant et al.
4 Letter from George Washington to Thomas Jefferson December 12, 1799
5 The Civil War Shelby Foote p. 946
6 ibid p. 948
7 (West Point-Thomas J Fleming page 303)
8 West Point—the first 200 years, John Grant et al
9 God, Country, Notre Dame-Office of Public Affairs and Communications
10 Inventing Modern Football-John S. Waterson American Heritage
11 Forward Pass p. 9
12 Carlisle vs. Army Lars Anderson p.191
13 Gridiron Grenadiers-Cohane p.12
14 ibid p.13
15 West Point-Thomas Fleming page 259
16 Gridiron Grenadiers-Tim Cohane p.14
17 ibid p.14
18 The NY Times Nov. 30, 1890
19 Notre Dame from Rockne to Parseghian page 5
20 Wake Up the Echoes p.16
21 ibid p.22
22 ibid p.23
23 ibid p.40
24 Shake Down the Thunder p. 24
25 The Big Game p. xii
26 New York Times October 19, 1913
27 Wake Up the Echoes p. 46

28 ibid p. 46
29 ibid p 42
30 Notre Dame vs. Army-Michael K. Bohn-McClatchey Tribune News Service
31 The Big Game p. 3
32 Wake Up the Echoes
33 Wake Up the Echoes p. 52
34 Notre Dame versus Army 1913, Fighting Irish Digital Media.
35 The Big Game p. 8
36 New York Times-November 12, 1913
37 Wake Up the Echoes p. 53
38 Notre Dame vs. Army Michael K. Bohn-McClatchey Tribune News Service
39 The Morning Call Allentown, PA-December 8, 1937
40 Wake Up the Echoes p.62
41 The Big Game p 42
42 ibid p. 79
43 New York Herald Tribune October 18, 1924
44 The Big Game p. 112
45 New York Daily News November 9, 1928
46 ibid
47 The Big Game p. 114
48 Gridiron Grenadiers p. 170
49 Wake Up the Echoes-Rappaport p. 306
50 The Big Game p. 117
51 ibid p. 118
52 ibid p. 121
53 ibid p. 133
54 ibid p. 350
55 Kansas Public Radio March 22, 2019 Bobbie Athon
56 ibid
57 Spirit of Knute 'Non Grounded'-Jeff Harrell April 2, 2021
58 Journal of Air Transportation World Wide Vol 5 No. 1
59 Bringing Up the Brass p. 153
60 Gridiron Grenadiers p. 188

61 The Big Game p. 133
62 Wake Up the Echoes p. 183
63 Being Catholic Being American p. 13
64 ibid p. 12
65 ibid p. 14
66 Reminiscences MacArthur p. 80
67 West Point Thomas Fleming p. 307
68 Duty, Honor, Country p. 261
69 West Point Two Centuries p. 173
70 ibid. p. 172
71 ibid p. 173
72 A Team for America p. 9
73 Hartford Courant Hartford Connecticut December 8, 1937
74 Gridiron Grenadiers p. 203
75 ibid p. 202
76 ibid p.205
77 War and Remembrance—Chicago Tribune December 8, 1991
78 Gridiron Grenadiers p.206
79 ibid p. 206
80 ibid p. 206
81 ibid p.207
82 ibid p. 218
83 ibid p. 218
84 A Team for America p. 16
85 ibid p. 17
86 ibid p.18
87 Democrat and Chronicle Rochester New York December 26, 1940
88 ibid
89 Gridiron Grenadiers p. 219
90 Shake Down the Thunder p. 79
91 Echoes of Notre Dame Football p. 127
92 Shake Down the Thunder p. 95
93 Shakedown the Thunder p. 98
94 ibid p. 104
95 ibid p. 105

96 ibid p. 45
97 ibid p. 45
98 The New York Sun, October 26, 1936
99 Shakedown the Thunder p. 158
100 ibid p. 212
101 Boston Globe Feb. 17, 1941
102 A Team for America p. 21
103 December 1941 p. 12
104 ibid p. 10
105 Gridiron Grenadiers p. 220
106 Leahy's Lads p. 10
107 ibid p. 76
108 ibid p. 33
109 December 1941 p. 370
110 Fields of Battle: Pearl Harbor, the Rose Bowl and the Boys Who Went to War
111 Los Angeles Times December 17, 2016
112 Assembly Magazine US Military Academy July 1942
113 The Navy V-12 Program—James G. Schneider p. 3
114 Football! Navy! War! Wilbur Jones p. 61
115 South Bend Tribune interview with Notre Dame President Theodore Hesburgh 1992
116 Navy Saves Irish from Sinking—Blue and Gold illustrated October 27, 2011 Lou Somogyi
117 Onward to Victory Sperber p. 97
118 Birth and Death of the Army Specialized Training Program Louis E. Keefer Army History Magazine Winter 1995
119 Football! Navy! War! p. 64.
120 From Playing Feld to Battlefield—Journal of Sports History Donald W Rominger Junior p. 258
121 The Great Marianas Turkey Shoot, Naval History and Heritage Command
122 The Big Game p. 104
123 West Point-Crane & Kieley
124 St. Louis Globe-Dispatch Nov 28, 1942

125 How Navy saved Notre Dame after World War II—the team's shared histories-BRYAN FITZGERALD @IrishCentral

126 Shake Down the Thunder p. 225

127 ibid p. 228

128 A team for America p. 64

129 The Coffin Corner Vol. 19, No. 4 Mike Gershman 1997

130 A Team for America p. 91

131 ibid p. 90

132 Mr. Inside and Mr. Outside p. 3

133 ibid p. 1

134 Gridiron Grenadiers p. 230

135 Mr. inside and Mr. Outside p. 3

136 ibid p.6

137 Glenn Davis, Obituary Mike Kupper March 10, 2005 Los Angeles Times

138 ibid

139 ibid

140 Being Catholic-Being American p.282

141 Leahy's Lads p. 59

142 ibid p. 59

143 Shake Down the Thunder p. 234

144 Leahy's Lads p. 62

145 A Team for America p.107

146 Leahy's Lads p. 72

147 ibid p.74

148 The Item-Sumter, SC April 21, 2009

149 ibid

150 A Team for America p. 127

151 Mr. Inside and Mr. Outside p. 52

152 Gridiron Grenadiers p. 246

153 NY Daily News Oct. 1, 1944

154 Mr. Inside and Mr. Outside p. 56

155 NY Daily News Nov 5, 1944

156 Fort WorthStar-Telegram Nov 5, 1944

157 Echoes of Notre Dame Football p. 74

158 The Big Game p. 250
159 ibid p. 252
160 Standard Speaker newspaper Nov. 10, 1944
161 The Big Game p. 236
162 Mr. Inside and Mr. Outside p. 74
163 The Big Game p. 261
164 Gridiron Grenadiers p.258
165 The Game for America p. 217
166 Gridiron Grenadiers p. 263
167 ibid p. 264
168 Leahy's Lads p. 81
169 ibid p. 94
170 Gridiron Grenadiers p. 266
171 Leahy's Lads p. 108
172 Mr. Inside and Mr. Outside p. 154
173 ibid p. 158
174 This Century
175 Army pamphlet 2– 210 History of Personnel Demobilization in the US Army
176 Being Catholic, Being American p. 343
177 The Austin American April 16, 1944
178 WWII Museum
179 The ND Scholastic
180 ibid
181 Gridiron Grenadiers p. 283
182 ibid p. 284
183 The Missoulian Sunday, September 1, 1946
184 Chattanooga Daily Times-Sept. 11, 1946
185 The Daily Oklahoman September 1, 1946
186 ibid p. 289
187 ibid p. 289
188 ibid p. 290
189 A Temporary Tribe NDU.edu
190 Being Catholic, Being American p. 386
191 Echoes of Notre Dame Football p.75

192 Gridiron Grenadiers p. 293
193 Onward to Victory p. 165
194 ibid p. 165
195 The ND Scholastic 10/11/46
196 Wake up the Echoes p. 262
197 Mr. Inside and Mr. Outside p. 188
198 Leahy's Lads p. 172
199 The Big Game p. 281
200 ibid p. 280
201 ibid p. 280
202 Mr. Inside and Mr. Outside p. 194
203 ibid p.194
204 ibid p. 194
205 Green Bay Press-December 6, 1946
206 NewYork Daily News December 31, 1946
207 The Big Game p. 282
208 The Notre Dame Scholastic Volume 88
209 Onward to Victory p. 161
210 ibid p. 162
211 Grant Pohlman text to the author
212 General Maxwell Taylor p.152
213 Sperber Shake Down the Thunder p. 501
214 When Pride Still Mattered p. 402
215 Being Catholic, Being American p.424
216 The Billings Gazette March 23, 1949
217 One Foot Down 5/26/2017
218 Inside Notre Dame Sports 5/25/2017
219 ibid
220 Shake Down the Thunder p. 274
221 ibid p. 279
222 Onward to Victory p.xxi
223 ibid p. 275
224 Onward to Victory p.485
225 Shake Down the Thunder p. 293
226 ibid p. 288

227 When Pride Still Mattered p. 101
228 ibid p. 117
229 Onward to victory p. 354
230 When Pride Still Mattered p. 129
231 ibid p. 130
232 Onward to Victory p.544
233 Poughkeepsie Journal May 6, 2004
234 Leatherneck Magazine December 2015 p. 50
235 Leader Telegram Eau Clair, WI May 1, 1946
236 National Museum of the United Staes Army
237 A History of the 106th by General Alan W. Jones CG
238 The Guns at Last Light p. 418
239 Ardennes 1944 p. 367
240 The Last Chalkline p. 376
241 Gridiron Grenadiers p. 157

www.ingramcontent.com/pod-product-compliance
Lightning Source LLC
LaVergne TN
LVHW091628070526
838199LV00044B/981